NORTHERN IRELAND POLITICS

NORTHERN IRELAND POLITICS

Edited by
Arthur Aughey and Duncan Morrow

LONGMAN
London and New York

Longman Group Limited
Edinburgh Gate
Harlow
Essex
CM20 2JE, England
and Associated Companies throughout the world.

Published in the United States of America
by Longman Publishing, New York

©Longman Group Limited 1996

First published 1996

ISBN 0 582 25346 2 PPR

British Library Cataloguing-in-Publication Data

A catalogue record for this book is
available from the British Library

Library of Congress Cataloging-in-Publication Data
Northern Ireland Politics / edited by Arthur Aughey and Duncan Morrow.
   p. cm.
  Includes bibliographical references and index.
  ISBN 0-582-25346-2
   1. Northern Ireland--Politics and government--1969-1994.
  2. Ulster (Northern Ireland and Ireland)--Politics and government.
  3. Northern Ireland--Politics and government--1994- I. Aughey,
Arthur. II. Morrow, Duncan.
  DA990.U46N67 1996
  320.9416'09'04--dc20   95-45047
                                       CIP

Set by 7 in 9.5 Times
Produced through Longman Malaysia, CLP

CONTENTS

PREFACE

In 1990 the late Professor John Whyte noted that there had been a dramatic increase in the amount of political research conducted in Northern Ireland since 1969. Much of this scholarship has been of high quality, increasing our knowledge of the complexities of the Northern Ireland 'question' and, more broadly, helping to establish a new platform of understanding about the problems of inter-group political conflict.

However, no single book exists which brings together the results of this scholarship and reflection in a form accessible to a wider readership. This book is an attempt to fill that gap. Our purpose is to provide a comprehensive introduction to politics in Northern Ireland which will prove useful to those who are studying politics in schools and universities. It is also designed to be accessible to those who are not engaged in full-time or part-time education but who are seeking a straightforward text on Northern Ireland politics written by those who are acknowledged in their respective fields of expertise.

The book is divided into six sections covering history, ideas, representation, administration, policy and society. There is also a postscript which assesses the most recent political initiative of the Framework Documents of February 1995. We have also tried to go beyond traditional history or politics texts on Northern Ireland by identifying new social movements and groupings not necessarily discussed in a context where so much attention is focused on the 'constitutional issue'. The chapters on Women, the Arts and Sport, for instance, examine themes which are often neglected in conventional political studies. The theme which emerges throughout the book is the extent to which change has been taking place in Northern Ireland irrespective of the long stalemate in constitutional politics. Indeed, it can be argued that these changes – in work, in cultural activities, in group representation – have been partly promoted by the peculiar administrative character of direct rule.

The authors of this book are the members of the Politics panel of the University of Ulster. All of them have published widely in the field of Irish and Northern Irish politics and have their own interests and perspectives. While the book is intended to be accessible and interesting to one reader it has certainly not been written in one voice. Each author has taken their own approach to their chosen theme and our approach as editors has been to seek to create a similar accessibility without destroying individuality. We hope that the different emphases add authenticity to a book about a subject in which there is and has been considerable and ongoing disagreement.

Arthur Aughey
Duncan Morrow

Jordanstown, June 1995

ACKNOWLEDGEMENTS

The editors are grateful to all those who have helped in the preparation of this book.

We would like to thank Janet Campbell, Jackie Darrah, Pauline Knox and Mary Williamson, the secretaries of the School of History, Philosophy and Politics at the University of Ulster, for typing and administration done on their behalf. We also appreciate the assistance provided by the Faculty of Humanities technicians, Rob Walker and Debbie Mathews, when dealing with tricky aspects of Microsoft Word.

The contributors to this book responded courteously and helpfully to all our requests for information and amendments to their manuscripts and made the whole exercise less painful than it might otherwise have been. Our editors at Longman were kind enough to give us reprieves on the deadline which equally made the production of the book a less nerve-racking experience.

It should be noted that the statistics in Chapter 18 were kindly provided by the RUC Central Statistics Unit, Lisnasharragh, Belfast. In Chapter 22, the census material, © Crown copyright 1994, is published by permission of the Controller of Her Majesty's Stationery Office; Figures 22.1–22.4 are reproduced from Doherty, P., 'Agape to Zoroastrian: religious denomination in Northern Ireland 1961 to 1991', *Irish Geography*, 26(1), 1993, by kind permission of the Geographical Society of Ireland.

Finally, both of us would like to express our gratitude to our families for their patience and forbearance.

Arthur Aughey
Duncan Morrow

LIST OF CONTRIBUTORS

Paul Arthur is Professor of Politics at the University of Ulster.

Dr Arthur Aughey is Senior Lecturer in Politics at the University of Ulster.

Dr Alan Bairner is Lecturer in Politics at the University of Ulster.

Dr Paul Doherty is Lecturer in Politics at the University of Ulster.

Dr Paul Hainsworth is Senior Lecturer in Politics at the University of Ulster.

Dr Duncan Morrow is Lecturer in Politics at the University of Ulster.

Dr Emmet O'Connor is Lecturer in Politics at the University of Ulster.

Henry Patterson is Professor of Politics at the University of Ulster.

Carmel Roulston is Lecturer in Politics at the University of Ulster.

MAPS

Map 1 Major towns and cities

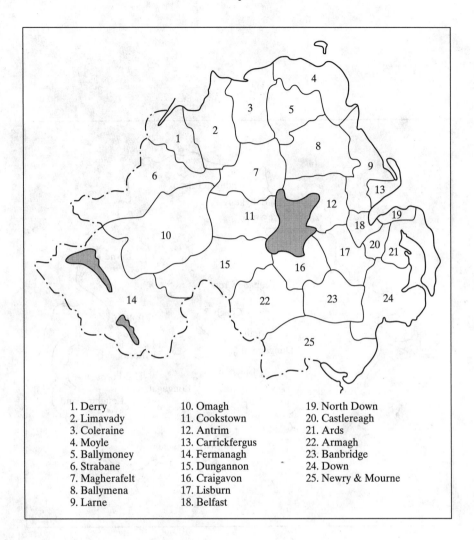

1. Derry
2. Limavady
3. Coleraine
4. Moyle
5. Ballymoney
6. Strabane
7. Magherafelt
8. Ballymena
9. Larne

10. Omagh
11. Cookstown
12. Antrim
13. Carrickfergus
14. Fermanagh
15. Dungannon
16. Craigavon
17. Lisburn
18. Belfast

19. North Down
20. Castlereagh
21. Ards
22. Armagh
23. Banbridge
24. Down
25. Newry & Mourne

Map 2 Local Government Districts since 1973

Map 3 Notable centres of political events, 1968–95

Section One

TWENTIETH CENTURY HISTORY

Chapter 1

NORTHERN IRELAND 1921–68
Henry Patterson

Although it was constitutionally part of the British state and its structures of devolved government bore many resemblances to the Westminster model, the Northern Ireland state departed in a number of ways from the norms of parliamentary democracy. From its creation until its destruction in 1972 it was ruled by a single party, the Ulster Unionists. This party was supported almost exclusively by Protestants who comprised two-thirds of the local population.

For writers from an Irish Nationalist perspective there was no mystery about the nature and the functioning of the state. It was an 'Orange State'. There was an organic link, from its development of a province-wide institutional form in 1905, between Ulster Unionism and the Orange Order. Established in 1795 by Protestant farmers and weavers in County Armagh, the Orange Order developed into a powerful force within Irish Protestantism, north and south, during the nineteenth century. For its largely aristocratic and gentry leadership, it was a means of mobilizing lower-class Protestants for the defence of the institutions of state, the established Church of Ireland and landed property. Its peasant and working-class mass membership saw it as a means of ensuring recognition by the Protestant élite of their 'rights'. These included preferential treatment in employment over 'Fenians' (radical Nationalists) and other 'disloyal elements'. By the end of the eighteenth century, Catholic and Protestant peasants in Ulster were well schooled in the development of secret organizations to pursue inter-ethnic competition for territory and economic resources.

These rural traditions were imported into an urban context as parts of the province around Belfast became the centre of Irish industrialization in the nineteenth century. The uneven development of capitalism within the island was a decisive factor in providing both the rationale for, and the dynamism of, Ulster Unionism. In Irish terms it was a unique success story. Even in British terms, Belfast was one of the fastest growing cities in the nineteenth century, expanding from 19,000 persons in 1801 to 349,000 in 1901. Its industrialists who controlled the key industries – linen, engineering and shipbuilding – boasted that it was the 'The Commercial and Industrial Capital of Ireland' and identified the key to its success as the Union with Great Britain and through it with the broader Imperial market.

3

A substantial section of the commercial class together with many tenant farmers were Presbyterians with a history of strained relations with the Church of Ireland. These groups had been the backbone of Ulster Liberalism which down to the 1880s had been the main electoral challenge to the Conservatives in the Ulster constituencies. They were traditionally contemptuous of Orangeism which was seen as both an appendage of Conservatism and, with its flamboyant and often aggressive sectarianism, an embarrassment to the Unionist cause in the rest of the United Kingdom. Nevertheless, Liberals and Conservatives would soon be forced into what was for some time an uneasy alliance by the emergence of a disciplined Irish Nationalist party under Parnell. This party won 85 Irish seats, 17 of them – a majority of one – in Ulster in the 1885 election and put the Irish demand for a limited measure of autonomy, Home Rule, at the centre of British and Irish political debate for the next four decades.

The alliance which supported Home Rule, British Liberalism and the Irish Parliamentary Party emphasized the sectarian component of Unionism while consistently under-estimating the seriousness of its opposition. Even if it was accepted that the Unionist argument was a purely sectarian one, this should have given its opponents more pause for thought. Irish Nationalism since the time of Daniel O'Connell had accorded a key organizational and leadership role to the Catholic clergy and there had been a strong tendency for many Nationalists to identify the 'nation' with the Irish Catholic population. This was particularly important in Ulster with its long history of sectarian competition and animosity. For many Unionists who had no involvement in Orangeism, the power of the Catholic Church in any Home Rule arrangement was and remained a major concern.

By the time of its most militant struggle against the Third Home Rule Bill (1912–14) the Irish Unionist cause had focused its point of resistance on the Ulster Unionist movement. This was inevitable given the latter's strength of numbers, popular mobilization and resources. However, it was also in Ulster that it was most likely that the negative and sectarian aspects of the Unionist cause would be most on display. Sectarianism was a component of both the main Irish political movements, but the degree to which it appeared in public was very much a matter of circumstance and often conflicting political calculations. The removal of the House of Lords' veto meant that the 1912–14 conflict over Home Rule was by far the most bitter and fraught with possibilities of serious violence. There was a rapid and substantial increase in membership of the Orange Order and the tone of Ulster Unionist argument reflected this. Even liberal Unionists emphasized the threat to their civil and religious liberties represented by Home Rule. There is no denying the specifically religious or sectarian tone of much of the controversy.

Yet an important section of the Unionist leadership was well aware of the dangers of their being seen as a movement fuelled by primordial and negative animosities. Thus, much effort was made to build up a grass roots movement through Unionist Clubs which were an alternative to the Orange Order. Ideological emphasis was given to the economically disastrous and socially regressive effects of a Dublin parliament dominated by the interests of peasants and other 'anti-industrial' elements. Politically the concern to avoid an identification of Ulster Unionism with Orangeism was influenced by the need to sell the Unionist case in Britain where most of its key supporters did not place Unionist fears of ill-treatment at the hands of Catholic Nationalist Ireland at the centre of their arguments. In Great Britain, supporters of the Union tended to stress the right of the majority in Ulster to be governed by the Crown-in-Parliament. In 1914 Ulster Unionism as a movement had an important Orange dynamic but both ideologically and in terms of political strategy it still felt the need to present itself in terms that connected with a broader and more positive identification with the United Kingdom. There was clear evidence of a conflict at its heart between a more parochial 'little Ulsterism' and a broader 'British Unionism'.

State formation

Developments after 1914 did much to ensure that when the Northern Irish state was established it would be heavily influenced by a populist sectarian dynamic. While in part this reflected an ever-present reality of the Unionist movement since its origins, it is important to register the circumstantial factors which ensured that the state had a predominantly populist, sectarian disposition.

By 1914 the Liberal government had been forced to reassess its Irish strategy by increasing evidence of the seriousness of Ulster Unionist opposition. In September 1912 some 250,000 signed the Solemn League and Covenant pledging themselves to use 'all means which may be found necessary to defeat the present conspiracy to set up a Home Rule parliament in Ireland'. In January 1913 an Ulster Volunteer Force was set up, highlighting the possibility of concerted resistance in arms, and the increasingly regionalist focus of Unionist opposition was clear when in September of that year the elements of a provisional government were set in place. In March 1914 the 'Curragh Incident', often known as the 'Curragh Mutiny', revealed that the British Army could not be effectively used to coerce the Ulster Protestants into a united Ireland and in April the Unionists organized a massive importation of arms at Larne. The Irish Parliamentary Party which recoiled from the underground physical force tradition in Irish Nationalism had little option but to sanction the emergence of an Irish National Volunteer force in response.

Partition was increasingly, if reluctantly, contemplated as a possible means of avoiding civil war and this immediately raised the question of minority rights under any partitionist structures in the north. Those leaders of constitutional Irish Nationalism like John Redmond and Joe Devlin, soon to become leader of northern Nationalists in the new Northern Ireland, who had reluctantly come to accept partition were adamantly opposed to partition plus devolution. They thought that the Catholic minority had less to fear from continued direct rule from Westminster than from a local parliament under Protestant control. However, this Irish Parliamentary Party élite would have its position undermined and then effectively destroyed during the war years by the emergence, after the 1916 Easter Rising, of the revolutionary Nationalist organization Sinn Féin. Sinn Féin was contemptuous of any notion of compromise with Ulster Unionism, exacerbating divisions on the island by demanding total independence and being prepared to contemplate the use of arms to obtain it.

The militarization of Irish politics in the second decade of the century would have very serious implications for the type of state structures that developed in Northern Ireland. Sinn Féin's replacement of the Redmondite party as the predominant force in Nationalist Ireland in the 1918 Westminster election and the gradual emergence of an armed struggle by the Irish Volunteers, rechristened the Irish Republican Army (IRA), deepened sectarian divisions in the north. It encouraged the Unionist political leadership to adopt strategies aimed at producing the maximum possible unity in the Protestant population whatever their harmful effects on Catholic/Protestant relations.

It has been argued that the Unionist political leadership would have preferred to combine partition with continued direct rule from Westminster: that the form of devolution included in the Government of Ireland Act was there for reasons of British strategy for an overall Irish settlement rather than because of Unionist demands. Evidence for this would seem to be the letter from Sir James Craig to Lloyd George where he accepted the Government of Ireland Act as 'a final settlement and supreme sacrifice in the interests of peace'. It is certainly true that Sir Edward Carson, who with Craig had spearheaded the pre-war mobilization against Home Rule, strongly favoured direct rule over devolution. But Carson was a southern Protestant who had tried to stand apart from the northern sectarian influences which had played such a role in Ulster Unionism. Direct rule, he believed, would have been a better framework for winning Catholic consent to partition than devolution with all its dangers of Protestant supremacism.

In fact the Government of Ireland Act of 1920 with its provision for a devolved legislature and a form of cabinet government would soon develop a strong appeal to the dominant group of Ulster Unionists. As the IRA destroyed British rule in three-quarters of the country, it became clear that the British government favoured negotiation with what it perceived to be the more moderate elements in the leadership of Sinn Féin. The widespread Ulster Unionist response was contempt and distrust for what was seen as British weakness and vacillation.

British government policy in the 1920–22 period was a subject of considerable internal debate and division. Its basic objective was to ensure that the more moderate elements in Sinn Féin would dominate in any new regime in the south. This in itself encouraged some members of the government led by Lloyd George to take a hard and critical line towards Ulster Unionism whose indulgence of sectarianism was seen to play into the hands of republican hardliners.

Distrust of British intentions exacerbated the Unionist leadership's disposition to look to local sources of support. It made use of traditional forms of pan-Protestant solidarity like the Orange Order and the more recently created structures of the UVF. The Unionist leadership was worried by a major outburst of class conflict in the Belfast shipyards and engineering plants in 1919. Just as land agitation had split the Protestant community in the nineteenth century, urban class conflict could lead to disunity in the face of the Nationalist threat. This became a significant, periodic concern of Ulster Unionism in the new century.

The apparent precariousness of its position in the period of state formation – 'besieged' by Sinn Féin and the IRA at a time when the British government's ultimate intentions were unclear and with recent memories of Protestant disunity – encouraged Unionism's most parochial and exclusivist dimensions.

Unionism in power

The Government of Ireland Act provided for a parliament with extensive powers over a range of important internal areas: law and order, local government, representation, education, social services, agriculture, industry and internal trade. The fact that the bulk of taxation powers and ultimate sovereignty were reserved to Westminster put major limits on the powers of the new regime. However, those powers that the new parliament did possess provided a substantial resource for those in the Unionist leadership who shared Sir James Craig's concern to maintain Protestant unity. Two areas in particular would serve to underline the fundamental biases of the state: security policy, and employment practices in the Northern Ireland Civil Service.

In a context of IRA attacks and intense inter-communal violence, the Unionist leadership incorporated an important element of Protestant vigilantism into the Northern Ireland security forces. This was the creation of a Special Constabulary, a paramilitary force to support the police and drawn exclusively from the Protestant population. This force, particularly its part-time component, the 'B' Specials, was a source of concern to some members of the British government because of its lack of discipline and propensity to sectarianism. However, attempts to professionalize it were successfully resisted by the Craig administration. In the two years between June 1920 and June 1922 428 people were killed and 1,766 wounded in sectarian conflict between Catholics and Protestants. Unionists then and since have explained the partisan nature of the state's security forces and a draconian piece of legislation like the Special Powers Act (1922) by reference to IRA activity and more general Catholic Nationalist hostility to the existence of Northern Ireland.

However, an important section of Northern Nationalist opinion did favour some recognition of the Craig regime and it is not adequate to explain the exclusivist features of the state as simply a defensive reaction to Nationalist hostility. Sir James Craig, who had spoken in 1921 of the need for 'broad views' and 'tolerant ideas' and later of the need for a 'fair deal' for Nationalists, never allowed such sentiments to intrude on his main priority of cementing Protestant unity, whatever the cost in Catholic alienation.

Thus even after the disappearance of significant IRA activity in the north and also, in 1925, of the threat to the territorial extent of the state in the operation of the Boundary Commission, there was no real evidence of a more relaxed approach to Catholics. Leading members of the Unionist élite like the Permanent Secretary to the Ministry of Finance and the head of the Northern Ireland Civil Service, Sir Wilfred Spender, were concerned that a continuing emphasis on the Protestant nature of the state would eventually turn Catholic alienation into rebellion and force British intervention. Spender and two successive Ministers of Finance were uneasy at the clear evidence of the exclusion of well-qualified Catholics from the NICS. However, the predominant practices and the resulting tone of the state were set by the increasingly parochial and sectarian disposition of Craig and the majority of his cabinet. In 1927 the Minister of Agriculture would boast publicly that his ministry employed only four Catholics.

Those members of the élite with a critical perspective could do little more than attempt to restrain the more florid excesses of Craig's patriarchal Protestant style which he openly admitted amounted to 'distributing bones' to Unionism's supporters. Spender's concern that the Catholic alienation caused by such policies might undermine the state by forcing British intervention would ultimately prove far-sighted. However, for decades Unionism would enjoy a position of effective insulation from the rest of the United Kingdom. Once the more militant section of Sinn Féin had been defeated in the Irish Civil War (1922–23), the principal objective of British policy was to hold Ireland at arm's length, following two generations of aggravation. Genuine concern about the Unionist treatment of the minority was secondary to the horror engendered in Westminster and Whitehall by any possibility of being drawn back into the 'Irish bog'.

This was clearly the case in the area of local government on which many subsequent Nationalist complaints of discrimination were to centre. Proportional representation had been included in the Government of Ireland Act as one means of protecting minority rights. In the 1920 elections Nationalists had gained clear majorities in such traditionally marginal authorities as Fermanagh and Tyrone County Councils and Londonderry Corporation. The Unionist response was to introduce legislation to abolish PR and, when the British government exercised its 'sovereignty' to delay the granting of royal assent, the Unionist government threatened to resign. Faced with being forced to take over direct responsibility for governing Northern Ireland, London backed down.

Ensconced in power, and relatively confident of London's reluctance to get involved, Unionism used northern Nationalism's policy of abstention to tighten the screw. By the use of the partisan Leech Commission, they gerrymandered local government electoral boundaries in 1923.

Whatever their initial qualms may have been, Craig and the majority of his cabinet had fallen in love with the devolved system of government. They responded to criticism of the discriminatory aspects of the state by referring to Nationalist violence in the south against Protestants in the 1920–22 period and their treatment thereafter as Dublin moved more explicitly towards the adoption of a Catholic constitution in 1937. While there was substance in these Unionist complaints, they simply avoided the core of the argument made by some of their own colleagues: that the attitude of many Catholics to the state was as much the product of their treatment by it as it was of Nationalist ideology.

War and the welfare state

The sectarian riots of 1935 in Belfast which indirectly prompted a Dominions Office inquiry into Unionist stewardship, and a late 1930s British interest in persuading Éamon de Valera into a possible war-time alliance, briefly disturbed the provincial assumptions of the Belfast government. The war, by putting an end to the high levels of unemployment which the region had experienced since 1921, allowed the combative traditions of the local working class to reassert themselves as Belfast felt the UK-wide surge towards Labour. Prime Minister Andrews' incapacity to deal coherently with this pressure forced him from office in 1943 only three years after he had replaced Craig. His successor, Basil Brooke, would remain in power for the next two decades, decades which saw the economic and social basis of Northern Ireland radically transformed.

The substantial defections to the Northern Ireland Labour Party (NILP) in the Stormont election in 1945 would prove decisive in determining the Unionist government's response to the introduction of the welfare state by the Attlee administration. Despite the opposition of members of his Cabinet and many in his parliamentary party, Brooke insisted that it be extended to Northern Ireland to prevent a haemorrhage of support to the NILP. Welfarism was an important factor in the strengthening of the Unionist Party's position in the post-war period. The extension of the welfare state was dependent on the agreement of the Treasury in London to underwrite it financially as was the adoption of new policies on industrial modernization and the attraction of new industry. Although this increasing financial dependence on the UK exchequer would ultimately reduce the northern state's capacity for pursuing policies that London disapproved of, this limit would not become apparent for almost two decades.

Unionism entered the 1950s with its position within the UK underwritten by the Ireland Act of 1949. This provided assurance that Northern Ireland would not cease to be part of the UK except with the consent of its parliament. The Attlee administration's underwriting of the Union represented London's (and Washington's) distaste for the southern state's neutrality in the Second World War. Buoyed up by the increasingly wide disparity between economic and social conditions north and south and by Dublin's international isolation, the Unionist government displayed little interest in a less exclusively Protestant state. The launch of an all-party Anti-Partition campaign by the Irish government in 1949 did little to encourage accommodation.

In 1950 the Minister of Education, who had raised grants available to Catholic schools for capital expenditure, was forced to resign by Orange pressure. In 1951 a Public Order Act was passed to enable the RUC to suppress 'inflammatory' Nationalist marches more effectively and in 1954, under Orange pressure, the Cabinet agreed to introduce a Flags and Emblems Act which obliged the RUC to protect the display of the Union flag anywhere in Northern Ireland. This was done against the advice of the Inspector General of the RUC.

The fifties were a decade in which the possibilities of a more inclusive approach by the regime were wasted. Unionism's position had never been stronger, while Irish Nationalism was at a low ebb with a major economic crisis in the south and the failure of the IRA's assault on the northern state (1956–62) to elicit significant support from Nationalists. By the end of the decade Seán Lemass had emerged as the new leader in the south, bringing with him a more flexible attitude to the north. Furthermore, there were signs of a more pragmatic and participationist attitude among northern Nationalists which seemed to presage the possibility of a new departure in Nationalist–Unionist relations on the island.

However, decades of Unionist Party rule had produced a style of leadership which focused obsessively on intra-Protestant relations to the virtual exclusion of changes within Nationalism. The capacity of the party to dominate Protestant politics was put in question by what was perceived to be its inadequate response to the increasing economic problems of the fifties. Employment in new industries did not expand fast enough to compensate for shrinking employment in agriculture and major crises for the staples of textiles and shipbuilding facing unprecedented international competition. Northern Ireland could not remain insulated from the post-war British consensus that governments had an obligation to provide full employment. With an unemployment figure four times the national average throughout the fifties, the administration led by the increasingly lethargic Viscount Brookeborough had lost large sections of Protestant working-class support to the NILP in the 1958 and 1962 Stormont elections. The unemployment problem and its political repercussions in the Protestant community obsessed the Unionist government as it entered the 1960s, the decade when Ulster Unionism would face its most serious challenge since the end of the First World War.

Brookeborough's failure to persuade the Treasury or Harold Macmillan's Conservative government to increase subsidies to Ulster industry sealed his fate and he was replaced by the Minister of Finance, Terence O'Neill, in 1963. O'Neill would subsequently criticize his predecessor for indolence and lack of vision. Yet, in the crucial first two years of his premiership he continued to strengthen his position primarily by winning back Protestant support lost to Labour. His main preoccupation was 'stealing Labour's thunder' (to use his own phrase) rather than allaying Catholic resentments. While capable of the occasional conciliatory gesture – such as a famous visit to a Catholic school – he espoused a rhetoric of planning and modernization by which Catholic grievances would be dissolved by shared participation in the benefits of economic growth. He saw no role for structural reform. In order to convince the Treasury of the need to increase financial assistance to 'transform the face of Ulster', O'Neill succeeded in raising Catholic expectations of change while at the same time deepening dependence on London. This made resistance to British pressure for reform more difficult.

Sir Wilfred Spender's warnings of the ultimate incompatibility between an exclusivist regime and economic dependence on the British exchequer, ignored for decades, would soon prove prophetic.

Further reading

Aughey, A., *Under Siege: Ulster Unionism and the Anglo-Irish Agreement*. Belfast: Blackstaff Press, 1989.

Bardon, J., *A History of Ulster*. Belfast: Blackstaff Press, 1992.

Bew, P., *Ideology and the Irish Question 1912–16*. Oxford: Oxford University Press, 1994.

Bew, P., Gibbon, P. and Patterson, H., *Northern Ireland 1921–1994: Political Forces and Social Classes*. London: Serif, 1995.

Buckland, P., *A History of Northern Ireland*. Dublin: Gill and Macmillan, 1981.

Farrell, M., *Northern Ireland: The Orange State*. London: Pluto Press, 1976.

Chapter 2

NORTHERN IRELAND 1968–72
Paul Arthur

Northern Ireland in 1968, like any other western liberal democracy, had free and regular elections. Admittedly it was the poorest region of the United Kingdom with the highest cost of living, highest unemployment and lowest (natural) life expectancy. But even these problems were being tackled by Captain Terence O'Neill, a Prime Minister who had self-consciously undertaken a modernization programme after he took office in 1963. And it was beginning to bear fruit: he was able to boast that the unemployment figures for March 1966 had been the lowest of any March since the war. In addition he had inaugurated what Richard Rose described as an 'era of good feelings' in which Catholics and Protestants in all kinds of localities were agreed that community relations were improving. But there was something artificial in all of this. When a visit by the Prime Minister to a Catholic school becomes particularly newsworthy it suggests that such gestures are unusual. When there are those who protest against such gestures one has to question the nature of the democracy in which it occurs.

The questioning of this 'artificiality' was not long in coming. The conditions on the streets of Northern Ireland by the end of 1968 showed that the very legitimacy of the regime was being called in question and Terence O'Neill was under siege from a militant civil rights campaign as well as from many of his erstwhile supporters. To add to his troubles he knew that conditions in Northern Ireland were being monitored by the international media and by Harold Wilson's Labour government. Not since the 1920s was the province under such close scrutiny. In virtually every decade since the 1920s there had been incidents of communal unrest but those beginning late in 1968 were different in three respects. In the past Unionism had remained united against any threat; in 1968 it was showing serious divisive tendencies. Secondly, the nature of the present protest was ostensibly about British rights and not about partition – in other words it was a reasonable phenomenon which deserved a reasoned response. Finally, Unionist reaction was being scrutinized by a British government who owed no favours to those in power in Belfast.

Some members of O'Neill's party realized that this was a challenge like no other and that it would have to be handled with sensitivity. Others had different motivations. There were those who simply wanted the removal of O'Neill. He had not been the easiest man to work with after the more 'gracious' ways of his

11

predecessor, Lord Brookeborough. He had insisted on highly professional standards from his Cabinet colleagues. He was Olympian in his manner and was surrounded by a coterie of close advisers. He had antagonized sections of his party through reshuffles and sackings. His present discomfort was seen as an opportunity to remove him as Prime Minister. Others had more ideological objections. They considered him too 'liberal', too accommodating towards enemies of the state, be they Catholics in general or members of the Republic's political establishment. 'O'Neill must go' was more about a demand for a radical change in policy than naked personal ambition. Those who supported O'Neill realized that he had little room for manoeuvre and that concessions would have to be offered to keep the Westminster government at bay. As a former Minister for Finance, the Prime Minister was ultra-conscious that the Treasury in London held Northern Ireland's purse strings. His enemies, long used to withstanding Westminster's blandishments, felt that if they stood their ground it would be the British government which would blink first. After all, successive governments in London had shown no signs of intervening in the past.

The crisis of 1968 was therefore different in kind to any which had preceded it. It was not simply a conflict between Unionism and the enemy within. It was to become just as much a fundamental debate within the Unionist family about (a) what type of Unionism was relevant for the late twentieth century; (b) what its relationship was to be with the sovereign powers at Westminster; and ultimately (c) the very identity of the Union. These questions were to unfold over the next few years. The immediate concern was with how the civil rights challenge was to be met. There was one view that it was a Republican-inspired conspiracy and that the only fitting response was to use the might of the law on it. More thoughtful souls recognized that civil rights represented a more subtle threat in that it was appealing across sectarian lines for the same standards for all. Moreover the civil rights movement adopted more sophisticated means of propaganda and had been careful to use a universal language of 'rights' which would strike a chord in any liberal democracy. Perhaps a proper response would be to concede its minimalist and reasonable demands to nip its potential in the bud. Hindsight suggests that this might have worked but that would be to ignore the conflicting noises which were crowding the stage at the time. It would also be to ignore the fact that the civil rights campaign, like Unionism itself, was not a monolith. And finally it would be to ignore the level of paranoia which existed in Northern Ireland politics.

Civil rights

On the surface the basic civil right demand was unanswerable: 'One Man One Vote' (we need to remember that this was the era before the feminist revolution). Northern Ireland was out of kilter with the rest of the United Kingdom in the matter of the local government franchise. A case could be made for arguing that the ratepayers' franchise was justified in an era when local government revenue was raised at source. But as the century proceeded more and more funding for local needs came from the central exchequer. So in 1947 the franchise in Great Britain was extended from ratepayers to all adults at local level for council elections. Not so in Northern Ireland where the business vote – which enabled some people to have up to six votes – was maintained and the franchise was not extended. That was the issue on which the civil rights movement began its campaign. The movement was an odd mixture of dissident voices within Northern Ireland. Some republicans were involved but so also were members of the Communist Party, Northern Ireland Labour Party, Nationalist Party, Liberal Party and various civil libertarians.

Moreover it had different geographical bases which reflected the plurality of its foundation. The Campaign for Social Justice (CSJ) launched in January 1964 was based in Dungannon around a group of 13 Catholic professional people. Its primary concern was with discrimination in the allocation of public housing and its method was the collection and publication of data on all cases of discrimination in jobs and houses. The first significant civil rights march took place in the Dungannon area in August 1968. The Northern Ireland Civil Rights Association (NICRA), which was to become the supervising body of all civil rights activity, originated in Maghera, County Derry in August 1966. It was formally inaugurated in Belfast on 9 April 1967 with a draft constitution of five objectives:

1   to defend the basic freedoms of all citizens;
2   to protect the rights of the individual;
3   to highlight all possible abuses of power;
4   to demand guarantees for freedom of speech, assembly and association;
5   to inform the public of their lawful rights.

These rather bland objectives were to be converted into concrete grievances as the campaign unfolded. NICRA was the body responsible for the protest in Derry on 5 October 1968 which led to serious unrest, allegations of policy brutality and the attention of the international media at what was going on in Northern Ireland. It was that rioting which led to the formation of the third strand of the campaign, the People's Democracy (PD).

One of the groups which participated in the Derry march was a loose conglomeration of students from The Queen's University of Belfast centred around the Young Socialist movement. They had been so shocked by police behaviour in Derry that they organized a picket outside the home of the Minister of Home Affairs, William Craig, the following day and a march to the centre of Belfast on 9 October. Out of this grew the People's Democracy, an unstructured and militant body, which quickly drew up six specific demands:

One man, one vote
Fair boundaries
Houses on Need
Jobs on Merit
Free Speech
Repeal of the Special Powers Act

The birth of the civil rights movement reveals several significant factors. One was its diversity. It cut across class, territory and, in some instances, creed. Even had the government so desired, it would not have been easy to enter into negotiation with this body since it was so disparate and since it was not clear who had final authority. Ostensibly NICRA was the governing body but it realized that its remit did not carry across the province. For example, serious differences arose on the handling of the Derry protest in October 1968. More radical elements in the socialist movement and the People's Democracy were intent on militant action. In addition the latter had much more freedom in terms of time and mobility; it could, and did, organize protests at very short notice, much to the embarrassment of the parent body. Nor could NICRA control a very strong sense of local autonomy. In Derry, for example, the Derry Citizens' Action Committee (DCAC) had been founded on 8 October in an effort to control local militants as well as all activity within its boundaries. After that, NICRA's role in the city was largely redundant.

Diversity was also apparent in the movement's aims and methods. All of the founding bodies had been inspired by the civil rights movement led by Martin Luther King in the USA. Hence the civil rights anthem was 'We shall overcome' rather than any Irish Nationalist song. Its method of non-violence was also based on US experience, but there the similarity ended. There was no tradition of non-violence in the Irish struggle. As well there were those, especially in the PD, who were conscious of direct action methods being used by the student movement, particularly in the 'May Days' of Paris in 1968. We have noted too how the aims shifted from a generalized sense of grievance to specific demands. In that respect 'civil rights' may be a misnomer: the programme sought civil, social and political rights which were perceived as a fundamental challenge to much of the government's programme. Finally there were those who noted the participation of republicans. Republican intellectuals had played a crucial role in the formation of NICRA and of its agenda. Some of them were members of the Executive. Some were identified as being prominent in the protests. But republicans themselves were sensitive to such charges and were careful to restrict their activities within the campaign.

The Unionist response

This was not the perception placed on the movement by the Minister for Home Affairs, William Craig. From the outset he viewed NICRA as a republican plot and that put a different construction on how it was to be contained. The civil rights movement was regarded as a Trojan Horse, as anti-partitionism by other means. On 5 October 1968, a civil rights march in Derry, which had been officially banned, ended up as a full-scale riot between marchers and police. Ultimately, it was Craig who was responsible for police action.

The Prime Minister, on the other hand, was under pressure from Downing Street to handle the affair sensitively. The next few months were to be a public relations disaster for the government. Ultra-loyalists led by the Free Presbyterian Moderator, the Reverend Ian Paisley, led counter-demonstrations against civil rights on the streets of Northern Ireland. These were noted for their lack of subtlety and hostility towards the media. They also turned on the Prime Minister with the slogan 'O'Neill must go'. This was the first sustained and public campaign against a Unionist leader since the foundation of Northern Ireland.

O'Neill realized too that he did not have the full backing of his Cabinet and he was forced to try to re-establish his authority. On 22 November, he unveiled a 'reform package' at the behest of Harold Wilson. In it, he promised an Ombudsman, the introduction of a points system in the allocation of houses, the reform of local government elections, the repeal of the Special Powers Act and the suspension of Derry Corporation. The announcement was not received positively by all factions. Moderates in the civil rights movement saw it as a victory for their dignified protests and a declaration of the Prime Minister's good intentions (hence there was a lull in civil rights activities). But the reform deal did not stem the tide of agitation mounting against O'Neill from a section of his own party.

O'Neill now went on the offensive through an emotional televised speech, warning Ulster people that they were on the brink of disaster. Moderate opinion responded, flocking to his support, and 100,000 people supported an 'I back O'Neill' campaign organized by the *Belfast Telegraph*. He went a stage further on 11 December 1968 when he sacked William Craig for expressing views about a uni-lateral declaration of independence (UDI). Immediately the DCAC pledged 'as an indication of their sincerity' to conduct their campaign without marches for a month.

But O'Neill's announcements amounted only to a stay of execution. The socialist element in the PD insisted on marching from Belfast to Derry in January 1969 as an exercise of a 'fundamental democratic liberty' which it likened to Martin Luther King's famous march between Selma and Montgomery in 1965. That was not the way it was perceived by loyalists who saw it as an arrogant invasion of their territory and so they harried and harassed it throughout. When the marchers were attacked by loyalists at Burntollet Bridge the inevitable result was deepening communal polarization and a further weakening of the Prime Minister's position. In response to growing civil rights agitation O'Neill set up a Commission (chaired by Lord Cameron) to enquire into the reasons for the civil disturbances. That decision resulted in the resignation of his Deputy Prime Minister, Brian Faulkner, followed two days later by another Minister. Finally 13 Unionist backbenchers met in Portadown to publicize their grievances with O'Neill. He replied by calling a general election for 24 February. The election was to be O'Neill's downfall. Although Unionists took 33 of the 52 seats, 11 of those went to anti-O'Neillites. Similarly the Nationalist Party lost three seats to Independent (civil rights) candidates. By the end of April, O'Neill had gone. In the subsequent by-election his seat was won by the Reverend Ian Paisley, the leading figure among O'Neill's ultra-loyalist critics. O'Neill's last service was to persuade his party on 23 April 1969 to accept the principle of one man, one vote for local government elections.

The consequences

We have dwelt on this period because it sets the scene for much that was to come. It was the beginning of the realignment of party positions in Northern Ireland when all the old certainties disappeared. It was also the beginning of an experiment in 'direct rule by proxy'. Two senior Whitehall officials now oversaw the conduct of government from offices in Stormont and reported directly back to London, a fact resented by Unionists who believed that their Prime Minister had become a mere puppet.

The fragile tranquillity of spring 1969 was broken in the summer. Although further political marches were declared illegal, an exception was made for Orange and other marches which were held to be traditional. Tension over this issue exploded in Derry in August 1969 when the RUC charged an angry, largely Catholic, crowd in the city's Bogside area. Riots broke out in Belfast, as crowds from the Protestant Shankill area descended on the neighbouring, Catholic, Clonard district. Given the breakdown in relations between the civil police force and the Catholic population and the general breakdown in law and order which now threatened, the British government reversed its policy of decades and agreed to the sending of British Army troops to Belfast, initially to stand between the Catholic population and the police.

Nevertheless, the British government still regarded Northern Ireland as a temporary problem. The Stormont government remained in place, now under the Prime Ministership of James Chichester-Clark. Nonetheless, Unionist resentment was growing. With the passing of time and the failure of the security initiatives of 1969–71, that resentment overflowed when direct rule was imposed in March 1972. This period therefore also represents the first sustained challenge to Stormont authority by Westminster and the first time since partition that Unionists 'lost'. That was to have a devastating effect on Unionism's sense of identity.

Unionists reacted with a mixture of belligerence and demoralization. William Craig had personified the first with his threats of UDI. Behind all the bluster serious questions were now being posed: what was the nature of the Union? What responsibilities and privileges did it carry? What actions were justified in opposing Westminster rule? These were questions which were still being asked more than two decades later. This was a period which saw the resurrection of 'Queen's rebels', those who were prepared 'to take all means necessary' to preserve their place in the Union. Hence, by 1972, the Ulster Defence Association (UDA) had emerged with its emphasis as a counter-terrorist organization. Whatever its self-perception, its formation indicated the degree to which politics had moved on to the streets and the legitimacy of the regime was now under threat from Protestants too.

Finally the period posed certain questions about the nature of the minority. The civil rights campaign had disorientated the majority population who were witnessing Catholic children of the welfare state articulating 'British' demands and winning the propaganda battle. In the past they could easily be dismissed as disloyal. Now it was more difficult so long as their campaign was non-violent. Once violence became part of the scene the campaign came under closer scrutiny. The original 'rights' claims were about issues of participation – 'how can we become accepted members of society?' – and of distribution – 'how can we enjoy the full civil and social benefits entailed in being citizens?'. In short the campaign produced a revolution in rising expectations. When these could not be delivered speedily enough the crisis became a more fundamental one of identity and legitimacy. Northern Ireland was now regarded as 'a failed political entity' and justice could be found only within Irish unity. These conclusions did not surface immediately but by the end of the 1960s they were coming to the fore and government responded with confused signals.

When the civil rights campaign started it aroused a certain degree of sympathy in a Labour government which believed that the answer lay in the reform package. The Wilson government persisted with that (and with a 'softly softly' security policy) until it lost office in May 1970. The incoming Conservative administration was more sympathetic to Unionism – after all the party took the Tory whip at Westminster – and more inclined to follow a security response. In addition, a reinvigorated IRA entered the scene after much recrimination about who was responsible for leaving the residents of the Falls Road open to loyalist attacks in August 1969. Furthermore, the IRA split into a more traditionally republican 'Provisional' movement which opposed the more Marxist 'Officials'. Over the next few years a battle was waged for supremacy in Catholic areas: the 'Provos' won. During 1970 much of their effort was expended on building up the IRA and in procuring weapons. In February 1971, after the first soldier was killed (by the IRA), Chichester-Clark declared war on the IRA and demanded an increase in troops from the British government. After many acrimonious discussions between London and Belfast on the nature of the security response Chichester-Clark resigned to be succeeded by Brian Faulkner in March.

Internment and its aftermath

Chichester-Clark's successor, Brian Faulkner, was considered to be the most professional Unionist leader. He had been waiting in the wings for almost a decade and was widely regarded as the last hope for Unionism, a man who could unite all wings of the party and offer dynamic leadership. Initially that promise seemed to be fulfilled but he over-reached himself when he persuaded the Heath government that the internment of known IRA leaders, without immediate trial, would bring a security dividend. On 9 August 1971, British Army troops were sent into many Catholic areas to implement the policy. It was a disaster (according to a future Chief Constable of the RUC). Many innocents, and few of the actual leaders, were detained. The Catholic population was alienated and those in leadership positions withdrew any remaining latent support from the Stormont system – especially after well-founded allegations of brutality were laid against the Army's treatment of internees. The policy was a disaster, too, for Brian Faulkner. Until then he had enjoyed the total confidence of Ted Heath. That trust disappeared and from then on Mr Heath made Northern Ireland one of his personal priorities.

Until internment, the British Prime Minister had been happy to leave Northern Ireland affairs in the hands of his Home Secretary, Reginald Maudling, while he (Heath) secured the United Kingdom's accession to the European Economic Community (EEC). When he had completed that goal and when he realized that he could not rely on the indolent Maudling, nor no longer trust the judgement of Brian Faulkner, he began to look at other approaches to the problem. One particular concern had been an over-reliance on a security, rather than a political, response. This failure was underlined by a series of official enquiries into the causes of the repeated civil disturbances – Cameron [Cmd 532] in 1969 and Scarman [Cmd 566] in 1972 – and into the role of policing in Northern Ireland – Hunt [Cmd 535] in 1969. All of these undermined security force morale, boosted IRA claims to be protectors of the Catholic community, and brought international opprobrium on British standards of justice. This was to be compounded by the events of 30 January 1972 when paratroopers opened fire on a civil rights demonstration in Derry, killing 13 unarmed civilians (a fourteenth was to die some months later) in what became known as 'Bloody Sunday'. The British government was now being internationally blamed for events in Northern Ireland without having complete political responsibility for policy.

Direct rule by proxy had to come to an end and Westminster had to take firm control, particularly in relation to security policy. On 22 March 1972 Stormont was prorogued and a week later the first Secretary of State for Northern Ireland, William Whitelaw, was in place in Stormont with his new team of direct rulers.

These events had been watched with great interest by the Irish government. They had protested at events in August 1969 when loyalist mobs had invaded Catholic West Belfast, at internment policy and allegations of Army brutality (allegations which they brought to the European Court of Justice) and at the impact of Bloody Sunday – which led to the destruction of the British Embassy in Dublin by an outraged mob. But they began playing a different role after September 1972 when Ted Heath invited Jack Lynch, Taoiseach (Prime Minister) of the Irish Republic, to a meeting at Chequers, and to a further meeting there with Brian Faulkner a few weeks later. The British government had begun to recognize officially that there was an 'Irish dimension' to the problem and perhaps also to the solution.

Conclusions

The events of 1968–72 will be seen as a watershed in the relationships between Britain and Ireland. After 1972 the United Kingdom and the Republic of Ireland entered the European Economic Community. It was the first time in that ancient asymmetrical relationship that Ireland was not treated as a subordinate. In the shorter term the Republic's interests were recognized in the 'Irish dimension' which was built into a White Paper of March 1973.

In 1968 Unionists appeared to be in complete control of their destiny and happy with their identity. They had existed as if they governed an independent state in close economic cooperation with the rest of the United Kingdom, a sort of 'sovereignty association'. By March 1972 they had witnessed untrammelled one-party rule disappear overnight. They were demoralized and divided and uncertain about their future. Some of their number had reverted to extra-parliamentary protest and the outlawed UDA was claiming over 25,000 due-paying members within six months of its formation. A law and order community was becoming schizophrenic.

During those same years the Catholic community had gained little in specific terms save the discomfort of their Protestant opponents and a growing self-confidence. There had been reforms posited on the civil rights programme but many of those were going to take years before they came on stream. They had moved from demanding British rights to questioning yet again the very existence of Northern Ireland. A struggle for civil rights had shifted to one of Nationalist demands. The air was filled with rancour and the sound of guns and drums and marching feet. Authority had broken down and a power vacuum was being occupied by the gunmen. When direct rule was imposed in March 1972 one commentator suggested that it would take between three and six months to put the house back in order. More than two decades later the complexity of the problem had at least been recognized as the British and Irish governments struggled to find a solution. 'One man, one vote' had taken on an existence of its own which no one had envisaged in 1968.

Further reading

Arthur, P., *The People's Democracy 1968–73*. Belfast: Blackstaff Press, 1974.

Arthur, P., *Government and Politics of Northern Ireland*. Harlow: Longman, 1987.

Arthur, P. and Jeffrey, K., *Northern Ireland since 1968*. Oxford: Blackwell, 1988.

Brett, C.E.B., *Long Shadows Cast Before*. Edinburgh: Bartholomew, 1978.

Hayes, M., *Minority Verdict*. Belfast: Blackstaff Press, 1995.

McAllister, I., *The Northern Ireland Social Democratic and Labour Party*. London: Macmillan, 1977.

Purdie, B., *Politics in the Streets: The Origins of the Civil Rights Movement in Northern Ireland*. Belfast: Blackstaff Press, 1990.

Rose, R., *Northern Ireland: A Time of Choice*. London: Macmillan, 1976.

Chapter 3

NORTHERN IRELAND 1972–95
Duncan Morrow

Introduction

By 1972, it was clear that the clashes over civil rights had brought Northern Ireland into its deepest crisis since partition. Not only had the Northern Ireland government resorted to emergency powers of arrest and internment without trial in defence of their position but by 1972 the British Conservative government had concluded that Northern Ireland's institutions were inadequate to the task of government in the province.

Certainly the security policies adopted by the Unionist government had failed even in their own terms. Far from quashing an emergent IRA, internment contributed to rapid recruitment and the escalation of political violence to a scale unknown in civil conflict in Britain or Ireland this century. In the course of 1972, the worst ever year for political violence, 467 people were killed, including 323 civilians. The atrocities of that year – Bloody Sunday, Bloody Friday, McGurk's Bar, Kelly's Bar, Callender Street, Abercorn – further deepened the spiralling crisis. Not only was the Provisional IRA now operating a full-scale terror campaign, but hardline, mass-membership Protestant paramilitary groups, such as the Ulster Defence Association (UDA) and Ulster Vanguard, made public shows of strength. Others tried to terrorize the Catholic community through a campaign of sectarian assassination.

Dilemmas and directions

After direct rule had been imposed, the new Secretary of State, William Whitelaw, like his successors, had to reconcile two fundamentally opposed positions. On the one hand he had to placate Unionist fears about threats to the state and to British sovereignty while simultaneously placating Nationalists who by 1972 were seeking radical reform, if not the abolition of Northern Ireland itself. After internment and Bloody Sunday, this task was an enormously difficult one for any British government.

The apparently irreconcilable goals of Unionism and Nationalism have been at the heart of the political problem in Northern Ireland. Following the eruption of political violence, the positions became more polarized than ever. Underlying trust, the irreducible component in political negotiation, was absent and terrorist bombs and emergency law did little to establish it. It was clear that military measures alone would not resolve the dilemmas. The main thrust of British policy for the next 20 years – security measures accompanied by repeated attempts at breaking the political log-jam – became established policy at an early stage. Nonetheless, there was always the danger that the one part of the policy would undermine the other.

The British government recognized from an early stage that long-term stability depended on the creation of political structures which could attract the support of the majority of both Unionists and Nationalists. This was easier said than done. Every attempt to rearrange the political framework met with objections from either one or the other. For republicans, indeed, all frameworks devised by the British were unacceptable, as the British presence was, of itself, the underlying problem. For Unionists, every attempt to bring anti-Unionists into power, whether in the form of Northern Irish Nationalists or through the formal involvement of the Republic of Ireland, diluted and threatened the Union itself.

Northern Ireland after 1972 was thus also a struggle about the sources and nature of political legitimacy. Unionists called for harsh measures to repress insurrection. Nationalists, ambivalent about or objecting to the claims to legitimacy of British rule in any part of Ireland, claimed a legitimacy for the Irish nation. Radicals in either camp claimed the right to decide who was and who was not a legitimate target for attack. A legitimacy which could transcend and combine these competing claims has been the holy grail of Northern Irish politics up to the present day.

Towards power-sharing

Following the collapse of a short-lived IRA ceasefire and the horror of Bloody Friday, Whitelaw sanctioned 'Operation Motorman', whereby troops forcibly entered the 'No Go' areas. The continuing IRA campaign enabled the main non-violent, or constitutional, Nationalist party, the Social Democratic and Labour Party (SDLP), to end its boycott of political talks. By the end of 1972, the British Prime Minister, Edward Heath, had met with Jack Lynch, Taoiseach (Prime Minister) of the Irish Republic, whose government was taking increasingly strong measures against the IRA.

A British government discussion paper, published in autumn 1972, attempted to reconcile the conflicting demands. Northern Ireland's position was guaranteed, dependent only on the support of the majority of the population in the province. However, the government suggested that Northern Ireland's government should take the form of inter-community power-sharing, whereby executive positions would be shared out between the parties in proportion to their strength. Nationalists were promised an 'Irish dimension'. These three elements – British sovereignty, Northern Ireland power-sharing and an Irish dimension – have been consistent threads in British policy on Northern Ireland ever since, albeit with significant changes in emphasis at different times.

The proposals were designed to appeal to various parts of the electorate. Crucially, while there was support in all places for some of the proposals, it was enormously difficult to maintain cross-community support for the package as a whole. This too was a pattern which was to reassert itself regularly. Thus the vast majority of Catholics boycotted the so-called 'Border Poll', a Northern Ireland-wide referendum held in March 1973, when 97.8% of those voting, representing 57% of all electors, indicated a wish to remain within the United Kingdom. At the same time, many Unionists baulked at proposals for an institutional Irish dimension.

Nonetheless, the government went ahead with its proposals. A White Paper in March 1973 [Cmnd 5259] proposed to devolve numerous powers back to an elected Assembly in Northern Ireland while retaining security and various other powers in the hands of a Cabinet-level Secretary of State. The Executive of the new Assembly had to satisfy the Secretary of State that it commanded wide cross-community support. There was to be a new Council of Ireland to regulate matters of common interest between Northern Ireland and the Republic.

The proposals met with a mixed response. Brian Faulkner, the leader of the Ulster Unionist Party, was cautious but willing to examine them. The SDLP and Alliance Party welcomed them. However, the proposals were rejected outright by a whole range of Unionists – Paisley's Democratic Unionist Party (DUP), the Vanguard Unionist Progressive Party (VUPP), the Orange Order, the UDA and dissident members of the Unionist Party itself. In elections for the Assembly, held on 28 June 1973, the profound nature of the split in Unionism was revealed. While Faulkner's Official Unionists gained 24 seats, anti-power-sharing Unionists combined won 26. Nonetheless, with 19 SDLP seats and eight for Alliance, Whitelaw determined to continue in the hope that the split among Unionists would give Faulkner enough room to manoeuvre.

Following negotiations throughout the summer and autumn, Whitelaw announced the formation of a power-sharing Executive in November 1973. With Brian Faulkner as Chief Executive and the SDLP leader Gerry Fitt as his deputy, the Executive met for the first time on 1 January 1974. In the interim, Whitelaw was surprisingly transferred from the Northern Ireland Office and replaced by Francis Pym. Negotiations between the Executive parties and the British and Irish governments at Sunningdale in Berkshire led to further agreement on the formation of a Council of Ireland.

In agreeing to a Council of Ireland, however, Faulkner's fragile hold on the Unionist Party was broken. In early January 1974, the Ulster Unionist Council rejected the Sunningdale Agreement. Riots broke out in the Assembly chamber. When Heath called a snap General Election for 28 February, the anti-Sunningdale Unionists and loyalists, organized as the United Ulster Unionist Council (UUUC), won 11 of the 12 Northern Ireland Westminster seats and 51% of the popular vote.

The power-sharing Executive was now in terminal decline. Despite support from Wilson's incoming Labour government, only disagreement among the anti-Executive Unionists delayed the final crisis. In May, a group of loyalist workers with close links to the UDA and other paramilitaries and calling themselves the Ulster Workers' Council (UWC), forced the hand of Unionist politicians by declaring a general strike. Closing off streets and turning people back from work, the strikers shut down all of the key Northern Irish industries. Loyalist bombs killed 32 people south of the border, the largest single total in any bombing. The British Army did not move against the strikers. On 28 May 1974, Faulkner withdrew his Unionist members from the Executive and the power-sharing experiment collapsed.

Picking up the pieces

The collapse of the Executive enraged the Labour government but left them powerless to engage in further immediate experiments. Direct rule was now the 'option of last resort' in Northern Irish politics. While rule from London was now becoming the norm, the psychological distance between Belfast and London was, if anything, greater than ever. As a result, the British government still regarded direct rule as a temporary, if prolonged, measure.

In the aftermath of the strike, the Labour government replaced the Assembly with a Constitutional Convention. Elections to the Convention were called for May 1975. The UUUC confirmed its majority status, winning 55% of the vote and 47 of the 78 Convention seats. In spite of the split between William Craig, leader of VUPP, and the rest of the UUUC over his suggestion of voluntary power-sharing arrangements, the hardline group within the UUUC had a controlling voice. Their majority report of November 1975 recommended an effective return to Stormont, allowing only for Catholic chairmanships of committees. As these proposals were entirely unacceptable to Nationalists and to the British and Irish governments, the Convention was wound up in March 1976.

The end of the Convention represented the end of constitutional experimentation for six years in Northern Ireland. Roy Mason, who replaced Merlyn Rees as Secretary of State in 1976, focused instead on technocratic measures, especially in the fields of law and order and social and economic policy. Security policy had already been tightened in the face of the first concerted bombing campaign by the IRA in England in late 1974. Following major bombs in London, Guildford and Birmingham, the Labour government passed the Prevention of Terrorism (Temporary Provisions) Act (PTA) in 1974. Intended as a temporary measure, the PTA was renewed annually every year up to and including 1995. Among its provisions, the most controversial in Northern Ireland was the introduction of 'internal exile' by which suspected terrorists could be refused entry to England, Scotland and Wales and returned or expelled to Northern Ireland.

By late 1975 detention without trial was ended in Northern Ireland, and from early 1976 the 'special category status' extended to those convicted of political offences was abolished. Despite protests by both republicans and loyalists, this measure did not seem to be extraordinarily controversial. Within five years, however, it had come to dominate the political agenda. The most significant social phenomenon of this period was the emergence of the Peace People in 1976. During 1976 and 1977 numerous large marches for peace were held. Increasingly, the Peace People became bogged down in internal disputes and jealousies, especially over the award of the Nobel Peace Prize in 1977, and the difficulty of translating a general revulsion against political violence into a coherent political programme.

The litany of bombing and shooting continued, although the numbers being killed declined after 1976. At the same time, the economic situation deteriorated, marked by increasing unemployment. Both of these factors may have contributed to the failure of a second general strike called by the United Ulster Action Council (UUAC) headed by Ian Paisley in 1977. Because of the active participation of paramilitaries, the Ulster Unionists refused to support the strike call. Despite its failure, the 1977 strike brought a new realignment of Unionism into focus. With the disappearance of the Vanguard and Faulkner's UPNI, the DUP emerged as the real rival to the Ulster or Official Unionist Party.

Ten men dead

The return to power of the Conservatives in Britain in 1979 was accompanied by increasing political controversy over the loss of special category status for paramilitary prisoners. For several years, republican prisoners in the Maze prison had been refusing to cooperate with the prison regime, demanding the return of 'political status'. The so-called blanket protest was broadened in October 1979 into a public campaign for 'five just demands'. In spite of a judgement against the prisoners by the European Commission of Human Rights in 1980, there were numerous and growing protest marches with increasing appeal to Nationalists including those usually unsympathetic to the aims of the IRA. In late October, seven republican prisoners in the so-called H-Blocks of the Maze prison declared a fast to death. In a climate of mounting tension, the strike was abandoned before Christmas following an apparent last-minute agreement. However, on 1 March 1981, Bobby Sands resumed the fast, accusing the government of failure to deliver on promises.

Five days after the beginning of the hunger strike, the independent Nationalist MP for Fermanagh–South Tyrone died. Following massive lobbying, Sands stood as a hunger-strike candidate. Under intense pressure not to split the Nationalist vote, the SDLP ultimately agreed not to put up a candidate of their own and recommended only that people abstain from voting. However, in an 87% turnout, Sands was elected by a majority of 1,500 votes, demonstrating the ability of the strikers to appeal to Nationalists far beyond the bounds traditionally associated with violent republicanism. The result electrified Northern Irish politics. Across the world, attention focused on the H-block dispute. Neither hunger-strikers nor the government were willing to compromise. Despite various visits and personal requests to end the hunger strike, Sands died on 5 May 1981. Nearly 100,000 people took part in his funeral procession in Twinbrook.

In the course of the next four months, nine further hunger-strikers died, followed each time by riots and increased IRA activity. By September, however, the families of hunger-strikers were increasingly intervening to stop the fasting, often at the instigation of Dungannon priest Father Denis Faul. Following discussions between prisoners and the new Secretary of State, James Prior, the strike was called off in October 1981.

The hunger strike again transformed the political landscape of Northern Ireland. Provisional Sinn Féin had abandoned the policy of electoral abstention and adopted a twin-track strategy of seeking an electoral mandate while continuing to support a sustained campaign of violent resistance, the armalite and ballot box strategy. Building on the groundswell of Nationalist support from the hunger strikes and the mass mobilization which it created, Provisional Sinn Féin sought to turn the momentum into political capital.

The political situation was now almost completely polarized. In both Unionist and Nationalist circles the radicals appeared to be in the ascendant. Following the opening of talks between the British and Irish governments in 1980, Ian Paisley led a series of demonstrations throughout Northern Ireland which he called the 'Carson trail', warning of an imminent sell-out of the Union. In local elections in May 1981, the vote of the DUP narrowly exceeded that of the UUP. When in November 1981, the UUP MP for South Belfast, Robert Bradford, was assassinated by IRA gunmen, Unionist anger threatened to boil over.

Breaking the deadlock?

If 1972 represented the bleakest year in military terms, then 1982 might be said to have been the bleakest in political terms. The DUP sought devolution without power-sharing. The Ulster Unionists sought either full integration into the United Kingdom or the implementation of the report of the Constitutional Convention. The Alliance Party sought devolution with power-sharing. The SDLP sought a copper-fastened Irish dimension while Sinn Féin demanded British withdrawal. James Prior's plan for 'rolling devolution', whereby power would be gradually handed over to a local Northern Irish assembly once cross-community cooperation had been established, led to elections in October but did not provide a solution. Sinn Féin captured over 10% of the vote, largely at the expense of the SDLP. Both Nationalist parties boycotted the Assembly from the outset, the SDLP protesting against the unwillingness of either Unionist party to share power. In the general election of June 1983, the president of Provisional Sinn Féin, Gerry Adams, was returned as MP for West Belfast as Sinn Féin further raised its share of the vote.

In the face of the impasse and the electoral rise of Sinn Féin, both British and Irish governments increasingly looked to each other. In November 1981, the governments set up the Anglo-Irish Intergovernmental Council (AIIGC) to facilitate regular meetings between civil servants and ministers. Furthermore, the SDLP was urgently looking to Dublin to provide support against Sinn Féin. It was rewarded when Garret Fitz Gerald established the New Ireland Forum in May 1983. The exclusion of Sinn Féin on the grounds of their support for political violence and the refusal of Unionist parties to participate restricted the Forum's range. Nonetheless, the combination of the Forum's deliberations and the increasingly frequent meetings between British and Irish government officials represented a real shift in approach to Northern Ireland. Instead of seeking internal cross-community agreement first, both governments were now engaged in a process which would try to build from agreement at intergovernmental level and only latterly depend on local cooperation.

Initially it appeared that the intergovernmental process had fallen at the first hurdle when Margaret Thatcher ruled out any of the Forum's proposed options for progress – Irish unity, federal Ireland or joint sovereignty between London and Dublin – and Charles Haughey, the leader of the Irish opposition, rejected the Forum's willingness to compromise on Irish unity. Nonetheless, the seriousness of the security situation had been brought home when, in October 1984, the IRA came within a whisker of killing the British Cabinet, including Margaret Thatcher, in a bomb at Brighton. The British interest in Irish cooperation over security and judicial questions thus coincided with the need on the Irish government side to deliver some recognizable progress to constitutional nationalism. Unionists in Northern Ireland were almost totally unprepared when Thatcher and Fitz Gerald signed the most important Anglo-Irish Agreement since partition at Hillsborough Castle on 15 November 1985.

Britain and Ireland say yes

Under the Agreement, there was to be an Intergovernmental Conference with a permanent Anglo-Irish secretariat based at Maryfield just outside Belfast. One of the ironies of the Anglo-Irish Agreement was that it established that part of the Sunningdale Agreement which had been so controversial, an Irish dimension, while leaving local arrangements undefined. These innovations, and the fact that a supposedly staunchly Unionist Prime Minister had signed the accord without any prior consultation with Unionists, inflamed loyalist anger. Republicans too were unhappy with the Agreement, particularly with the concession by the Irish government that sovereignty over Northern Ireland would only change if a majority inside the North so desired.

Unionists engaged in a campaign aimed at destroying the Agreement. Under the slogan 'Ulster says no', the largest protest demonstration seen since partition, between 50,000 and 100,000 people gathered outside Belfast City Hall. All UUP and DUP MPs resigned their Westminster parliamentary seats in protest. However, despite an increased Unionist vote, the SDLP gained a seat in the by-elections. Furthermore, the SDLP could claim that the Agreement had contributed to the decline in the Sinn Féin vote. Extra-parliamentary tactics were also fraught with danger for Unionist politicians. The civil disturbances of the 'day of action' on 3 March 1986 resulted in embarrassment for the Unionist leadership. Indeed, by adopting abstentionist tactics the Unionist parties looked increasingly like Sinn Féin. The refusal to strike a rate in district councils was easily overcome by the Northern Ireland Office striking one for them.

Although taken aback by the scale of the protest, the British government held firm. Cross-party support at Westminster and in the Dáil, (the lower house of the Irish Parliament), international approval of the accords and the practical benefits to both governments of security and political cooperation outweighed the costs of local opposition. Indeed, the very strength of the Agreement was that it could not be brought down by mass loyalist protest, as had happened in 1974.

Endgame in Ulster?

As the heat went out of the protest against the Agreement, a number of events again turned the spotlight on Nationalism. In a referendum on divorce in the Irish Republic in July 1986, 63.5% voted against reform of the constitutional ban. This seemed to reinforce the cultural cleft which divided Ireland, despite the Anglo-Irish Agreement. When in November 1987 a huge bomb exploded at the Remembrance Day ceremony in Enniskillen killing 10 civilians, there was worldwide condemnation of IRA activities. Events surrounding the shooting dead of three IRA volunteers in Gibraltar by British Army special agents (SAS) further underlined the antagonisms not far below the surface of politics in Northern Ireland.

By 1988 the steam had also gone out of Sinn Féin's attempt to establish itself as the leading Nationalist party in Northern Ireland. Talks between the leaders of the SDLP and Sinn Féin ended inconclusively, but it was clear that changes were taking place in Sinn Féin thinking. Unionists too were having to rethink their strategy. Furthermore, the number of people killed by terrorist violence was considerably smaller than the totals of the mid-1970s. By 1988 the economic and social doom and gloom of 1982–83 had been replaced by relative economic buoyancy. Public investment in housing and infrastructure was bearing fruit as the physical landscape of Belfast and other towns was transformed. Unemployment was falling. The retail and service sector boomed with the opening of numerous new shopping complexes.

Political progress remained slow, however. Following 'talks about talks' in 1989 and 1990 with the constitutional parties, a formal talks agenda was agreed by Secretary of State Peter Brooke. It was divided into the three separate strands recognizable since 1973: internal Northern Irish arrangements; North–South arrangements; and relations between the United Kingdom and the Republic of Ireland. To enable all parties to feel secure, the meetings took place on the basis that 'nothing is agreed until everything is agreed'. To meet Unionist objections, meetings of the Intergovernmental Conference were suspended for the duration. The talks stalled in 1991 but were resumed in Spring 1992 under a new Secretary of State Sir Patrick Mayhew. They ended inconclusively in November.

Political interest shifted to renewed talks between John Hume and Gerry Adams. Failure to publish the outcome of the talks caused considerable nervousness among Unionists. The combination of the Hume–Adams talks and the threat of open sectarian warfare galvanized the governments into action. Following a series of meetings, the Prime Ministers of the United Kingdom and the Republic of Ireland launched the Downing Street Declaration in December 1993.

Conclusions

The Declaration clearly heralded another potentially decisive moment in Northern Ireland politics. The strategy initiated in the Anglo-Irish Agreement in 1985, seeking an accommodation of the constitutional parties, was now regarded as inadequate in Dublin and London. On the other hand, the importance of the Dublin–London axis was unchanged. Now the governments signalled their interest in a comprehensive settlement including the paramilitaries. For the first time since 1969, the governments held out the prospect of an end to political violence with the prize of a lasting potential agreement not far behind. Publicly, however, the key question of legitimacy remained to be resolved. The search for a government acceptable to all the people has not yet come to a conclusive end.

Further reading

Arthur, P., *Government and Politics of Northern Ireland*. Harlow: Longman, 1987.

Bardon, J., *A History of Ulster*. Belfast: Blackstaff Press, 1992.

Bew, P. and Gillespie, G., *Northern Ireland: A Chronology of the Troubles 1968–1993*. Dublin: Gill and Macmillan, 1993.

Hadfield, B. (ed.), *Northern Ireland: Politics and the Constitution*. Buckingham and Philadelphia: Open University Press, 1992.

O'Dowd, L., Rolston, B. and Tomlinson, M., *Northern Ireland: Between Civil Rights and Civil War*. London: CSE Books, 1980.

O'Malley, P., *Uncivil Wars*. Belfast: Blackstaff Press, 1983.

Wichert, S., *Northern Ireland since 1945*. Harlow: Longman, 1991.

Wright, F., *Northern Ireland: A Comparative Analysis*. Dublin: Gill and Macmillan, 1987.

Appendix 3.1 Secretaries of State for Northern Ireland

Conservative	1972–73	William Whitelaw
	1973–74	Francis Pym
Labour	1974–76	Merlyn Rees
	1976–79	Roy Mason
Conservative	1979–81	Humphrey Atkins
	1981–83	James Prior
	1983–85	Douglas Hurd
	1985–89	Tom King
	1989–92	Peter Brooke
	1992–95	Sir Patrick Mayhew

Section Two

IDEAS AND MOVEMENTS

Chapter 4

UNIONISM
Arthur Aughey

Unionism and partition

Unionism as a self-conscious political identity and as a set of commitments may be said to have its origins in the transformation of political life which took place in Ireland in the 1870s and 1880s. As Irish Nationalists effectively mobilized the Catholic electorate in the name of self-government or Home Rule so defence of the Union of Great Britain and Ireland became the rallying cry for the majority of Irish Protestants. In the process, constitutional politics became party politics and party politics became almost exclusively confessional politics. The partisan passions of this constitutional struggle were most acute in Ulster where Protestantism and Unionism had an effective popular basis. The distinctiveness of Ulster (the nine counties) from the rest of Ireland – its Protestant majority and its industrialized economy around Belfast – was, as far as Irish Unionists were concerned, the political exception which disproved the case for Home Rule. While Irish Unionists could argue a good general case for the economic and political benefits of Ireland's remaining within the Union and the value of remaining at the heart of the British Empire (much as, though in very different circumstances, it is argued today that a member state should not leave the European Union), Ulster Unionists could point to the practical evidence of their province's undoubted prosperity. Protestant Ulster's popular resistance to constitutional change was to be the Unionist tactic for preventing Home Rule for Ireland as a whole.

Ulster Unionism, then, was but one part of a wider political identity which embraced both southern Irish and British Unionism. In the battle over Irish Home Rule in the first two decades of the twentieth century, Ulster Unionists were strong enough to prevent the detachment of the *six* counties of what is now Northern Ireland from the United Kingdom. But in the process the wider Unionist identity was diminished and Unionism's intellectual appeal significantly weakened. Therefore, claims that the partition of Ireland represented an historic 'victory' for Unionism need to be severely qualified. Partition can just as well be understood in terms of the disintegration of the powerful British–Irish Unionist alliance as it can be understood in terms of Unionist success. Or, more to the point, it could be interpreted as both failure *and* success.

That the partition of Ireland was a success for Unionism ignores the experience of southern Unionists (and, in particular, the fate of Ulster Unionists in the three counties of Monaghan, Donegal and Cavan). The cost of the exclusion of Ulster from the Home Rule settlement might be, as the Conservative leader Bonar Law once confided to the Liberal Prime Minister Asquith in 1913, that southern Unionists would be 'thrown to the wolves'. Indeed, the settlement which emerged in the 1920s did leave southern Unionists outside the Union. The old Anglo-Irish Ascendancy was left to fend for itself within the new Catholic democracy of the 26-county Free State. And abandoned by the North, one of the ironies of history is that the sufferings of southern Protestants as recounted in Northern Ireland's Unionist newspapers – their intimidation, their murder, their flight, their falling numbers – enabled the Ulster Unionist Party to consolidate its own regime in the difficult years before the Second World War.

The simple view of Unionist success also ignores the weakening of British Unionism and the profound consequences which that was to have for the character of the state in Northern Ireland. Defence of the Union had been an affair which had absorbed much of the energy of the British Conservative (and Unionist) Party for the best part of a generation. The settlement arrived at in 1920–21 was one defined by a British Conservative willingness to compromise in Ireland rather than to seek a Unionist victory. In the end it was all rather messy. Old allies were ditched; Home Rule was given to a six-county Ulster (which never asked for it in the first place); and concessions were made to Irish Nationalist ambition – such as dominion status for the 26 counties – which would have been inconceivable a decade earlier. While maintenance of the Union remained a matter of absolute principle for Ulster Unionists, it had become of diminishing significance for most politicians at Westminster. This distinction between principled Ulster Unionism and pragmatic British Unionism has been a constant theme of Northern Ireland's history. It lies at the heart of Unionist suspicions of the intent of successive British governments, suspicions greatly increased by the developments which have taken place in the last 25 years.

It is another irony that 'success' for Ulster Unionists – who had fought against Home Rule for Ireland – was to mean that they alone became responsible for the conduct of Home Rule as originally envisaged for Ireland. This was one consequence of the effective mobilization of popular Protestantism in the north, though one which Unionist leaders did not originally desire. But despite the famous claim by the leader of the Ulster Unionists, Sir James Craig (later Lord Craigavon), that Home Rule for Northern Ireland was only reluctantly accepted in the interests of peace, few Ulster Unionists by 1920 disputed its necessity or its possibilities for their own security. Unionism was to be the exclusive *governing* ideology in Northern Ireland until the prorogation of the Stormont Parliament in 1972. This experience engendered a definite style of Unionist practice.

Unionism in power

The practice of Unionism has been 'conservative' in the precise sense of devotion to the conservation of the constitutional link between Great Britain and Northern

Ireland. For much of its history Ulster Unionism has been closely attached to the Conservative Party as well. Most Unionists believe that the settlement of the 1920s should have been acknowledged as the final chapter of the Irish question. And it is very noticeable how frequently the language of finality and permanence recurs throughout the history of Unionist politics. Thus for Craig the Government of Ireland Act of 1920 was 'a final settlement'. Seventy years later, William Ross MP spoke of the Talks process, set in train by the former Northern Ireland Secretary of State, Peter Brooke, as involving deliberation about a 'final conclusion' to political initiatives about the future of Northern Ireland. Finality means, as it has always done to Unionism, successful resistance to the ambitions of Irish Nationalism and a permanent guarantee for Northern Ireland as part of the United Kingdom. How did Unionists confront the disturbing and threatening challenge of Irish Nationalism after 1920? The conservative disposition of Unionism issued in a style of politics which was both rational in the circumstances and, for most of this century, reasonably successful in its own terms. There were two broad aspects to it, political unity and political parity.

The first imperative was to achieve and to maintain, as far as possible, Unionist unity. Only on the basis of effective Unionist solidarity could Nationalist 'conspiracy' to subvert the status quo be confronted. This was the task of the Ulster Unionist Party which governed Northern Ireland from 1921 to 1972. Unity was secured, firstly, within the structure of the party's own organization by its association with all bodies of Unionist opinion, particularly with the Orange Order. These associations ensured a popular base for Unionist politics, a well-organized structure and a cross-class alliance of interests. Secondly, it was secured by way of the effective mobilization of the Unionist vote on the issue of the border, an issue which became the focus of every election in Northern Ireland. Thirdly, the patronage of Unionist political authority under the devolved Stormont system was used – where it was possible to use it – to ensure that loyalty to Unionism received its reward and disloyalty went unrewarded. One consequence of this Protestant Unionist unity, mobilized as a governing bloc, was the perpetuation of Catholic disaffection. However, there were also tensions within Unionism itself between the cautiously conservative and the radically populist elements of that alliance. With the onset of the Troubles in the late 1960s, Unionism experienced organizational and political division very broadly along the fault lines of that tension and this has characterized its history of the last 25 years.

The second broad aspect was political parity, a principle which meant that as far as possible Northern Ireland should keep in step with the major legislative developments in the rest of the United Kingdom. This principle of parity was designed to disprove the assertion which the Unionist leader Sir Edward Carson had made about the danger of Irish Home Rule, namely that there could be no half-way house between Union and separation. The Irish Free State *had* become ultimately a Republic, abandoning the British connection. Unionism, by contrast, was determined to ensure that devolved government at Stormont would not mean this sort of disengagement from the rest of the United Kingdom. In welfare and expenditure terms, Unionist governments had to struggle against the parsimonious instincts of the British Treasury in London. It was only after the end of the

Second World War that parity of public service provision was conceded by London. Arguably, it has been only since the onset of direct rule in the 1970s that Northern Ireland has made up the historic gap in public spending between it and the rest of the United Kingdom. In the end, the tasks of devolved government were limited ones for Unionism, albeit dominated by two priorities: firstly, ensuring control of security and physical protection, and secondly, holding Ulster for the Union.

The character of Unionism

There is significant diversity of opinion about what precisely defines Unionism. Scholars recently have debated the priority of religion, nationality, colonialism and citizenship in Unionist politics. Moreover, there is quite a diversity of opinion among Unionists themselves about what it is that constitutes their identity. Some critics have argued that there exists a 'crisis' of Unionist identity precisely because of this diversity. Many Nationalists argue that this crisis can only be resolved once Unionists become part of the Irish nation. Is it possible to define what is common to and what has, at times of crisis, tended to hold together this diversity within Unionism?

Distilling this complex political brew, one could argue that at the heart of the Unionist understanding appear to be two distinct though practically interrelated ideas. The first holds that membership of the United Kingdom represents a clear and unequivocal definition of British political status. To live in Northern Ireland, in other words, ought to mean that one is accorded equality of citizenship with everyone else who lives in the United Kingdom. Unionists have been insistent that this represents the minimum acknowledgement of their 'Britishness'. The particular circumstances of Northern Ireland might demand special treatment (especially on security issues) but special treatment must not threaten its status. Some might articulate this position in terms of an ethnic identity, of the rights of the 'Protestant people' in Ulster and of the British way of life. It has been also articulated in terms of the statehood of Northern Ireland, understood as the acceptance by the majority of the authority of the Crown-in-Parliament and therefore of the full legitimacy of Northern Ireland's position within the United Kingdom.

For instance, it was not 'Britishness' as an ethnic identity which Unionists pledged themselves to maintain under the famous Covenant of 1912 but something much more civic, namely the 'cherished position of equal citizenship in the United Kingdom', a notion embracing both 'civil and religious liberty' and 'material well-being'. For Unionists to choose the Union as opposed to a separate Irish state was not seen, at that time, in terms of replacing their Irish identity with an exclusively British one. It was to assert that it was possible and sensible to be both Irish and loyal to the Union. On the other hand, critics have argued that this status claimed by Unionists has involved the denial of an equal status to Nationalists and therefore inevitably involved a culture of Protestant supremacy. In this context is usually cited the famous remark by Craigavon in 1933 that he was glad to preside over a Protestant parliament and a Protestant state.

Craigavon made that remark in response to the claim by Éamon de Valera, leader of the governing party in the south, Fianna Fáil, that Ireland was a Catholic state. As he explained his position in the Northern Ireland House of Commons some years later, Craigavon argued that while he accepted that the government of southern Ireland should be carried on along lines which were appropriate to its Catholic majority, it was surely right that the government of Northern Ireland should be conducted in a manner appropriate to the wishes and desires of its Protestant majority. For Unionists like Craigavon, the settlement of the 1920s had divided Ireland effectively into zones of majoritarian democracy. The southern parliament embodied Catholic majoritarianism (which it defined as Irish) and the northern parliament embodied Protestant majoritarianism (which it defined as British). The premiership of Terence O'Neill in the 1960s and his meeting with Seán Lemass was a tentative step towards changing those assumptions on both sides. The end of Unionist political control in the 1970s painfully shattered the assumption of Unionist hegemony so clearly expressed by Craigavon 40 years previously.

The second idea is that this Unionist British status, founded on the democratic will of the majority, ought to be durable. This attitude is fixed in terms of the justice of the constitutional arrangements guaranteeing Northern Ireland's place within the Union. In other words, there ought to be no change in the status of Northern Ireland unless and until there is a change in the 'general will' of the people (understood as the 'consent of the majority'). In practice, this has meant a determination on the part of Ulster Unionists to accept no political initiative which could be judged to attenuate the British citizenship of those who live in Northern Ireland. And this determination has also provided a mandate to Unionist politicians to reject any set of arrangements based on the idea of the natural *political* unity of the island of Ireland. For the Ulster Unionist there is today (unlike a century before) no natural political unity in Ireland. There are, depending on whether culture or politics is stressed, two nations or two states on the island of Ireland.

This popular mandate goes some way towards explaining the behaviour of Unionists in recent periods of crisis such as 1973–74 and 1985. In both instances, the Council of Ireland as proposed by the Sunningdale agreement of 1973 and the Conference and Secretariat as laid down by the Anglo-Irish Agreement of 1985 were judged – rightly or wrongly – to be institutions formed on the assumption of the natural political unity of Ireland. To accept the 'natural' political unity of the island is by definition to concede the illegitimacy of the Unionist position. The majority of Unionists came to give their support to those who opposed these initiatives, successfully in the first instance, unsuccessfully in the second instance. This attitude has been repeated in the reception of the Framework Documents of February 1995.

These two ideas, status and durability, provide the key to understanding the meaning of self-determination within Unionist politics. The key statement of Unionist self-determination is that membership of the United Kingdom ought to be a clear definition of political status and that that status should be durable and properly acknowledged. Thus the exercise of self-determination in this form has been negative rather than positive. It has been about avoiding separate political development within the British state rather than about encouraging it. As such, Unionism has advanced an idea of self-determination which is the opposite of that of Irish Nationalism. Nationalists demand self-determination for the (Irish) people as a means of establishing a constitution whose purpose is to distinguish and to differentiate a specific political community (the people of Ireland from the people of Britain). Although there have been, of course, demands made by Protestant groups for Ulster independence at regular intervals in the last 25 years, this notion of self-determination has never been electorally popular within Unionism.

Devolved government at Stormont, as we have seen, only worked for Unionists so long as it operated on the basis of holding Northern Ireland close to the prevailing policies of the rest of the United Kingdom and preventing separate development (the parity principle). For separate development has been understood as movement towards Irish unity. Once the old Stormont system collapsed, how best to secure the maintenance of the Union became a contested issue within Unionism. If, in the changed circumstances of the last quarter of the twentieth century, it was not possible to reconstruct Stormont as a 'bulwark' of the Union then it might be possible to democratize direct rule and achieve proper integration into the British state. 'Integrationism' thus became a powerful argument within Unionism in the 1980s and 1990s.

The thrust of integrationist argument has been this. If negative on the idea of self-determination, certain Unionist arguments could be interpreted as a positive commitment to the idea of the Union as a multi-national state and one capable of respecting cultural diversity as well as ensuring proper levels of individual welfare. This was the substance of the claims advanced by the Campaign for Equal Citizenship (CEC) in the 1980s. In this formulation, Unionism could present itself not as a political anachronism but as relevant to the changing character of the United Kingdom. This is a tradition which can be traced back to the liberal Unionists at the turn of the century, and to some of the views of Sir Edward Carson. It is a tradition which was never wholly submerged in the passions of Northern Ireland politics.

The challenge to Unionism today

Since 1969 Unionism has been on the defensive. Because, as we have argued, Unionism is essentially conservative in constitutional outlook this is not a surprising conclusion. There has developed the impression that Unionists have lost control over their own destiny. Many Unionists feel that their position is being bartered away in secret deals between the British and Irish governments. This helps to explain the behaviour of Unionists from the Anglo-Irish Agreement of November 1985 to the Framework Documents of 1995.

The Unionist response was based on a sense that what they understand the Union to be – a definitive measure of their status and a durable constitutional arrangement – is being transformed by the Agreement into something very different: the very opposite in fact. In this view of things, Northern Ireland's constitutional status after November 1985 has become re-expressed as a political process that is designed to ensure movement towards a framework which would be substantially Irish and only residually British; in other words, from the Union as Unionists understand it towards some form of all-Irish arrangement, be it joint authority, federal Ireland or unitary state, the solutions of the New Ireland Forum Report of 1984. Rather than being durable, the Union, it is feared, could become a transitional form designed to edge Northern Ireland out of the United Kingdom. This would involve some means of getting around the principle of majority consent in order to facilitate British disengagement from Northern Ireland. These notions of process and transition are largely Nationalist notions and seem to promote a negative view of the Union (the illegitimate British presence) attached to a positive idea of Irish national self-determination (the historic destiny of the Irish people).

Thus, the avowed and laudable purpose of the Agreement was to foster a change in the cultures of both Ulster Unionism and Irish Nationalism to enable opposing identities to be accommodated within a balanced set of political institutions. Unionists did not perceive a new balance in these arrangements. They perceived a new imbalance which, it was argued, privileged the Nationalist 'aspiration' to Irish unity at the expense of the Unionist 'right' to be British. This is what James Molyneaux, the former leader of the Ulster Unionist Party, meant when he argued in the House of Commons during the debate on the Agreement that only 'rights can be guaranteed, not aspirations'. For the fear informing this argument is that the 'aspiration' to Irish unity would become transformed into a 'right'. And that is what some Unionists believe to have happened eight years later under the formulation of the Downing Street Declaration of December 1993 where it states that a united Ireland 'as of right' may be the outcome of policy 'over a period'. The Democratic Unionist Party has taken this to be the mark of another attempt to 'sell-out' the Union. Many Unionists believe this to have been confirmed in the details of the Framework Documents of 1995.

These critics can also point to the language of the Declaration which talks of two different collective entities – the 'people of Ireland' and 'the people of Britain'. On two counts this language offends the sensibilities of Unionism. Either Unionism has proposed that it is exclusively British and not Irish; or it has proposed that it is possible to be both Irish and British. To suggest, as the Declaration does, that Unionists are exclusively a part of the 'people of Ireland' is deeply disturbing to many.

Conclusions

At the beginning of this century Unionists in Ireland and Great Britain looked to Ulster as the means by which to avoid Home Rule for Ireland. There were two facts about the north which appeared to undermine the Nationalist case. In the first place, Ulster (the traditional nine counties) had a Protestant majority which did not identify itself with the Catholic Nationalist cause. In the second place, the north, and in particular the Belfast region, was the most prosperous and did not identify itself with the Catholic Nationalist cause. In the second place, the north, and in particular the Belfast region, was the most prosperous and industrially advanced area of Ireland. It had prospered under the Union and its industrial and commercial interests were opposed to any Home Rule settlement which might jeopardize their place in the British and imperial markets.

In Northern Ireland today Unionists are still in a majority and are still opposed to any weakening of the link with Great Britain. Even Irish Nationalists also acknowledge that the strength of the Unionist case is partly the strength of their numbers. The strength of Unionism is not simply the argument of numbers alone. That strength lies in the existence of the Union itself. However suspicious Unionists may be about the Anglo-Irish Agreement, the Downing Street Declaration and the Framework Documents, the essential structure of the Union of Great Britain and Northern Ireland remains a fact.

On the other hand, of course, Northern Ireland's industrial and commercial significance has withered. It can be seen no longer, as it was only a generation ago (by both Unionists and Nationalists), as the great engine-room of Irish prosperity. Ironically, the economic and welfare dependency of employers and citizens in Northern Ireland today has probably meant a strengthening rather than a weakening of the economic argument for the Union. The present level of British public expenditure necessary to support living standards in Northern Ireland is something which all parties are keen to maintain.

The resources of Unionism today – political, institutional and economic – are much weaker than they were at the beginning of this century. Nevertheless Unionism remains an essential factor in any settlement envisaged for Northern Ireland.

Further Reading

Aughey, A., *Under Siege: Ulster Unionism and the Anglo-Irish Agreement*. Belfast: Blackstaff Press, 1989.

Bell, G., *The Protestants of Ulster*. London: Pluto Press, 1976.

Bew, P., Gibbon, P. and Patterson, H., *1921–94 Northern Ireland, Political Forces and Social Classes*. London: Serif, 1995.

Bruce, S., *God Save Ulster! The Religion and Politics of Paisleyism*, Oxford: Oxford University Press, 1986.

Bruce, S., *The Edge of the Union, The Ulster Loyalist Political Vision*. Oxford: Oxford University Press, 1994.

Coulter, C., 'The character of Unionism', *Irish Political Studies*. 9, 1994.

Foster, J.W. (ed.), *The Idea of the Union*. Vancouver and Belfast: Belcouver Press, 1995.

Kennedy, D., *The Widening Gulf: Northern Attitudes to the Independent Irish State*. Belfast: Blackstaff Press, 1988.

Todd, J., 'Two traditions in Unionist political culture', *Irish Political Studies*. 2, 1987.

Whyte, J., *Interpreting Northern Ireland*. Oxford: Clarendon Press, 1990.

Wright, F., 'Protestant ideology and politics in Ulster', *European Journal of Sociology*, 24, 1973.

Chapter 5

NATIONALISM
Henry Patterson

Irish Nationalists in the province of Ulster entered the twentieth century optimistic about their political future. Like Nationalists throughout the island, they were relying on the Irish Parliamentary Party in alliance with British Liberals to deliver a substantial form of self-government for the island as a whole. The opposition of Irish Unionism and particularly of Ulster Unionists to Home Rule tended to be dismissed as a mixture of bigotry and the defence of vested interest. However when the depth and strength of the Ulster Unionist mobilization forced the question of partition to be taken seriously by the Liberal Government in London and the leader of Irish Nationalists, John Redmond, the major dilemmas of northern Nationalism quickly surfaced.

The decision by the leader of Northern Nationalism, Joe Devlin, MP for West Belfast, to support Redmond's acceptance of partition, even on a temporary basis, produced a major schism which continued to divide Nationalists within the new state. The division to some extent mirrored the broader process by which the moderate constitutionalists were displaced by the militants of Sinn Féin in the process of 'militarization' of Irish politics beginning with the 1916 insurrection. Ulster was the only province where the older parliamentary Nationalist tradition did not succumb totally to the assault of Sinn Féin.

Sinn Féin's leadership was even less inclined than the Redmondites had been to seek a compromise with Unionism. For Éamon de Valera, the Unionists were a 'rock on the road' to a united and sovereign Ireland and the use of force was legitimate to clear them out of the way. However, the use of force in the IRA's struggle to destroy British rule in the rest of the island would contribute powerfully to the deepening of communal divisions in the north. The Nationalism of many Catholics in Belfast and the east of the province was affected by an intense fear that partition would mean not simply separation from the rest of the Irish nation but their submission to a form of 'Orange' rule. For them militant rhetoric or deeds on the part of Sinn Féin could have distinctly negative effects.

Devlin had reflected these fears when he had been prepared to contemplate partition if it was combined with the continuation of Irish representation at Westminster and the partitioned area continuing to be directly ruled from Westminster. However, such a willingness to approach a complex problem with a

39

degree of flexiblity was anathema to the dominant forces in Irish Nationalism and Ulster Unionism after 1916.

Nationalists marooned

Nationalism entered the new state divided and increasingly demoralized. In the first elections for the Northern Ireland parliament in May 1921 Sinn Féin obtained almost double the first preference votes of the Devlinite candidates. However, much of this vote reflected a view that Sinn Féin was the most capable of opposing partition, a calculation soon shown to be mistaken. Sinn Féin was also substantially stronger in the border counties of Fermanagh and Tyrone, Derry city, south Armagh and south Down. Here Nationalists expected that the Boundary Commission clause in the Treaty would transfer them to the southern state and maintained a distrust of Devlin for his willingness to consider a six-county partition settlement even on a temporary basis.

Many hoped that a Northern Ireland shorn of at least two of its counties and its second city would be unviable and they were for a time encouraged by the leaders of Sinn Féin in the south not to recognize the new state. Their MPs refused to enter the new parliament, councils under their control declared their allegiance to the Dáil and for a brief period primary school teachers had their salaries paid from Dublin. But even before their hopes in the Boundary Commission were dashed, northern Nationalists of both camps were to learn that political leaders in the south did not put the partition issue or the situation of the Catholic minority in Northern Ireland at the top of their list of priorities.

The Sinn Féin party in the south split on the Treaty, which ended the Anglo-Irish war, but the bitter Civil War which followed revolved around the issue of the sovereignty of the new 26-county state with partition a marginal concern. Sinn Féin and IRA members in the north supported the pro-Treaty side overwhelmingly. The Civil War effectively removed the IRA as a military force from the north as its members went south to fight. It also strengthened the position of the more moderate Nationalists who had argued that Sinn Féin's national leadership had never understood the north and that their extremism and support for violence actually worsened the position of northern Catholics.

For Devlin and his supporters, abstentionism was a recipe for deepening the impotence and marginality of northern Catholics. Despite the argument of apologists for the Unionist regime, the sectarian and exclusivist features of the Northern Ireland state were not simply the unfortunate response of a 'beseiged' majority to a minority united in opposition to the very existence of the state. In fact, given the intensity of the violence attending the period of state formation (1920–22), particularly in Belfast, and in which the Catholic population suffered disproportionately, the very existence of a Nationalist constituency for recognition of the state was remarkable.

Partition plus devolution had been the nightmare scenario of even the most moderate of Nationalists whose fear of rule by Protestants considerably outweighed their dismay at being separated from their co-religionists on the rest of the island. Sir James Craig, Northern Ireland's first Prime Minister, had declared in February 1921 that 'The rights of the minority must be sacred to the majority . . . it will only be by broad views, tolerant ideas and a real desire for liberty of conscience that we here can make an ideal of the parliament and the executive.' Already minority attitudes to the new regime had been coloured by the sectarian violence unleashed in the Belfast shipyard expulsions in July 1920: in the next two years over 8,000 workers, the majority Catholic, lost their jobs through intimidation and 23,000 were driven from their homes. For the minority, this was a state-sponsored 'pogrom'. This interpretation ignores the degree to which Protestant violence was itself regarded as a response to IRA actions and also exaggerates the degree to which events were orchestrated from above. Nevertheless, the failure of any Unionist leader to condemn the expulsions and the involvement of members of the new state's security forces in sectarian violence reinforced the conviction that partition was incompatible with justice for the minority.

Despite this, there was from the mid-1920s a serious attempt by northern Nationalists to work within the new parliament. This reflected the temporary weakening of border Nationalist militancy. The Civil War, the agreement of the Dublin and Belfast governments to ignore the Boundary Commission report and a widespread tendency to see militancy as actually worsening the minority's position all tended to strengthen the position of those who argued that abstentionism simply allowed untrammelled Unionist rule. Yet participation brought few benefits. Whatever his earlier statements or his own personal inclinations, Craig did little to discourage a tendency for government ministers to openly proclaim the 'Protestant' nature of the state and ignore the existence of a significant sector of Nationalist opinion which sought redress and reform within the system. The participationist tendency was undermined by the predominant strategy of Protestant populism followed by Ulster Unionism in power. From the mid-1930s only two Nationalist MPs regularly attended the Stormont parliament.

Yet abstentionism was fraught with problems. Northern Nationalism looked increasingly to Dublin to resolve its dilemmas, but the response was little more helpful than at the time of the Boundary Commission. Requests from northern Nationalists to be allowed to sit in the Dáil and for Fianna Fáil to organize in the north were brusquely rejected as de Valera made it clear that his priority was the attainment of a fully sovereign 26-county state.

A policy of abstentionism also had implications for Nationalism's ability to maintain province-wide support. By the 1930s the entry of Fianna Fáil into constitutional politics in the Free State had completed the process whereby the former Sinn Féin support base in the north had shifted towards a grudging accommodation with the Devlinites with the formation in 1928 of a new Nationalist organization, the National League. However, the National League was still unable to transcend the division between those Nationalists who still bitterly resented inclusion in the northern state and were contemptuous of participation in its institutions and the more pragmatic current which saw abstentionism as a recipe for powerlessness.

Nationalism's social philosophy

The problem for the participationists was not simply the sectarian character of the state. Nationalism proved incapable of developing a specific social and economic programme which might have spoken to the needs of the working-class Catholic community or have made cross-communal alliances with Labour and Independent Unionist critics of the Unionist Party. Devlin had long propounded a form of working-class Nationalism reflecting his constituency in Belfast and from time to time talked of a populist alliance crossing the sectarian divide. But after his death in 1934 the tone of the party was set by the Catholic lower middle-class of solicitors, publicans and hoteliers who, with the clergy, dominated what political organization existed. One result was embarrassment and a retreat from Belfast in the face of the onset of social democratic politics and the welfare state in the post-war period. Already in the 1920s a leading northern Nationalist had warned the infant Fianna Fáil party that unless a widening gap in living standards since partition was dealt with, it 'could act as a barrier to National Unity'. The Nationalist MP, Cahir Healy, would return to the theme in 1939 when he warned de Valera of the erosion of the 'national spirit' in Northern Ireland by 'the English dole system and the other social services'. The gap became a chasm with the extension of the welfare state to the province after 1945; northern Nationalism became more stridently anti-partitionist at the same time as it effectively conceded that it had nothing to offer working-class Catholics in the state's capital city.

The war years, 'The Emergency' as it was termed in a neutral Irish state, were the high point of de Valeran Nationalism. Spurred on by the dictum that 'England's difficulty is Ireland's opportunity', some Nationalists in the north looked to a possible German victory as a means of realizing unity. They included Cahir Healy, a fervent anti-communist and admirer of the British fascist, Oswald Mosley, and the Archbishop of Armagh, Cardinal Macrory, who had been a Sinn Féin supporter. More disturbingly for the Nationalist mainstream was the increasing evidence that the 1930s had seen a recrudescence of the physical force Nationalism of the IRA. Beneath the formal unity of the National League there remained the unresolved tension between abstentionism and participationism.

The decade after the war witnessed an increasing disparity between the traditional structures and objectives of Nationalism and domestic and international conditions. Northern Catholics benefited from the new National Health Service and the Butler Education Act. Well aware that their material conditions were much better in the north than they would be in the south, their Nationalism increasingly reflected more their communal identity in a state which remained stubbornly Protestant than an active commitment to a united Ireland.

Outside Belfast post-war Nationalism threw its energies into a new Anti-Partition League whose objective was to pressurize the Labour government to reopen the partition question. The campaign, which was taken up and re-echoed in the south in the All-Party Anti-Partition campaign launched in 1949, got an unsurprisingly negative response from London where Ulster Unionism benefited from the south's neutrality in the war. Just as the increased British subvention to extend the welfare state to the north and aid its process of industrial diversification materially strengthened the Unionist position, the Ireland Act of 1949 provided a symbolic strengthening of the Union.

In the 1950s northern Nationalism was characterized by a clear division between a rural and small-town Nationalist Party which clung to anti-partitionism despite the failure of the post-war campaign and a Belfast-based mix of parties which paid lip-service to republican socialism. The very substantial electoral support for Sinn Féin in the Westminster elections of 1955, when it won two seats, demonstrated little about Catholic support for republicanism but quite a lot about the minority community's sense of embattled distance from the Northern Ireland state. When the IRA launched an armed campaign against the northern state on the back of Sinn Féin's electoral successes, it soon became apparent that it had wrongly assumed that antagonism to Unionism meant opposition to the very existence of the state itself. Here it shared with the Nationalist mainstream a pronounced tendency to confuse questions of democracy and civil rights with the national question.

Civil rights

It was only when Nationalism was able to separate the issues of reform from those of the very right of the state to exist that it emerged as a major threat to Unionist hegemony. The forces that produced this change came from outside the old assumptions and structures of Northern Ireland. British welfarism has been credited with a large degree of responsibility through its role in creating a new middle class of university-educated Catholics impatient with the negative politics of the Nationalist Party. New organizations appeared at the end of the 1950s and early 1960s such as National Unity and its successor, the National Democratic Party.

In the early 1960s young modernizers like John Hume demanded that northern Nationalism develop a positive agenda for change within Northern Ireland as a precondition for an ultimate unity that would have to be based on consent. Hume and other modernizers developed a critique of a Nationalist Party that lacked the attributes of a modern political party: there was no structure of branches and no party conference. Crucial to the challenge to the Nationalist Party was the emergence for the first time of a credible strategy for reform of the state. Two decades of effectively social democratic government in Britain had undermined the insulation of Northern Ireland from the rest of the United Kingdom which partition plus devolution had encouraged. The sharp rise in support for the Northern Ireland Labour Party (NILP) at the end of the 1950s reflected popular expectation that the government had an obligation to produce similar economic conditions, particularly full employment, to those which existed in the rest of the UK. These pressures increased the already large degree of dependence of the Unionist administration on British Treasury goodwill and reduced their capacity to resist pressure for reform from London. For the first time in the history of the state it began to appear possible to enlist the support of London in pressuring for change in the structures of the northern state while leaving the question of its ultimate constitutional status to one side.

At the time and since, Ulster Unionists accused the civil rights movement of being a Trojan Horse for what was essentially an unchanged anti-partitionist agenda. This ignores the strong sense of many in the leadership of the movement that it did indeed mark a departure from the failed strategies of constitutional anti-partitionism and physical force republicanism. However, the majority of them remained committed to unity as an ultimate objective and thus still underestimated the depth of grass-roots Unionist resistance to the goal of Irish unity no matter how it was expressed. Nevertheless, at its core, the demands of the civil rights movement – 'British rights for British citizens' – represented a radical departure from traditional Nationalist language. The fact that many in the leadership and the mass base of the movement saw the demands as a means of undermining the state does not detract from this shift. The civil rights movement contained important elements of change as well as undeclared continuity.

The violence of August 1969 contributed to the re-emergence of Nationalist traditionalism. Many observers believe that this reflected not so much the emergence of a hidden agenda as the continued hesitation on the part of the Labour government about introducing direct rule from Westminster. If direct rule had been introduced after 1969 (as Harold Wilson had threatened), the reformist and modernizing element in the civil rights movement might have remained in control. Whatever the case, the arrival of British troops, welcomed initially as a protection against Protestant violence, soon became interpreted as a prop for a divided and unreconstructed Unionist regime. This was the context for the rebirth of physical force Nationalism in the north as the miniscule IRA, which had been unprepared for August 1969, was inundated by young Catholics looking for the weapons and training necessary to defend their areas.

A direct product of the civil rights movement's brief but spectacular mobilization of the Catholic community was the creation of a new party, the Social Democratic and Labour Party (SDLP) in 1970. As its name suggested, although a Nationalist party it sought to transcend the limited reach and strategic bankruptcy of its predecessor. However, the party's determination to bring the majority of northern Catholics into one electoral bloc demanded a reflection of more traditional currents of opinion.

Traditionalism was also encouraged by the communal polarization associated with the intensifying violence and the re-emergence of the IRA as a paramilitary force with significant popular support. As the Unionist regime disintegrated and the British government was drawn back reluctantly into direct involvement in the affairs of Northern Ireland, an increasing amount of the violence flowed from confrontations between the working-class Catholic communities of Belfast and Londonderry and the British Army. It was from these communities that the Provisional IRA emerged. It was created in 1969 from dissidents in the existing republican movement who accused it of failure to defend northern Catholics from state and sectarian violence and of subordinating its military role to Marxist politics.

From civil rights to national rights . . . and back again

Within the first four years of its existence the SDLP displayed the degree to which it still faced the dilemma which had divided northern Nationalism since the formation of the state: participation versus abstentionism. Thus, even before internment a willingness to participate at Stormont was overtaken by the pressure of events: the shooting dead of two civilians by the Army in Londonderry in July 1971. Refused an inquiry, the party withdrew from Stormont. Internment solidified the abstentionist position as the SDLP supported mass protests such as a rent and rate strike.

Faced with a fast-growing republican movement whose campaign of bombings and shootings was aimed first to destroy Stormont and then to force the British government to negotiate a withdrawal from the province, abstentionism put into question what the SDLP's difference from republicanism, except the rejection of violence, really was. There were two responses. The first was an attempt to map out a stage of constitutional transition. This was done in 'Towards a New Ireland', its first substantial constitutional policy document, published in September 1972. This proposed an interim form of goverment by condominium – joint Dublin/London rule, leading eventually to unity. This reflected the influence of the more traditional Nationalist components of the party in the west of the province plus the undoubted desire not to cede ground to the Provisionals. Its radicalism outstripped what the British government was then prepared to contemplate and was scarcely more favourably received in Dublin, where such direct involvement was regarded with horror by most of the political élite. It was also regarded as too extreme by the Belfast-based Labourites like Fitt and Devlin who saw the introduction of direct rule as creating the basis for a new form of participation by Nationalists in Northern Irish political life.

The second approach reflected the clear evidence that the British wanted to restore institutions of government to the north based on some form of 'power-sharing' between Unionists and Nationalists. For participationists like Fitt the basic aim was to get a share in governmental power and to use this to ensure equality of treatment. However, if the more Nationalist component of the party could not make progress on the condominium proposal, they were able to ensure that the SDLP demanded not simply power-sharing but a substantial 'Irish Dimension'. This would be a Council of Ireland with ministers from both a new northern government and Dublin, and charged with the task of increasing north–south cooperation in a range of areas as part of a process of 'harmonization' which would create the conditions for ultimate unity. However, it was precisely this combination of power-sharing and an 'Irish Dimension' which proved fatal to the Sunningdale Agreement in 1974.

After the collapse of the Executive, the SDLP continued to have its participationist and more radical Nationalist currents although it was the latter which increasingly set the tone of internal party debate. The more Nationalist elements demanded a more traditionalist posture, calling for a British declaration of intent to withdraw, bringing the party close to the position of the IRA. John Hume, who was soon to become leader of the party, began the process of setting out a new approach altogether. This, while turning its back on the hope of a power-sharing settlement, sought to distance itself from the Provisionals. By attempting to mobilize external pressure – from the United States and the European Community – Hume sought to persuade the British government to adopt an inter-governmental approach with Dublin which could, if necessary, introduce changes over the heads of the Unionists. Hume had moved from the traditional Nationalist argument, still the basis for the 'armed struggle' of the Provisional IRA, which saw the end of British involvement in Ireland as the key to unity, towards the idea of a transition period in which Britain would remain in Northern Ireland as a guarantor of the Unionist 'identity' at the same time as Dublin represented the Nationalist 'identity' in some form of joint authority. This was a return to the ideas of 'Towards a New Ireland' although these were now presented in a more gradualist manner.

By the late 1970s the leadership of the Provisionals was in the hands of a new generation of northern republicans led by Gerry Adams. They had become convinced that a purely military campaign could never force a British withdrawal and that the Armalite had to be complemented by electoral success. Despite successes during and after the hunger strikes of 1981, the politicization of Sinn Féin did not bring the major gains predicted by Adams. In particular, Sinn Féin was unable to get support in the south while in the north its links to the IRA remained an obstacle for the majority of Catholics.

Conclusions

After two decades of 'armed struggle' it was clear that the IRA, which had been the major agent of deaths in the conflict, had not achieved its objective. There was some evidence that a new and much expanded Catholic middle class might live with direct rule from London if it was supplemented with the 'green tinge' of the Anglo-Irish Agreement. As at the formation of the state, many northern Nationalists remain more concerned about rule by Protestants than they have been about partition. In the 1990s many northern Nationalists appeared to look to Dublin, not as a potential ruler of the north, but rather as their guarantor within a state which would remain within the Union for the foreseeable future.

The IRA's declaration of a 'complete cessation' of military operations on 31 August 1994 and Sinn Féin's increasingly clear willingness to negotiate on an agenda short of its maximum programme, brought northern Nationalism back to an effectively reformist agenda, similar to that of its founding figure Joe Devlin. Devlin had been prepared to contemplate partition if Catholic interests were protected by direct rule from Westminster and the continuation of Irish representation there. The separate development of the Irish state made the latter condition inoperable but it is now the Irish government that is seen to be the guarantor of northern Catholic interests within the northern state. Ultimately, northern Nationalism may have proven to be driven more by the needs of communal defence and interest than by a desire for Irish unity.

Further reading

Boyce, D.G., *Nationalism in Ireland*. London: Routledge, 1991.

Farrell, M., *Northern Ireland: The Orange State*. London: Pluto Press, 1976.

Mallie, E., *The Provisional IRA*. London: Corgi, 1988.

O'Connor, F., *In Search of a State: Catholics in Northern Ireland*. Belfast: Blackstaff Press, 1993.

O'Halloran, C., *Partition and the Limits of Irish Nationalism*. Dublin: Gill and Macmillan, 1987.

Patterson H., *The Politics of Illusion: Republicanism and Socialism in Modern Ireland*. London: Hutchinson Radius, 1989.

Purdie, B., *Politics in the Streets: The Origins of the Civil Rights Movement in Northern Ireland*. Belfast: Blackstaff Press, 1990.

Chapter 6

LABOUR AND LEFT POLITICS
Emmet O'Connor

In a region famous for its lack of consensus, a united, secular trade union movement functions where divisions are deepest – among the working class. The efficient secret, and the secret inefficacy, of Northern Ireland trade unionism lies in mass non-active participation in the movement, and its dominance by a self-selecting élite committed to labourist values. This has given union leaders the freedom to adopt a studied neutrality on sensitive political questions and place a paramount emphasis on organizational interests.

Sectarianism is a root and prop of unity. Because Catholics were marginal to its workforce, industrializing Ulster produced one predominantly Protestant trade unionism, rather than two confessional ones. Economic ties within the United Kingdom encouraged integration with British labour, and unions absorbed the culture that went with it, so that an initially Protestant, but increasingly mixed, trade unionism became overlain with a secular class ethos. Unionism has been hostile to labour for its tinge of socialism and anti-partitionism. However, though a few overtly 'Ulster' trade unions have been formed, Unionism was too conservative to compete effectively with labourist unions on ideological or material terms. Protestants have not generally challenged the policies of their unions. Whenever they felt the need for industrial political mobilization, such as in the 1974 Ulster Workers' Council strike, they set up separate shopfloor organizations. Catholics have sometimes asserted Nationalist politics where they made up a majority, but being usually in the minority, as deferential as Protestants to the myths of British labourism and as dependent on the British economy, they too have rarely rocked the boat. For its part, the so-called 'sleeping giant' of trade unionism is acutely aware of the limits of solidarity, and knows that it dare not confront Nationalism or Unionism beyond well-understood conventions.

The dislocation of labour values from the wider political culture is tolerated as another reflection of Northern Ireland's fractured condition. People in Northern Ireland are used to living between contexts – Catholic, Protestant, local, Irish, United Kingdom (UK) – and adjusting the response code in each; and used too to bureaucratic governance. Moreover, Northern Ireland is a province, not a country. Even before direct rule, many of the decisions affecting the economy, labour law, and wage bargaining were in reality taken in London, thereby diminishing the importance of local control. Indeed, it has been a consistent aim of trade unions to strengthen links with pay bargaining in England, Scotland and Wales as a means of raising wage rates.

The material basis of labour's industrial unity has no equivalence in politics. Ambiguities in the fragile solidarity nursed in the mid-1960s were exposed in 1969. While many Catholic and Protestant workers believe they share a common interest, scarcely a handful can agree on what it is, beyond obvious points like pay and conditions.

Trade union organization

Largely confined to craftsmen up to the Second World War, trade unions acquired a mass base when the war brought near-full employment for the only time in the history of Northern Ireland. After 1945, union membership grew more rapidly than in Great Britain, reaching 263,000 in 1970 (55% of employees), and a peak of 283,000 in 1983 (61% of employees, compared with a UK average of 53.5%). By 1989, these figures had fallen to 247,000 (49% of employees, compared with 39% in Great Britain). Membership was broadly based, though density was higher for males (51%) than females (47%), for manufacturing employees (55%) than non-manufacturing employees (47%), and for Catholics (51%) than Protestants (46%). Most of the larger British unions are represented in Northern Ireland, roughly in proportion to their total size, so that though their number is being trimmed through mergers, there are many minnows in the pool. Of 93 unions in 1987, 83 were UK based (with 77% of trade unionists), five were Northern Ireland based (with 16%), and five were Republic based (with 7%). Local unions are disappearing and the only sizable survivor is the Northern Ireland Public Service Alliance, a legacy of Northern Ireland's separate administration under Stormont. The few Dublin-based unions have maintained a small northern presence since pre-partition times. Since 1970, general and craft unions have suffered serious decline, while public sector unions have enjoyed dramatic growth.

Pay bargaining for public sector workers is conducted on a UK basis, or on a regional level where employees come within the authority of the Northern Ireland Office (NIO); in many instances regional agreements provide for parity with comparable groups in Great Britain. Private sector wage bargaining has become more integrated with UK machinery, but local wage determination still applies to a large minority. In 1985, local private sector wage agreements covered 15% of all employees. Wage levels in Northern Ireland moved closer to the UK average in the 1960s and 1970s but, for private sector workers, the differential has since been increasing. Nearly 40% of the workforce were classed as low paid in 1988.

Strike activity similarly may be UK or local. Contrary to the prevailing image, Northern Ireland is comparatively strike prone, recording 30% more strikes per 100,000 employees than the UK average in the period 1958–84. The fact that Northern Ireland workers are occasionally exempted from UK industrial action, and that most stoppages are small and involve manual workers in a few industries around Belfast, may explain the impression of unions in Northern Ireland as non-militant. While UK disputes make news, local disputes between 1980 and

1984, for example, accounted for 88% of strikes and 55% of strike days. Cross-border strike activity or wage bargaining is not common, even for members of unions based in the Republic.

Much of Northern Ireland's industry was lost in the years 1970 to 1994. The proportion of workers engaged in manufacture tumbled from 34% to 18%; unemployment rose from 5% to 13%. So why did trade union density increase up to the mid-1980s? Primarily, the political climate cushioned the impact of recessions and Thatcherism. Both Labour and Conservative governments treated Northern Ireland as a special case. Public employment grew to a peak of 43% of employees in 1986, boosting jobs in a sector of high union density. Privatization policy was implemented more slowly and selectively, and even after the conventional time lag in extending Westminster legislation to Northern Ireland, not all provisions of Conservative labour laws were put on the Northern Ireland statute book. Notably, the Labour Relations Agency, roughly analogous to the Advisory Conciliation and Arbitration Service (ACAS) in Great Britain, retained authority to investigate and conciliate in recognition disputes. The repeal of equivalent powers in Great Britain by the Employment Act (1980) contributed to a decline in union density. Labour–state relations were and are friendlier in Northern Ireland, where the government's chief enemy has been the paramilitaries. In the propaganda war for the representation of Northern Ireland as a 'normal society' plagued by a few terrorists, unions have been cited by the Northern Ireland Office as evidence of social 'normality', and praised for their opposition to sectarianism and violence. Unions have also enjoyed a positive public image, in respect of their industrial role at least. People tend to blame the government or the paramilitaries for industrial decline, and value unions as a means of keeping pace with wage rates in the rest of the UK. For example, in an attitude survey of UK employees in 1990, 55% of Northern Ireland respondents agreed that trade unions were necessary to protect workers, compared with 41% in Great Britain.

Some of these factors are now changing. Union membership is falling. As privatization measures have percolated through the system, public sector employment has been reduced to 35% of the total; since the mid-1980s the leading growth sector has been private services, and there has been an increase in part-time employment. The implications for unions are evident from the 1989 Labour Force Survey, which showed that 69% of employees were unionized in the contracting area of public administration, compared with 19% in the growth area of distribution, hotels, and repair, and 28% in the case of part-time workers. The Industrial Relations Order of 1993 substantially ended Northern Ireland's exemption from key sections of Conservative labour legislation. Labour's wage bargaining strategy of tracking British rates is under pressure from the government's policy of promoting regional differentials and a diversification of trade and investment beyond Great Britain. A permanent peace would intensify all of these trends, and diminish the propagandist value of trade unions for the NIO. A branch-based movement, semi-detached from its London leadership, is ill equipped to meet these challenges and the need for a more proactive trade unionism is likely to enhance the importance of the Northern Ireland Committee (NIC).

The Northern Ireland Committee

The Northern Ireland Committee (NIC) of the Irish Congress of Trade Unions is the policy-making body of trade unions in Northern Ireland. All-Ireland representation in a Dublin-based Congress predates partition and suits British unions, some of whom still have branches in the Republic. The cross-border connection has become integral to labour's sense of itself as pluralist, and there is the fear that an 'Ulster TUC', sometimes mooted, would split the movement. Before the 1940s, Northern Irish unions had little to do with Congress. Wartime growth, and a pragmatic recognition of the requirements of a separate jurisdiction, led to the appointment of the NIC in 1944. Although technically a committee of Congress, the NIC is autonomous and elected by a biennial conference of affiliates. It has 15 members, and a staff of seven, directed by Congress's Northern Ireland Officer. Northern trade union delegates attend the conferences of Congress but, by convention, do not vote on motions affecting only the Republic. In 1994, there were 33 unions affiliated to the NIC, with 214,000 members (92% of the total).

In most respects, the NIC's work is analogous to that of any TUC. Along with servicing its affiliates directly, its distinguishing function is to maximize labour input into public policy. Some 38 trade union representatives sit on 32 public bodies or committees, of which the most important are the Northern Ireland Economic Council, the Labour Relations Agency, and the Fair Employment Commission. Opportunities for influencing public policy have increased since the introduction of direct rule. The Stormont parliament tended to follow Westminster labour law 'step by step', with minor modifications that were usually to the detriment of trade unions. Direct rule has led to a more regional approach to administration, and the creation of new non-governmental organizations (NGOs) to offset the 'democratic deficit'. The NIC's influence on the Northern Ireland Office reached its zenith during the tenure of the 1974–79 Labour government, and it lobbied successfully to have the Trade Union and Labour Relations Act (1974) and the Employment Protection Act (1975) extended to Northern Ireland in 1976. Conservative industrial relations acts have been extended to Northern Ireland under three orders, made in 1982, 1987, and 1993; and though the NIC might take credit for slowing down and amending the process, the desire of the Northern Ireland Office to consult both the NIC and the Confederation of British Industry in Northern Ireland (CBI-NI) was a factor in the delays, and employer advice eventually carried more weight.

Ever since the confrontation between the Heath government and the TUC in 1971, the question of developing a different industrial relations system in Northern Ireland has surfaced intermittently. During consultations on the application of the Employment Act (1982) to Northern Ireland, the chairman of the Labour Relations Agency proposed a tripartite standing conference of the Agency, the NIC, and CBI-NI to review local industrial relations. Underpinning the conference would have been an agreement that the CBI-NI would withdraw its demands for the extension of the 1982 Act in return for a trade union commitment not to join UK strikes in which they had no formal interest. It is likely that the Northern

Ireland Office would have sanctioned the arrangement, though CBI-NI backing was less certain. In any case, the NIC's 1984 conference rejected the no-strike concession, and 'Tebbit's law' was applied to Northern Ireland in 1987 with few changes. Since 1987, the decline in union membership and the example of 'social partnership' in the Republic, where tripartite programmes have given Congress an input into government policy, has renewed interest in the idea of 'social partnership' for Northern Ireland. But the CBI-NI is unenthusiastic and it is doubtful if NIC affiliates would be willing to pay the price of weakening pay bargaining links with Great Britain.

Politically, Congress has held to the view that it would not be 'appropriate' for it to express opinions on the constitutional status of Northern Ireland. Unions have taken pains to avoid exacerbating inter-communal tension, and neutrality is a reason, though but one, for the virtual absence of overt sectarian conflict from the shopfloor during the recent troubles. The NIC has evolved a coherent stand on specific issues. In addition to papers on job creation and economic reconstruction, it has published programmes supporting civil rights, and condemning internment, discrimination, and intimidation, and sponsored campaigns against violence, all without disruption. Membership detachment is typified by the 1974 Ulster Workers' Council strike. Protestant workers ignored NIC appeals to return to work, but remained as committed to their unions after the strike as before; the NIC bore the humiliation stoically, and carried on. Similarly, Catholic and Protestant workers have happily marched to NIC rallies against *all* violence and walked home again with their politics intact.

One area where NIC work has intersected with politics is in relation to fair employment. On paper, trade unions have a vintage record of hostility to sectarian discrimination; in practice, they have rarely acted against it. The NIC's satisfaction with the Fair Employment Act (1976), despite scant improvement in Catholic under-representation in employment, seemed to critics another example of union reluctance to confront the issue. During the early 1980s, the NIC came under mounting pressure to endorse the MacBride principles, which called, *inter alia*, for affirmative action for equality. Characteristically, the push came not from Catholics within the movement, but from external groups, including senior trade unionists in the Republic. To avoid further embarrassment – for the MacBride principles were associated with republicans, and fiercely opposed by the Northern Ireland Office – the NIC's 1985 conference adopted a stronger commitment to equality; and it is in fact in this area that the NIC has been most influential with the government, which introduced a tougher Fair Employment Act in 1989. The NIC subsequently appointed an anti-intimidation officer and launched an anti-intimidation programme, 'Counteract'.

Left politics

Essentially, the left has responded in two ways to the divisions of Northern Ireland. One was to try to unite workers around 'bread and butter' politics and to avoid divisive issues. The other was to face the constitutional question directly. By and large, Protestants have preferred the first. Catholics, seeing their condition as bound up with the character of the state, have gravitated to the second.

The first approach was tried in its purest form by the Northern Ireland Labour Party (NILP) from its foundation in 1924 up to 1949. The early NILP was mainly Protestant, but drew a mixed vote, and up to the 1940s many Protestant socialists were against partition. It took no position on the constitution. Until its demise the party also had trade union affiliates on the British Labour model: something of organizational, rather than vote winning, advantage. The NILP never won a Westminster seat, or more than three of the 52 seats at Stormont before 1949, when anti-partitionists decamped to the Irish Labour Party and the remnant adopted a pro-Union stance. After a lean decade, the NILP won four Stormont seats in 1958 and 1962. Emboldened, and encouraged by the apparently reformist Unionism of Terence O'Neill, members queried party reticence on sectarianism. Branches were restarted in Catholic areas. In 1966 the NILP underwrote a 'Joint Memorandum on Citizen's Rights' with the NIC, and in 1968 it formed a Council of Labour with the Republican Labour Party and the Irish Labour Party. However, the liberal drift had possibly lost the party two Stormont seats in 1965 and leaders were worried at the erosion of its working-class Protestant base by Paisleyite reaction to O'Neill. A cautious response to the crisis of August 1969 offended Catholic supporters, without reassuring Protestants. One of its two remaining MPs, elected, untypically, for the Catholic Falls constituency, joined the Social Democratic and Labour Party (SDLP) on its foundation. It was a measure of NILP desperation in 1970 that it could simultaneously blame Harold Wilson's Northern Ireland policy for alienating Protestants from Labour and apply, in vain, to merge with the British Labour Party.

Adopting a more Unionist line in the early 1970s did not help the NILP to compete with the main Unionist parties, and possibly lost it the liberal Unionist vote to the newly formed Alliance Party. David Bleakley, co-opted to the last Stormont government as Minister of Community Relations, was the NILP's only voice in the Northern Ireland Assembly of 1973–74, and in the 1975 Constitutional Convention. The party failed to contest the 1982 Assembly elections. Efforts to revive labourism since then have taken two forms. One has promoted cross-community radicalism within a regional politics, as in the case of United Labour (1978–87), the Labour Party of Northern Ireland (1984–87), the Newtownabbey Labour Party, and Labour '87, which absorbed these groups along with most of the shrunken NILP. The NILP's trade union affiliations did not transfer to Labour '87. The second, formerly led by the Campaign for Labour Representation and now by Labour in Northern Ireland, has aimed to persuade the British Labour Party to organize in Northern Ireland. Neither approach has met much favour at the polls. In the local elections of May 1993, 13 'Labour' candidates won 2,786 votes (0.4% of the total), and only one was elected.

Left mobilization on the Catholic side is a story of displacement of the conservative Nationalist Party, from Belfast after 1945 and Northern Ireland after 1970, without managing to transcend its rationale. The Irish Labour Party was strongly represented in urban Nationalist areas from 1949 to 1958. Thereafter its Northern Ireland organization shrivelled to a few branches and was wound up in

1972. Following his election to Stormont in 1962, Gerry Fitt reorganized Belfast's Nationalist labourites into the Republican Labour Party. Fitt's vigorous style, and integration of Catholic grievances with socialist attacks on Unionist 'Toryism', set a headline. When the new wave of anti-Unionist politicians thrown up by the civil rights movement came together in 1970, they formed the SDLP as a moderately socialist party, under Fitt's leadership. However, the SDLP soon became better known as the main Nationalist party, nearly monopolizing the Catholic vote before Sinn Féin contested elections in the 1980s, and distinguished by its demand for cross-community power-sharing and opposition to violence. The fall of the power-sharing executive in 1974, in which the SDLP held four portfolios, soured the party's belief that Northern Ireland could be reformed through internal agreement primarily. Fitt resigned in 1979, when the SDLP insisted on links with the Republic as part of any new constitutional settlement, and under John Hume the party has placed a priority on cross-border structures. Although the recognized affiliate of the Socialist International in Northern Ireland, the SDLP's leftist credentials are questioned by critics of its predominantly middle-class composition and Nationalist agenda.

The remaining Catholic vote is divided largely between Sinn Féin, the Workers' Party, and Democratic Left, all structured on an Ireland-wide basis. The events of 1969 split the republican movement between a 'red' faction, the Officials, and the 'green' Provisionals. The Official Irish Republican Army (IRA) called a ceasefire in 1972, and Official Sinn Féin evolved into the Workers' Party, losing out in Northern Ireland to the Provisionals for its pointed rejection of Nationalism for class politics, but gaining ground in the Republic. Democratic Left was founded in 1992 by reformists unable to persuade the Workers' Party to abandon Marxism – Leninism and alleged links with the ostensibly moribund Official IRA. When the initial Nationalist revolt yielded to a protracted armed struggle, dependent on Catholic working-class areas, Provisional Sinn Féin restyled itself in revolutionary socialist colours. Largely an IRA propaganda and welfare auxiliary in the 1970s, Sinn Féin entered electoral politics during the 1981 hunger strike, beginning a process of politicization of republicanism that culminated in the 1994 ceasefire. As with the SDLP, Sinn Féin's socialism is overshadowed by its Nationalism, and even the Workers' Party and Democratic Left have failed to attract significant Protestant backing. In the May 1993 local elections the SDLP won 22.1% of the vote, Sinn Féin 12.4%, the Workers' Party 0.8%, and Democratic Left 0.4%.

Conclusions

Trade unions in Northern Ireland face two overriding challenges. For most of the past 20 years they enjoyed a markedly more favourable employment structure and legislative framework than their counterparts in Great Britain. These advantages are now being eroded. It is likely that Northern Ireland trade union density will remain above the UK average, but that the decline in membership will persist in the short term. Peace will mean a slimmer public sector, intensified efforts to regenerate the economy through the development of private services and trade beyond the UK, and the adoption of a more regional approach to the governance of Northern Ireland. This will create difficulties for a movement geared to strengthening ties with wage bargaining in Great Britain. It may also offer unions an opportunity to make a greater input into public policy through NIC participation in a regional 'social partnership'. The second challenge is that the unity of Catholic and Protestant workers within the trade union movement, no mean achievement, has been sustained through membership detachment rather than participation. In all probability unions will choose to leave well alone.

Since the NILP became politically irrelevant in the aftermath of August 1969, working-class politics has become more polarized than ever before. The prospects for rebuilding the cross-community support garnered by the NILP before 1949 and again in the mid-1960s are remote. Catholics have found putting their grievances first a more effective means of redress than pursuing common 'bread and butter' politics; Protestants, feeling threatened by the success of Catholic mobilization, have rallied to Unionism in response. Moreover, there is little space for an exclusively social democratic agenda. Nonetheless, the near absence of labour politics within the Protestant community is an historical anomaly, given the record of Protestant support for the NILP up to the 1970s. An easing of inter-communal tensions would create opportunities in this respect.

Further reading

Arthur, P., *Government and Politics of Northern Ireland*. London: Longman, 1994.

Boyd, J. and Black, H., 'Industrial Relations', in R.I.D. Harris, C. Jefferson and J.E. Spencer (eds), *The Northern Ireland Economy; A Comparative Study in the Economic Development of a Peripheral Region*. London: Longman, 1990.

Connolly, M. and Loughlin, S. (eds), *Public Policy in Northern Ireland: Adoption or Adaptation?* Belfast: Policy Research Institute, 1990.

Cradden, T and Erridge, A., 'Employers and trade unions in the development of public policy in Northern Ireland', in R.I.D. Harris, C. Jefferson and J.E. Spencer (eds), *The Northern Ireland Economy; A Comparative Study in the Economic Development of a Peripheral Region*. London: Longman, 1990.

Chapter 7

IN SEARCH OF COMMON GROUND
Duncan Morrow

Northern Ireland came into existence in the midst of political turmoil. From the outset it was divided into well-defined groups who opposed one another on the most profound political question of all: should Northern Ireland exist? Central to that issue was the question of whether part of Ireland should still remain within the United Kingdom when the rest of the island became independent. For Unionists, whose *raison d'être* involved defending the Union with Great Britain, the answer to both questions was a clear yes. For Nationalists, whose *raison d'être* was the removal of British rule in Ireland, the answer was equally clearly no. From the beginning, political life in Northern Ireland was therefore cast as a struggle for survival. Although in times of relative calm this sense of fundamental conflict was less apparent, the basic division between Unionists and Nationalists, and the fear it engenders, has remained central to all political life.

The 1960s saw important changes in Northern Ireland. The economy prospered, the welfare state began to erode the most serious poverty and social changes across Europe and North America had increasing influence on the province. Most importantly, the political atmosphere appeared to promise less sectarian politics. The emergence of the Civil Rights Association (NICRA) appeared to suggest that many Nationalists were coming to terms with the existence of Northern Ireland. However, the events of 1968–72 destroyed any hope that these changes would lead to immediate stability. The collapse of the power-sharing experiment in May 1974 signalled the end of local cross-community political initiatives. In the context of serious political violence, residential segregation and mutual recrimination, the concept of a 'middle-ground' between Unionism and Nationalism appeared unrealistic and foreign. At the same time, all hope of a political solution which did not rely entirely on the suppression of one group or another depended on the discovery of and agreement on a common point of departure. This was particularly true for at least three categories of people in Northern Ireland for whom this division gives rise to particular difficulty: those born outside the North, those in or from mixed marriage backgrounds and those who reject the attitudes of their backgrounds without having embraced a new identity. There is evidence that all of these have been growing categories since the outbreak of violence in 1969. For these people and for many who shared doubts about aspects of their traditional political identities, the desire for a common ground became ever more pressing as violence continued. The identification of what the 'common ground' might be has therefore remained central to politics in Northern Ireland even if it has remained elusive. The fact that it has not yet been agreed does not detract from its importance in a democracy.

Middle and common ground

In liberal democratic states, communities and societies are bound together on the basis of commonly held systems of authority within agreed territories. What marks democracies out from other systems are the underlying assumptions that authority is expressed in the form of laws which are equally applicable to all and that the authority of the government is based on the consent of the governed. Democratic politics takes place against the backdrop of these common assumptions. Its practical limits are defined by what is possible within their parameters. The rules and systems which arise out of them form the 'common ground' of political societies, and allegiance to them enables political coherence and a common sense of belonging, even if people disagree about policy matters.

Within any political system, political differences are inevitable. Disputes in democracies are limited by common allegiance to the system of authority and its procedures. Political differences are resolved through voting by the electorate and by elected representatives, and defeat at an election does not mean a withdrawal of consent for the system itself. Since the French Revolution of 1789, political parties have often been described as parties of 'the left', 'the right' and 'the centre'. In this context, 'the centre or middle ground' is understood as somewhere between two other important positions. 'Middle ground' is thus part of a spectrum of views and is not the same as 'common ground' in the sense of a system of political order to which everybody belongs no matter what their political views.

Northern Ireland politics has traditionally lacked both a common ground and a large middle ground. The system of legal authority has been a matter of sometimes violent dispute from the very beginning. The absence of an assumed common ground on the nature of the state and the legitimacy of the system accounts for the chronic instability at the core of political life in Northern Ireland. At the same time, Northern Ireland has been part of the United Kingdom and bordered and claimed by the Republic of Ireland. Both of these states have established stable liberal democracies where the common assumptions of legal–rational authority and the principle of consent are taken for granted. Northern Ireland is therefore in the curious position of lacking stable liberal democratic assumptions internally while the political struggle is about which liberal democratic state should have legitimate authority in Northern Ireland. The concepts of liberal democracy are therefore still the basis on which politics are judged and assessed even though a locally functioning liberal democracy remains elusive. The object of dispute is, therefore, neither governmental form nor competing ideological claims on the nature of humankind but the bonds of identity and affection usually described as 'Nationalism'. The question at hand remains: to which nation or state does Northern Ireland belong?

Instead of operating within a common framework, political groups in Northern Ireland have been prepared to fight to ensure that politics will be conducted within their framework rather than accept the framework proposed by the others. For instance, those who rejected a British framework, the minority in Northern Ireland, did not simply accept defeat as part of the political process but maintained their allegiance to an all-Irish political framework in which they feel part of the national majority. Even though many may feel ambivalent about parts of their allegiance, they feel bound to choose.

Such disputes are particularly difficult to resolve in politics because there is no commonly agreed basis through which they can be resolved except by the domination of one group by the other. Historically, such disputes have usually been resolved by force, with the winner establishing their system in the face of the defeat of the loser. People who in other respects are very different find themselves united by their choice about which system is the legitimate system. Where two or more choices attract widespread loyalty, the potential for violence and political polarization along the axis of this division is very great indeed. Furthermore, where there is a long history of violence along this axis, there are real reasons for fearing and rejecting all cooperation with those 'on the other side'. Northern Ireland has suffered from all of these problems with the important qualification that there has been no easy winner or loser. In addition, attempting to resolve this dispute by force is contrary to the principles of the political system in force in both Britain and Ireland, liberal democracy. The result has been a complex political problem, where the principles of force and the principles of democratic consent have both been present while the use of force has compromised progress on the basis of democratic discussion.

Sovereignty

Systems of political authority are embodied in the state. To have final authority is to be sovereign. Sovereignty, by extension, is therefore final. Disputes in Northern Ireland are thus crucially issues of the political sovereignty and authority of the state. The sovereignty of one state or another is therefore not just one issue among many but the keystone of political authority. Where two or more claims to sovereignty compete, common ground is often lost in the competition. Common ground is found within sovereignty or where there are clearly agreed places where one system is sovereign and other places where another is sovereign. Such places can then be separated by mutually recognized borders. The fact that the border of Northern Ireland is not fully recognized by many of the people who live within that border means that sovereignty remains in dispute, at least at an inter-personal and inter-communal level. Seeking common ground is therefore a difficult and delicate process.

The absence of any recognition of the sovereignty of the British state in Northern Ireland by many Irish Nationalists has meant a tendency to polarize all politics between those who accept and those who reject that state. As a result, even though there may be many practical issues either on which there is cross-community agreement or where different political divisions, such as class divisions or divisions between men and women, might be expected to emerge, there is a permanent tendency for the debate about sovereignty to reassert itself. Voting in Northern Ireland has thus been much less to do with 'issues' than to do with the assertion of identity and sovereignty. More importantly, common ground on problems of agriculture, social services and hospital closures does not necessarily lead to greater unity on the underlying question of sovereignty.

From 1969 until the ceasefires of 1994, Northern Ireland endured political violence justified by this dispute. In the context of such violence, the search for common ground becomes even more difficult.

Even though people wish peace, they find it impossible to make peace if sovereignty does not rest, ultimately, with their side of the dispute. Between 1976 and 1978, large numbers of people from all parts of Northern Ireland gathered for public marches to demand peace. The 'Peace People' tapped into the strong desire of Northern Irish people for an end to political violence. The inability of the Peace People to make the leap from emotional movement to political breakthrough is a classic illustration of this problem and led to a deep cynicism in Northern Ireland about the possibility of real common ground.

While people are being killed, entering into political negotiations with associates of those responsible for the deaths of one's own allies can easily be seen as betrayal rather than as a search for an honourable compromise. There is a long tradition in Northern Ireland that compromise or accommodation is tantamount to betrayal of the dead and injured. In such traditions, common ground can only be established through the acceptance of the sovereignty of one's own system by one's opponents, by force if necessary. In this view, common ground can only be established once this shift has taken place but never before.

In theory at least, common ground in Northern Irish politics could be established through the acceptance by everyone of either British or Irish sovereignty. Common ground might also mean neither of these things. Other proposals have been widely canvassed at different times: independence for Northern Ireland on the basis of a common Northern Irish identity, joint sovereignty between Britain and the Irish Republic, or even the creation of a special region of the European Union. Events in Northern Ireland since 1974 suggest that the British and Irish governments may be increasingly moving to accommodate one another before presenting an effective *fait accompli* to the Northern Irish population. The implicit claim is that common ground in Northern Ireland cannot be exclusively Unionist or Nationalist but must be something new. As such, neither Unionism nor Nationalism is held to hold out enough to provide a new consensus.

These claims remain highly controversial in Northern Ireland. They have not become established as the explicit policy of any local party. Nonetheless, they have clearly been influential in the wider shaping of events. Furthermore, there have been many local initiatives which, while usually remaining unspecific on the constitutional issue, have attempted to build groups and institutions on an explicitly cross-community basis.

The remainder of this chapter will be concerned with policies and groups which have explicitly sought common ground outside the traditional confines of Nationalism and Unionism and, confusingly, are therefore sometimes described as the middle groud of Northern Irish politics. Some of these are explicitly concerned with constitutional questions. Others, while unspecific about the constitutional politics of Unionism and Nationalism, are usually clearly disturbed by the human and societal implications of the absence of common ground between Unionists and Nationalists.

In search of common ground through politics

Upon the abolition of Stormont in 1972, power in Northern Ireland passed directly to Westminster. Since then, successive British governments have been concerned to produce institutions in and for Northern Ireland which would foster political stability. Both Conservative and Labour governments at Westminster were convinced of the need for local administration which would avoid the pitfall of being seen as a purely Unionist institution. This ran up against the opposition of Unionist parties, who regarded such prescription as anti-democratic, and of republicans, who regarded devolution as a diversion from the central problem of British presence in Ireland. In the context of widespread political fear and violence, all radical initiatives were likely to be severely tested.

British initiatives to resolve the Northern Irish dilemma of producing workable and acceptable political institutions have taken two main forms. The first, and increasingly important, strand emerged in tentative form in the power-sharing experiment of 1973–74. This involved a power-sharing or consociational model of internal political organization, where Unionists and Nationalists would share executive positions, and institutional links with the Irish Republic. The latter have proved both the most controversial with Unionists and the most significant. The 'Council of Ireland', vaguely defined within the Sunningdale Agreement of 1973, precipitated loyalist opposition which led ultimately to the collapse of the whole power-sharing experiment in 1974. Nonetheless, the principle of cross-border cooperation at the highest political and administrative level was the central feature of the Anglo-Irish Agreement of 1985, the Downing Street Declaration of 1993 and the Framework Documents of 1995. Indeed, the Anglo-Irish Agreement in many ways reproduced the Sunningdale model in reverse, whereby the 'Irish dimension' was formally institutionalized while arrangements for devolution were left vague and ill defined. Widespread Unionist opposition to the Agreement was, ultimately, powerless to prevent this process. Although both governments have consistently denied any attempt to produce joint sovereignty over Northern Ireland by both Britain and Ireland, the British and Irish governments now consult and share views at regular intervals through the Anglo-Irish Conference and the Anglo-Irish Secretariat based outside Belfast.

The second, and probably weaker, strand of British initiative involved the encouragement of local parties in Northern Ireland to reach their own consensus beyond simple Unionism and Nationalism. The Constitutional Convention of the mid-1970s produced no consensus and reproduced the split between Unionists and Nationalists which had dominated the Stormont system. Likewise, when the SDLP did not take their seats in the Northern Ireland Assembly between 1982 and 1986, all hope that the devolution of minor issues might 'roll forward' and collect new powers failed. The Brooke–Mayhew talks of 1991 and 1992 reproduced the same split between the Assembly parties and the SDLP and ended inconclusively. The British government produced further proposals for local devolution in the Framework Documents in 1995.

Behind all of these British government proposals lie two key presumptions. The first is that common ground in Northern Ireland is dependent not only on simple majority numerical support but on the broad support of both communities. As such, there can be no serious transfer of power back to local institutions until this condition is met. Between 1974 and 1995 no agreed devolved structures materialized for Northern Ireland. In the interim, rule by the British government in ever-closer consultation with the Irish government appears to represent the least-worst political option for both governments. The second presumption is that Northern Ireland is not identical with the rest of the United Kingdom. Even Conservative governments which have strongly opposed devolution of power from Westminster to Scotland and Wales have supported special institutions for Northern Ireland. This appears to be largely inspired by the conviction that common ground must first be built between communities in Northern Ireland if stability is to return. Political emphasis is therefore automatically placed on inter-community relationships and policies designed to reduce competition in the social and economic arena. The dilemma for Unionist and Nationalist parties is that it appears to direct them towards placing their relationships with one another above their constitutional loyalties, which runs counter to their historical structure and instinct.

The result is a complex political stalemate. On the one hand Anglo-Irish institutions function with a degree of political normality. At the same time there is very little local accountability or participation in these institutions. Despite loud Unionist protestations in the mid-1980s, by 1990 the majority of all communities appeared willing to passively acquiesce in these arrangements if not to support them actively. This explains the evidence that the number of people who vote for political parties which are moderate on the question of the border is much smaller than the number of people who say that they are ambivalent about being categorized in total as Unionist or Nationalist.

The absence of active local political support for these combinations of Anglo-Irish and inter-community political institutions has made democratization of the structures very difficult. Common ground is therefore created actively between the British and Irish governments but only passively, if at all, at local level. Local political leadership therefore assumes no responsibility for governance and all parties have a tendency to become parties of opposition rather than parties of government. Social and economic policy changes arising from the Anglo-Irish/power-sharing model have been implemented under direct rule from Westminster but political cooperation between Nationalist and Unionist parties has not increased. Such local political cooperation as exists takes place instead at the level of community groups and semi-government bodies popularly known as 'quangos'.

Community relations and equity: the search for parity of esteem

In 1971, David Bleakley of the Northern Ireland Labour Party (NILP) became the first and only non-Unionist Party member of the Stormont government as Minister for Community Relations. In his short period of office, he established the Community Relations Commission with the brief of improving relationships between the various communities in Northern Ireland. Although the Commission was abolished in 1974 by the power-sharing executive, it represented the first public acknowledgement that community divisions in Northern Ireland were endemic and therefore central to public policy. Indeed, there were few issues in Northern Ireland which were not entangled in hostilities and fears linked to the political instability. Between 1972 and 1995, numerous agencies were established by government to specifically address issues of controversy between the communities.

Perhaps the most controversial was the Fair Employment Agency (FEA) established in 1976 to address issues of discrimination in the labour market. Persistently high levels of unemployment among Catholics reflected numerous historic factors and showed little sign of change. In 1971, Catholic men were still two and a half times more likely to find themselves unemployed than their Protestant counterparts. However, from the outset, the FEA was attacked by Republicans as toothless and cosmetic and by Unionists as interfering and irrelevant.

The question of discrimination in employment continued to dog British governments, especially in the United States. In the 1980s numerous US companies came under pressure to support specific programmes of affirmative action for Northern Ireland involving minimum quotas of Catholic employment, known as the McBride Principles. State legislatures in various American states passed motions supporting the Principles as the only basis on which companies with headquarters under their jurisdiction could invest in Northern Ireland. In the light of this growing pressure, the government replaced the FEA with a Fair Employment Commission (FEC) as part of a general toughening of Fair Employment legislation in 1989. Under the new legislation companies were not specifically forced to adopt targets or quotas but all companies with more than 25 employees (since reduced to 10) were compelled to register, monitor and publish their employment records with regard to perceived religious origins. Interviewing and appointment procedures were made more rigorous while penalties for companies found guilty of religious discrimination were sharply increased.

The history of the FEA/FEC illustrates some of the difficulties involved in changing established patterns by legislation. According to the 1991 census, Catholic men remained more than twice as likely to be unemployed as their Protestant neighbours. At the same time, some questioned the economic wisdom of imposing labour market restrictions on an already fragile economy. In a static labour market, new jobs in one community can only be created by increasing unemployment in another. Resistance in the community which fears increased unemployment is therefore to be expected. At the same time, frustration at perceived slow progress is equally likely to appear within the community which has been historically disadvantaged. Monitoring returns showed that overall statistics from employment in large companies often disguised a number of effectively segregated workplaces. The potential that the FEC is resented by everyone is therefore considerable. At the same time, it is difficult to see how parity of esteem can be seen to be delivered while large gaps in unemployment levels remain. In 1995, the FEC reported improvements in the numbers of Catholics employed at high levels in the public and private sectors in Northern Ireland since the introduction of Fair Employment legislation. Clearly, addressing issues of equity does not necessarily mean the establishment of common ground across traditional barriers. Indeed, it appears at times to necessitate bringing divisions more sharply into focus.

Employment was not the only field to be tackled as part of a general policy to promote equity at all levels in Northern Ireland. As part of the response to the civil rights movement, policies ending all discrimination in voting and housing had been passed by the Stormont government. In addition, a Northern Ireland Ombudsman was appointed to look into cases of maladministration. Under direct rule, the government established a Standing Advisory Committee on Human Rights (SACHR) to examine issues of justice and rights and a Central Community Relations Unit (CCRU) within the Northern Ireland Office to advise on community relations issues across the range of policy areas. In education, the introduction of the Education for Mutual Understanding (EMU) programme was intended to ensure that all schools in Northern Ireland's divided education system addressed issues of cultural diversity and pluralism through changes in the curriculum and the encouragement of inter-school contact. This was paralleled by increasing parental support for integrated schools at primary and secondary levels. The first such school was established in Belfast as Lagan College in 1980. By 1995, 2% of children in Northern Ireland were being educated in integrated schools.

In 1990, a new Community Relations Council was given funding to encourage cross-community contact and the implementation of community relations policy in all important areas of society in Northern Ireland. The Council invested in local community groups which were willing to undertake work towards greater community understanding throughout Northern Ireland while also supporting projects to develop and protect all cultural traditions. It further relied on the work of numerous organizations which had become established over time as agencies of genuine inter-community relationship such as the Corrymeela Community (churches and community groups) and Counteract (trade unions).

The public sector infrastructure in support of equity and improved inter-community relations has thus grown enormously since 1969. Indeed, this level of support for political and cultural pluralism has few parallels outside Northern Ireland. At times, particularly in the area of fair employment, this has been controversial, highlighting the gulf which exists between two traditional political communities. Other initiatives, including educational changes, have been widely accepted, indicating that political division and an absence of political progress does not necessarily undermine the broad argument for consciously improving community relations. Nonetheless, the development of community links does not necessarily produce a new common political framework unless the quality and strength of the relations produced are powerful enough to demand loyalty beyond previous political allegiances. Historic antagonisms remain powerful political motivators. Better community relations are not a certain guarantee that new political initiatives will be successful. However, without improvements in the relations between communities, new political structures are unlikely to prove lasting.

Conclusions

In its essence, the political problem in Northern Ireland *is* the absence of common ground. Politics in the province is therefore about the establishment of that necessary framework which provides limits and form to political life. All other issues are ultimately secondary to this question. The absolute demands of sovereignty and the fears associated with the sovereignty of 'the others', whoever they may be, makes political life in Northern Ireland appear deeply intransigent. This apparent intransigence may have more to do with the fact that politics and politicians in other western states never have to address the issue of establishing a common basis of identity and loyalty from which constructive and even cooperative politics can emerge. They simply take such common allegiance for granted. Nonetheless, intransigence gives the further impression that there are no moderates, no middle ground.

By 1995, the Northern Ireland population appeared tired of the polarization and violence associated with the attempt to ensure that the battle for sovereignty was won. The ceasefires of 1994 brought 25 years of violence to an end but they did not of themselves create the common ground on which to build a stable future. Nonetheless they did enable a new climate in which such a future might be easier to build.

Further reading

Boyle, K. and Hadden, T., *Northern Ireland: The Choice*. London: Penguin, 1994.

Community Relations Council, *Annual Reports*. 1990 onwards.

Connolly, M. and Loughlin, S. (eds), *Public Policy in Northern Ireland: Adoption or Adaptation?*. Belfast: Policy Research Institute, 1990.

Fair Employment Commission, *Annual Reports*. Belfast, 1990–95.

McKeown, C., *The Price of Peace*. Belfast: Blackstaff Press, 1987.

Whyte, J., *Interpreting Northern Ireland*. Oxford: Clarendon Press, 1990.

Wichert, S., *Northern Ireland since 1945*. Harlow: Longman, 1991.

Section Three

PARTIES AND ELECTIONS

Chapter 8

POLITICAL PARTIES:
(1) ELECTIONS AND STRATEGIES
Paul Arthur

Any study of the party and electoral systems in Northern Ireland would need to concentrate on the two contrasting periods of 'BCRC' and 'ACRC' – that is, Before the Civil Rights Campaign and After the Civil Rights Campaign. The aftermath of that campaign produced a seismic shift in Northern Ireland's politics. Until the late 1960s there was a deadening predictability about election results and the health (or otherwise) of the party system. The fact of the matter was that Unionism was never under threat and that the Unionist Party had never held less than 32 of the 52 seats in the Stormont Parliament. They were assisted in their success by an electoral system which was harsh on smaller parties. Originally elections were to be conducted under the single transferable vote (STV) system of proportional representation (PR). Government had recognized the anomalies of the British model of 'first past the post' in deeply divided societies – hence the insistence initially that elections be conducted under STV in both parts of Ireland. This was felt to be a means whereby the Protestant minority in the south and the Catholic minority in the north would get more equitable representation at local and national level.

The precise nature of the electoral system had little real significance in the south because the Protestant electorate was so small and fragmented. From time to time Protestant candidates stood and were elected but for the most part they were absorbed into the mainstream parties. In the present Irish Parliament, for example, there are three Jewish TDs and one Muslim TD (which is totally disproportionate to the size of either community) representing the three major parties of Fianna Fáil, Fine Gael and Labour but only two Protestants representing Fine Gael and the Green Party. Not since the 1960s has there been a TD elected solely on a Protestant ticket. The situation in Northern Ireland could not have been more different. There the government was acutely conscious of the impact of religion on voting patterns; and following the second general election for Stormont in 1925 alarm bells were sounded.

In 1921, 40 Unionists and 12 anti-partitionists were elected in the first general election. Four years later the combined forces of the Nationalist Party and Sinn Féin remained at 12 but the Unionists lost eight seats to Labour, Independent Unionists and a farmers' candidate. In addition two members of the government failed to get re-elected, and no Unionist headed the poll in Belfast. All of the seats were lost in the greater Belfast area in an election which the Unionist leader (and Prime Minister) Sir James Craig had attempted to sell as being about territory with his slogan of 'Not an inch'. The Unionist electorate had shown more sophistication by voting for those who were more concerned with their material needs. The government had a ready-made remedy. Section 14(5) of the Government of Ireland Act (1920) made provision for the alteration of the electoral system after three years provided that the number of MPs remained the same and that in any redistribution of seats population was considered. It had not been implemented immediately, possibly because Labour was in control at Westminster in 1924 and Unionists feared its intentions. The shock of 1925 gave the desire for electoral change a new momentum. The Northern Ireland government realized that PR had allowed the electorate a measure of choice incommensurate with Unionist Party ambitions.

By 1929, when the third general election took place, STV had been abolished and whatever excitement and surprise that elections held disappeared. The Unionist Party now had all the appearance of being a monolith. Single-issue movements such as temperance candidates could make no headway in the new system. There was a real challenge at the 1938 general election when a new party, the Progressive Unionists, contested 12 constituencies, all of them against UUP candidates. None of them were successful – indeed the UUP increased its percentage. Not until the 1960s when first the Northern Ireland Labour Party (NILP) and then the Protestant Unionists began to fight elections against UUP candidates did the UUP have any flavour of a contest. Many seats remained uncontested: between 1929 and 1969 37.5% of the seats were returned unopposed. Terence O'Neill, for example, entered Stormont in 1946 when he won an unopposed by-election and did not fight his first opponent until 1969 by which time the whole regime was under question. Unionists usually won three-quarters of the seats with slightly more than half the electorate's support. Two groups were seriously disadvantaged – Labour and independent Unionists: the latter won 29.1% of the total vote in 1938 but won only three seats. The UUP managed to co-opt or absorb all pretenders to its throne, that is until the arrival of the Reverend Ian Paisley.

A similar picture could be seen on the Catholic side. There had been some sort of contest between Sinn Féin and the Nationalist Party in the early days. However, the Nationalist Party became the largest opposition and there was very little competition between Nationalists and Sinn Féin. The Nationalists were a party of local notables lacking in central organization and even a manifesto. They concentrated on contesting seats at Stormont. It was not until the 1960s when the first winds of change began to blow that they adopted both. Meanwhile Sinn Féin concentrated on Westminster where they won two seats in 1955 – although both MPs were disqualified because they were felons. With the exception of the very first election, the Nationalists did not even contest enough seats to be in a position to form a government. Opposition politics became sullen, plaintive and fragmented. The nature of the fragmentation could be seen in the creation of a Republican Labour Party in 1964 when Republican and Irish Labour merged and two one-man parties became one two-man party. The party which might have broken this trend was the NILP when it became a real force in Protestant working-class Northern Ireland from the early 1960s. It won four seats in the late 1950s, consolidated them in 1962 and increased its percentage in 1965, but thereafter NILP was on a slippery slope to oblivion. Part of its problem was that, paradoxically, it had raised rights issues which did not seem relevant to its largely Belfast Protestant working-class constituents. It was feared that reforming the franchise would be advantageous to Catholics. So whereas the NILP had raised such issues prior to the formation of the civil rights movement, it was the latter which was to change the political landscape in Northern Ireland. What had appeared such an innocuous item on the political agenda – One Man, One Vote – was to have a profound impact on the party system. That led to a reform of the electoral system which impacted yet again on the party system. The predictability and artificial stability of party competition disappeared between 1969 and 1972. The party system itself underwent significant change over the next 25 years.

Consequences of change: Unionists

The first victim was the UUP itself. It was the established party in Northern Ireland in formal existence since 1905 but with firm roots going back to the 1880s and the period of major democratic reform. During those years it consolidated its grip on virtually the whole of the Protestant community working in close liaison with the Orange Order. To reinforce its grip on the Protestant working class the party had formed the Unionist Labour Association in 1918. Here then was a very broad church united to the cause of the Union but with a potential to divide on denominational as well as socio-economic lines. In the years between the mid-1920s (when Northern Ireland's position within the United Kingdom seemed secured at last) and the late 1960s there was an unquestioning acceptance of the Union and its material benefits. That was the problem. Little thought was given to the nature of the Union and the power relationships which existed within it.

These questions came to the fore after the first serious civil rights disturbances in 1968. What followed appeared to be 'interference' from London and an undermining of the authority of the Northern Ireland government. In fact what was being tested was precisely where power lay between Belfast and London and what were the responsibilities (as well as the privileges) of a devolved government. The UUP split on these issues. There were those who felt that Westminster had no right to intervene, that in effect a convention had been established which created virtual sovereignty for Northern Ireland. The anger of this group was compounded by the perception that it was a Labour government (with an Irish unity agenda) which was forcing the pace. Others had an anti-O'Neillite agenda. They believed their Prime Minister was too liberal or too haughty or too interventionist. In short, their motives were mixed but many of them were jealous of their local power base. They had witnessed the loss of some powers under O'Neill and now they were expected to make concessions which would hand over local government control to Nationalists in some areas. A third group was fundamentalist in its outlook. It held the civil rights campaign to be a Romish plot designed to drive Protestant Ulster into a united Ireland. The leader of this group, the Reverend Ian Paisley, already had established the Protestant Unionist Party.

All of these forces were in evidence at a general election called in February 1969 by Terence O'Neill in a vain attempt to shore up his authority. His difficulty was personified in the contest for his Bannside seat where he was challenged by the People's Democracy leader, Michael Farrell, as well as the Reverend Ian Paisley. He won the seat and the election but the UUP had split into 22 pro-O'Neill Unionist MPs and 11 anti-O'Neill Unionist MPs. This was the party's worst result since the foundation of the state. It was only a matter of months before O'Neill resigned along with one of his supporters – the two ensuing by-elections were won by Protestant Unionists. He had been Prime Minister for six years; his two successors were to last for less than two years and one year respectively. His predecessors had held on to office throughout 1921–40, 1940–45, and 1945–63 respectively. The life span of a Unionist leader served as a barometer of the fortunes of Unionism. Another victim of that election was the Nationalist leader, Eddie McAteer. He fell to the civil rights leader, John Hume, and the Nationalist Party was reduced to only five MPs.

The fortunes of O'Neill and McAteer were reflected in the changing party system. The UUP was to remain largely intact after 1970 but it never regained its former glory. Indeed there were even disputes over its name. Officially it retained the title of UUP but for much of the following 20 years it was known as the Official Unionist Party (OUP) to distinguish it from the plethora of unionist parties which emerged in the aftermath of the introduction of PR. All of them were intent on claiming both 'Ulster' and 'Unionist' in their titles. We shall pursue that maze later. For the moment we note that the UUP spent much of its time protecting its own flanks from an invigorated fundamentalism and, to a lesser extent, from liberals concerned with what they considered to be the malign influence of the Orange Order. The latter were closet O'Neillites, some of whom helped in April 1970 to found the Alliance Party, a party of the Union rather than a unionist party. That message may have been too subtle for an electorate weaned on a diet of Orange and Green.

Alliance became more of a nuisance than a challenge to the UUP. The same could not be said for the wider fringes of loyalism. The effect of the introduction of PR for local elections was that no fewer than 13 parties contested the 1973 local council elections on a unionist or loyalist ticket, reflecting both the post-direct rule confusion among Protestants and an intense localism. PR then created a multi-party system and a growing intra-community competition. The split in Unionism which emerged in February 1969 was carried over into the 1974 power-sharing Assembly in which the Faulkner Unionists were outnumbered by 27 anti-power-sharers. In the elections for a Constitutional Convention of May 1975, 47 loyalists were elected under the umbrella of the United Ulster Unionist Council. The UUUC had been formed in January 1974 to oppose power-sharing and any interference by the Irish government in Northern Ireland's affairs. It collapsed in 1977 following a 'constitutional stoppage' led by the Reverend Ian Paisley and loyalist paramilitaries in an effort to persuade the government to restore Stormont and to be proactive against the IRA. That signalled Protestant disarray with divisions between integrationists and devolutionists, between militants and moderates. For the first time since 1921 no single party dominated their community. Ian Paisley's Democratic Unionist Party (DUP) sought that domination by seeing off rivals like William Craig's Vanguard Unionist Progressive Party (VUPP) and then by challenging the UUP for outright control. The former had been achieved by 1976, the latter never. We can trace the intensity of competition between the DUP and UUP by comparing the party share of first preference votes at the local council level during 1973–93 (Table 8.1). They illustrate the rapid rise of the DUP until 1981 and then a relatively moderate decline. It would be foolish to suggest that this trend is irreversible

Table 8.1 Electoral performance of Unionist parties: percentage share of first preference votes at local council level

	1973	1977	1981	1985	1989	1993
DUP	4.3	12.7	26.6	24.3	17.7	17.3
UUP	41.4	29.6	26.5	29.5	31.3	29.4

Consequences of change: Nationalists

Nationalist politics also underwent a sea change whereby the long established Nationalist Party became redundant. Three independents, all of them from a younger civil rights-oriented generation, had been elected in 1969. They were to become the backbone of a new party, the Social Democratic and Labour Party (SDLP), formed in August 1970. Its cumbersome name suggests a difficult gestation but it was sending the clear message that it was not a warmed-up version of the old Nationalists and that it had a distinctive social and economic policy. It was committed to a card-carrying membership, political organization, and a belief in constructive political action, all of which served it well in more trying times. It was akin to the Nationalists in that it desired Irish unity but the emphasis was firmly on consent. This outlook was apparent in a political strategy which recognized the limitations of a purely internal solution to the Northern Ireland problem. Following the failure of power-sharing in 1974, the Constitutional Convention in 1975 and the Atkins Conference in 1980–81, the SDLP continued to contest elections within Northern Ireland but much of their propaganda was directed at an influential international audience.

The dynamism of the SDLP, illustrated in Table 8.2, has to be contrasted with the more cautious approach of traditional Nationalism and the militancy of armed republicanism. The Nationalist Party had been superseded by the civil rights movement but attempted some sort of comeback through the Irish Independence Party (IIP) founded in 1977. This party took less than 4% of the poll in 1979 and again in 1981 (for district councils). After 1982, with the electoral rise of Sinn Féin, the IIP became a footnote in history. There had been no SF electoral presence in the 1970s because it eschewed the ballot box in favour of acting as a support group for the IRA. All of that changed as a result of republican hunger strikes in 1980–81 when SF realized the efficacy of the 'armalite and ballot box' strategy. This policy, which was summarized by *Republican News* as 'while not everyone can plant a bomb, everyone can plant a vote', was to be remarkably popular. Working from an electoral base of zero, the party took just over 10% of first preference votes at the 1982 Assembly elections and 13.4% at the 1983 general election when Gerry Adams was returned as a Westminster MP. Now they had become a serious threat to SDLP dominance, winning as much as 40% of the Catholic vote. That threat was countered through the Anglo-Irish process beginning with the Agreement signed in 1985.

Table 8.2 Electoral performance of Nationalist parties: percentage share of first preference votes at local council level

	1973	1977	1981	1985	1989	1993
SDLP	13.4	20.6	17.5	17.8	21.0	22.0
SF	n/a	n/a	n/a	11.8	11.2	12.4

Conclusions

What conclusions may be drawn from this survey? The first is one of current complexity. Before the 1970s, elections were noted for their predictability and the party system for its lethargy. There were little local skirmishes but a dominant one-party system and a majoritarian electoral system operated against change and genuine political dialogue. The appearance of normality and stability had created complacency in both Belfast and London. The civil rights campaign acted as the midwife of change, a transformation which the old party system could not handle. One-party dominance gave way to multi-party confusion and an electoral system which helped to compound these difficulties. Between 1921 and 1972 Northern Ireland elections operated under the 'first-past-the-post' model. That system continued for Westminster elections, but STV was introduced for local and Assembly elections *and* for direct elections for the European Parliament when Northern Ireland was treated as one huge constituency.

The second concerns the nature of party debate. There was little need for such debate either within or between parties before the onset of the Troubles. Everything seemed inevitable. There was no reason to expect either fundamental political change or alternating governments. So there was no need for political thought. The Troubles transformed all that. Unionists, for instance, needed to come to terms with their new relationship with the government in London, then with the minority, and finally with changes in Anglo-Irish relations. More importantly it raised questions about identity: what did it mean to be British or Irish? Was the cost of staying within the UK or moving to Irish unity too high in terms of the responsibility entailed? Were there any lessons to be learned from the European experience? Were Unionists being abandoned? Would Nationalists need to rethink their fundamental tenets? Above all, how could relationships between Unionists and Nationalists be reshaped so that they could appear less threatening? All of these questions have been fed into the political debate and have played some role in shaping the nature of current party politics.

The third concerns the questions of leadership and of personality. Both come into some sort of conjuncture in the European elections where two men have dominated the scene since 1979 – Ian Paisley and John Hume. Both of them have topped the polls in their respective political communities. With Northern Ireland being treated as one constituency for European elections, the opportunity has arisen to marry strong personality and strong organization – hence the dominance of Paisley and Hume. But we should not confuse personality with leadership. For far too long Northern Ireland has produced weak political leaders. Personality has often masqueraded as leadership. That is not true of all leaders. Some have displayed acumen and vision. But they are the exception. It will be interesting to see whether the trauma of the past 25 years can produce more measured, mature leadership.

Further reading

Arthur, P. and Jeffrey, K., *Northern Ireland since 1968*. Oxford: Blackwell, 1988.

Aughey, A., *Under Siege: Ulster Unionism and the Anglo-Irish Agreement*. Belfast: Blackstaff Press, 1989.

McAllister, I., *The Northern Ireland Social Democratic and Labour Party*. London: Macmillan, 1977.

Seldon, A., *UK Political Parties since 1945*. London: Philip Allan, 1990.

Chapter 9

POLITICAL PARTIES:
(2) STRUCTURES AND PLATFORMS
Arthur Aughey

Party system

As we saw in the previous chapter Northern Ireland has its own distinctive party system. It is dominated by the competition between varieties of Ulster Unionism and varieties of Irish Nationalism. The major sociological factor in electoral mobilization remains not social class but religious background. Support for Unionist parties is overwhelmingly Protestant and support for Nationalist parties is overwhelmingly Catholic. Nevertheless, while the argument between Unionism and Nationalism dominates political life, the divisions within Unionism and within Nationalism have often been as deep and sometimes as bitter. A number of parties over the years have tried to canvass on a non-communal basis but they have met with only limited success.

Unionist political parties

There has been both fragmentation and cooperation within Unionist politics since the early 1970s. This has been mitigated by the traditional political wisdom that only Unionist unity could prevent the undermining of Northern Ireland's constitutional position within the United Kingdom. In the late 1970s and early 1980s, the UUP and the DUP became keen rivals for the Unionist vote. After 1985, this rivalry transformed itself once more into cooperation when both parties opposed the Anglo-Irish Agreement. However, bitter personal and political divisions opened up again following the conflicting responses of the two parties to the Downing Street Declaration of December 1993. The publication of the Framework Documents in February 1995 may have created the conditions for renewed cooperation.

Party organization

For most of its history the Ulster Unionist Party maintained a direct organizational link with the British Conservative (and Unionist) Party. It was the convention that elected representatives of the party at Westminster would take the

Conservative whip. It was only after the Conservative government of Edward Heath prorogued the Unionist-controlled devolved legislature in Belfast in 1972 that the Ulster Unionists began to organize themselves as a distinct party in the House of Commons. In 1986 the Unionists withdrew from the National Union of Conservative and Unionist Associations following the signing of the Anglo-Irish Agreement. The relationship with the Conservatives has been severely strained over the last decade. The expectation of Unionist leaders that they would be fully consulted on Northern Ireland policy in return for supporting the Conservatives at Westminster was not fulfilled.

Ulster Unionism is organized within the umbrella of the Ulster Unionist Council. One of the constitutional objectives of that Council is to link together members and their parliamentary representatives in order to settle policy, to express opinion and to advance and defend the interests of Unionism. The Council, which usually meets only once a year, is a large body consisting of party members and their leaders. There is provision for the attendance of between 600 and 700 delegates from Westminster constituency associations as well as representatives from other affiliated bodies. These bodies include the Orange Order, the Young Unionist Council, the Ulster Unionist Councillors' Association and the Ulster Women's Unionist Council. Despite this potentially large attendance, the quorum for the transaction of Council business is only 200 members.

The Council elects the leader of the party and has a significant role in the election of the Executive Committee and of the party officers. The Executive Committee is composed of the party leader, party officers and representatives of the party at Westminster, as well as members elected from the constituency delegates and representatives of affiliated bodies at the Council. It meets at least four times a year and is responsible for the general administration of party business and the consideration of policy. The Executive Committee appoints the Secretary to the Council who acts as a business manager. The Party Officers are charged with the conduct of party business between meetings of the Executive Committee and, in consultation with the leader, help to formulate party policy. An annual conference is held under the auspices of the Unionist Council to debate proposals submitted by associations and affiliated bodies.

The Democratic Unionist Party is a product of the current Troubles. As its original formulation put it, the DUP was to be 'right wing in the sense of being strong on the Constitution, but to the left on social policies'. What this formulation leaves out is the influence of the Free Presbyterian Church in the party's organization, finance and culture and, of course, the dominant influence of Ian Paisley, the leader of that church and leader of the party. The DUP's electoral image has always been one of Protestant populism first and foremost. As a result, it is largely an anti-establishment party. The DUP expresses a tradition strongly rooted in Protestant dissent which asserts that the (Protestant) people of Ulster have an inalienable right to determine their own political future.

The DUP's structure rests on local branches based on district council and Westminster constituencies. These constituencies have their own associations responsible for electing their respective officers and selecting candidates for council or Westminster elections. There is provision for a Central Delegates Assembly consisting of members elected by and from each local branch and the party executive whose tasks are to ratify all party manifestos and to select the party's candidate for election to the European Parliament.

The day-to-day business of the DUP is conducted by the Central Executive Committee which is composed of four members elected by and from each of the Westminster Constituency Associations plus the leader and deputy leader. The Executive Committee elects annually the party officers and (in the absence of a local assembly) the leader and deputy leader. The Executive Committee organizes the annual party conference which any member of the party may attend.

Electoral performance

In the early 1980s the junior member of the 'Unionist family', the DUP, seemed set to overtake in popularity the senior member, the UUP. Electoral competition between the two parties entered a new phase following the result of the first direct election to the European Parliament in June 1979. The DUP leader, Ian Paisley, came top of the province-wide poll. This vote, confirmed in all subsequent European elections, has allowed the DUP leader to claim a mandate to speak for the (Protestant) people of Ulster and that his own party therefore best represents the will of the (Protestant) people.

This, however, may misinterpret somewhat the nature of the Unionist vote. At one level, that vote expresses opposition to the idea of a united Ireland. Because the DUP is understood to embody that opposition in an uncompromising way, the European elections have something of the character of a referendum on the constitution about them. Undoubtedly, the DUP leader has profited from this. But that *negative* statement – no to a united Ireland – is not necessarily the same thing as a thorough declaration in favour of the DUP as a party or of its policies. If the Unionist vote is seen as a *positive* commitment to the Union, as it might be in local or Westminster elections, then the DUP is not necessarily seen as the best vehicle for that commitment. Indeed, the UUP has traditionally fulfilled that role.

In 1981 the DUP certainly appeared to be in the ascendant. But by 1982 the UUP had begun to recover its dominant position in the elections to the new local assembly established by the Secretary of State, James Prior, when it increased its vote to 29.7% while the DUP's fell back to 23%. The trend was confirmed in the Westminster election of 1983.

In response to the Anglo-Irish Agreement, the two parties concluded an electoral pact in January 1986 which lasted until the general election of 1992, largely to the electoral benefit of the UUP. This offended many DUP activists and was a source of division within that party. Pressure from within the DUP to end the pact became irresistible by the time of the general election of 1992. But even with a larger number of candidates the DUP's vote rose by only 1.4% over its 1987 vote to 13.1%. Although the UUP vote did fall three percentage points to 34.5%, this may be put down as much to the intervention of a new rival, the Conservative Party, as to competition from the DUP. The 1992 general election and the 1993 district council elections confirmed the UUP's status as the dominant Unionist party even though Paisley once more topped the poll in the European election of 1994.

In 1995 the UUP had nine Westminster MPs, one Member of the European Parliament and 197 district councillors. The DUP had three Westminster MPs, one MEP and 103 district councillors.

Policy

The main debate within and between the Unionist parties for much of the 1970s and 1980s was about the relative merits of a strong devolved system of government for Northern Ireland (the DUP position) or a more limited form of administrative devolution within a reformed structure of direct rule from Westminster (the UUP position). However, neither party foresaw an active or direct role for the Irish government in any political settlement in Northern Ireland. When the British and Irish governments negotiated the Anglo-Irish Agreement without any consultation with the Unionist parties and gave the Irish government a consultative role in the affairs of Northern Ireland, Unionists in both parties were left unprepared.

The challenge facing the two Unionist parties after November 1985 was twofold. Firstly, they had to try to reaffirm the United Kingdom status of Northern Ireland which Unionists believed had been compromised by the Agreement. Secondly, the UUP and DUP had to confront the possibility of an ever-deepening process of Anglo-Irish cooperation by proposing a new relationship between the two states which would more satisfactorily guarantee their interests. In the words of the joint manifesto of 1987, Molyneaux and Paisley wanted 'an alternative to and a replacement of the Anglo-Irish Agreement'. Differences between the two parties remain on what that alternative or replacement should involve, though there does exist much common ground.

Central to the strategy of both parties has been the demand that the Irish Republic should remove the territorial claim to Northern Ireland contained in Articles Two and Three of its constitution. The goal of Unionist policy is to compel the British government to reassert, in Paisley's words, the 'integrity of the state' by pressing the Irish government to confirm clearly and absolutely Northern Ireland's present status as a part of the United Kingdom. Both the UUP and the DUP have envisaged the establishment of a different British–Irish Agreement, with Northern Ireland integral to the British position. This would involve, among other things, a devolved legislature for Northern Ireland guaranteeing a proportionate role for the minority. Crucially, internal Northern Irish arrangements would have to be agreed before there could be any guaranteed formal cooperation with the government of the Irish Republic.

Following the issue of the Downing Street Declaration of December 1993 divisions between the Unionist parties increased. The DUP rejected it immediately as a 'sell-out'. The UUP, while neither welcoming nor endorsing the Declaration, did not reject it entirely and announced their willingness to let it 'run its course'.

The same was not the case with the Framework Documents which were published by the British and Irish governments in February 1995. Both the UUP and the DUP rejected them as unacceptably Nationalist in tone and intent. At the same time, while there was a broad consensus against the Documents there was still little clear unanimity, especially within the UUP, about how they might best be opposed.

Nationalist political parties

It was not until August 1970 that Nationalists in Northern Ireland constructed for themselves a recognizably modern party organization. The Social Democratic and Labour Party (SDLP) was formed at that date and replaced the moribund Nationalist Party. The SDLP indicated that it was willing to participate in the government of Northern Ireland on a power-sharing basis so long as the Irish government were to play a role in cross-border institutions. However, the collapse of the power-sharing arrangement in 1974 encouraged the SDLP to turn towards a rather different strategy in the 1980s and 1990s under the leadership of John Hume.

In part, this shift had to do with the emergence of an electoral rival to the SDLP within the Catholic community. That party was Sinn Féin (known until the 1990s as Provisional Sinn Féin), the political wing of the Provisional IRA, which began contesting elections during the hunger strike of 1981. The emotional impact on Ulster Catholic opinion of the hunger strike campaign by republican prisoners provided an opportunity for Sinn Féin to seek popular legitimation for the 'armed struggle' of the IRA. There were two immediate reasons for Sinn Féin developing an electoral strategy. Firstly, the hunger strike had created an opportunity to gain not only local but world-wide legitimacy for the IRA's campaign. Secondly, popular momentum seemed to suggest that there was a possibility of overtaking the SDLP in share of the popular vote within the Catholic community and attaching that vote to the 'armed struggle'. Nationalist politics in the 1980s were dominated by the contest between this militant strategy and the SDLP's constitutional approach.

Party organization

The SDLP's constitution states the objective of organizing and maintaining a socialist party in Northern Ireland. Like the Labour Party in Britain it has provision for 'corporate' as well as individual membership which, so its constitution specifies, would include trade unions. Since the outset, the SDLP's Nationalism has been more prominent than its socialism and no trade union has ever affiliated. However, the SDLP does participate in international socialist bodies and is a member of the Socialist Group in the European Parliament. The organizational basis of the party is the local branch which has representation at district (council) executive and constituency council levels.

The annual Party Conference is designated the 'supreme governing authority in the Party' and is composed of delegates from the local branches, the General Council, district councillors, the women's group and the youth commission. There is now provision for the Leader and Deputy Leader of the Party to face annual re-election by the Party Conference. The Conference debates motions on party policy and elects the party officers and the members of the Executive Committee. The Executive is composed of the six party officers, ten delegate members, one member of the women's group, one member of the youth commission plus the Leader and Deputy Leader. Some 40% of the posts on the Executive are to be held by women.

The Executive meets at least nine times a year. It directs the business of the party, its financial and organizational matters, and acts as the standing committee of the General Council which is responsible for the development of policy and programmes between Conferences. The General Council is composed of the Executive, representatives of the constituencies and district councillors, MPs, MEPs, Leader and Deputy Leader. There is also a Central Council which meets once a year. It is a sort of mini-conference whose purpose is to provide a means of communication between the members and the central organs of the party between Conferences.

The formal policy-making body in Sinn Féin is also the annual Conference composed of delegates from its constituent branches and regional councils. The conference elects the President, officers and the National Executive. The National Executive is responsible for the effective conduct of party policy. A standing committee of the Executive conducts the administrative affairs of Sinn Féin.

Electoral performance

In local elections in October 1982 Sinn Féin polled 10.1% of the vote against 18.8% for the SDLP. By the Westminster elections of June 1983, the figures were 13.4% and 17.9% respectively. Most importantly, the president of Sinn Féin, Gerry Adams, took the West Belfast seat from the incumbent former leader of the SDLP, Gerry Fitt, who was accused of selling out to the British government. This was a victory of enormous symbolic significance. However, the prospect of political republicanism replacing constitutional Nationalism as the main organized expression of the Catholic community sent messages of panic through government circles in London, Dublin and Belfast.

The Sinn Féin advance has stopped since the Anglo-Irish Agreement in 1985, their vote stabilizing at 11–12% while the SDLP has continued to improve to about 23%. However, this development cannot necessarily be attributed to the Agreement alone. Sinn Féin's vote was at its highest in 1983 when the party had mobilized support among those who had formerly abstained from voting. By the general election of 1992 the SDLP continued to increase its vote to 23.5%, the second best performance in its history, while Sinn Féin's vote dropped back slightly to 9.7%. More significantly, Adams lost his Westminster seat in West Belfast to the SDLP candidate Dr Joe Hendron. In the European election of 1994 the SDLP leader John Hume recorded a personal (and party) best of 28.9%.

In 1995 the SDLP had four Westminster MPs, one MEP and 127 district councillors. Sinn Féin had 51 district councillors but no MPs or MEPs.

In 1979 Gerry Fitt resigned as leader of the SDLP claiming that the party had lost its social radicalism. He was replaced by John Hume, a veteran of the civil rights movement, who increasingly promoted a new policy position from that of the 1970s. Hume's policy was to reduce the priority of an 'internal settlement' with Unionists (which did not appear possible anyway) and to work primarily for an 'external' agreement between the British and Irish governments more favourable to Nationalists. The SDLP has pursued this policy consistently and with considerable success. The strategy emerged in two distinct ways. Firstly, there was an attempt to reformulate Irish Nationalism by the SDLP and the political parties of the Republic of Ireland through the Forum for a New Ireland, which held its first session on 30 May 1983. The report of the New Ireland Forum, which was published on 2 May 1984, refocused attention on the Irish dimension to the Northern Ireland crisis. The second strategy involved negotiations between the British and Irish governments for a joint political initiative which would help to undermine Sinn Féin and the IRA, stabilize Catholic politics and sponsor a settlement between Unionists and Nationalists. The Anglo-Irish Agreement was the most important consequence of these events.

After 1988 Hume sought to develop agreed Nationalist principles with Gerry Adams, the leader of Sinn Féin, in an attempt to establish a common strategy for an 'agreed Ireland'. The Hume–Adams proposals (never made public) were delivered to the two governments in 1993 and were widely believed to be important in forming the agenda on which the Downing Street Declaration of December 1993 was based.

Although Sinn Féin decided that it could not accept the Downing Street Declaration as an adequate basis for peace, the IRA declared a ceasefire at midnight on 31 August 1994. Shortly afterwards, Sinn Féin entered into preliminary dialogue with British officials demanding recognition of their electoral mandate without prior commitment to disarmament.

In the new circumstances brought about by both the IRA and the subsequent loyalist ceasefires, the British and Irish governments agreed their Framework Documents spelling out the potential outline of a comprehensive political settlement which many Unionists believe represents a further significant advance for the politics of constitutional Nationalism pursued by the SDLP for the last 25 years.

Non-communal parties

A number of parties have competed for the non-communal or non-sectarian vote in Northern Ireland. Some of these, like the Northern Ireland Labour Party, have been dissolved; others, like the Workers' Party and more recently Democratic Left and the Conservatives, have failed to make any significant electoral impact. The party which has carried the banner of self-conscious non-sectarianism throughout the period of the present Northern Ireland crisis has been the Alliance Party.

The Alliance Party was formed in April 1970 to promote the reform of Northern Ireland's political system. Its objective was to support those institutions of government which would be as inclusive as possible. In practice that meant supporting power-sharing. This position had both its possibilities and its dangers. On the one hand, the Alliance Party could be the balancing point between the two main political blocks. On the other hand, Alliance could be squeezed by the competition of the Unionist and Nationalist parties and its moderation discounted.

The collapse of the power-sharing Executive in 1974 was a tremendous blow to the Alliance Party. Its demise, and the failure of policy to resurrect something like it, has left the Alliance Party for the last 20 years in no-man's-land. The party has maintained a distinct presence in the district councils (44 seats in 1995), especially in the east of the province, but it has never won a Westminster or European Parliament seat. In the 1980s the party witnessed a slow attrition of its support, an unsurprising reality since the 1980s were years of polarization and sectarian bitterness. The party took 10% of the vote in the general election of 1987, falling to 8.7% in 1992 and to 7.6% in the district council elections of 1993.

Alliance generally welcomed the Downing Street Declaration and the Framework Documents. Furthermore, unlike any other party which accepts the Union, it has been willing to take part in the Forum for Peace and Reconciliation in Dublin set up by the Irish government under a provision of the Downing Street Declaration.

Conclusions

The Troubles since 1969 have witnessed some interesting patterns of party competition in Northern Ireland. The great division, of course, remains between those who support the Union of Great Britain and Northern Ireland and those who want to end that Union. As this chapter has shown, however, the politics of Unionism and Nationalism have also their internal distinctions and often bitter rivalries. These rivalries within and between Unionism and Nationalism have been embittered by two decades of political violence. The extreme uncertainty about the shape and nature of the political future of Northern Ireland means that new patterns of party competition may emerge in the next few years, but their precise form is still largely unpredictable.

Further reading

Aughey, A., *Under Siege: Ulster Unionism and the Anglo-Irish Agreement*. Belfast: Blackstaff Press, 1989.

Elliott, S., 'Voting systems and party politics in Northern Ireland', in B. Hadfield (ed.), *Northern Ireland: Politics and the Constitution*. Buckingham and Philadelphia: Open University Press, 1992.

McAllister, I., *The Northern Ireland Social Democratic and Labour Party*. London: Macmillan, 1977.

Patterson, H., *The Politics of Illusion: Republicanism and Socialism in Modern Ireland*. London: Hutchinson Radius, 1989.

Smyth, C., 'The DUP as a politico-religious organization', *Irish Political Studies*, 1, 1986.

Smyth, C., *Ian Paisley: Voice of Protestant Ulster*. Edinburgh: Scottish Academic Press, 1987.

Section Four

ADMINISTRATION

Chapter 10

DIRECT RULE
Arthur Aughey

What is direct rule?

A student of politics approaching the issue of direct rule in Northern Ireland is faced with something of a paradox. On the one hand, the main features of direct rule have been in existence since March 1972. Only very briefly, that is in the first five months of 1974 during the period of the Northern Ireland Executive, was the operation of direct rule replaced by a locally accountable, devolved administration. Direct rule has, therefore, been sustained for over 20 years. On the other hand, the assumption of most British politicians as well as most politicians in Northern Ireland has always been that direct rule is an exceptional form of government and not the norm. It has been commonly the opinion of many Members of Parliament, irrespective of party, that direct rule should ultimately be replaced.

Indeed, the view of successive British governments has been that direct rule is only a temporary expedient and certainly not a solution to the problems of Northern Ireland. The legislation giving effect to direct rule in 1972 was the Northern Ireland (Temporary Provisions) Act. The Labour government's White Paper of July 1974, *The Northern Ireland Constitution*, the document which paved the way for the Northern Ireland Act of the same year, made it clear that direct rule was envisaged as a set of 'temporary arrangements'. What defines these exceptional 'temporary' arrangements in terms of the assumed 'norm' of Northern Ireland politics?

The assumed norm is some form of devolved arrangement in which locally elected representatives would take responsibility for the day-to-day decisions and administration affecting the welfare of citizens in Northern Ireland. That was the sort of arrangement, the provisions of which were set out in the Government of Ireland Act of 1920, which direct rule replaced when the Northern Ireland Parliament was prorogued in 1972. It was the sort of arrangement which the British government tried to re-establish in 1973–74 under the Northern Ireland Constitution Act. And it has been the sort of arrangement towards which the British government has been disposed ever since, despite the failure of the power-sharing Executive. Direct rule has meant the Westminster Parliament taking back direct responsibility for matters which had previously been transferred to the devolved legislature at Stormont. These are responsibilities which Westminster had happily shed in the 1920s in order to conjure the Irish question 'out of existence'. Between 1921 and 1972 it had been the task of the Northern Ireland Parliament to ensure 'peace, order and good government'.

For almost the whole of this period of devolved government Westminster operated an effective policy of non-interference in Northern Ireland's internal affairs, even though Westminster retained ultimate sovereign authority. After the exercise of this sovereignty in 1972 – the introduction of direct rule – the relationship changed dramatically. The peace, order and good government of Northern Ireland was once again a matter for United Kingdom politicians and United Kingdom civil servants. What has become clear since 1972 is that there is no way back for the British government to the distant, 'hands off' policy which obtained under the 1920 Act. It is also clear that direct rule has undergone changes in its long 'temporary' existence. Direct rule itself, in other words, has a history.

Changes in direct rule

While it is possible to put a definite date to the institution of direct rule – 30 March 1972 when the Northern Ireland (Temporary Provisions) Act received its Royal Assent – there had been preparations already laid by the British government for such an (unwelcome) eventuality. From August 1969, when the Army was called to 'aid the civil power', the British government began to interfere in a systematic way in the formulation and administration of policy in Northern Ireland. The Labour Home Secretary, James Callaghan, and after June 1970 the Conservative Home Secretary, Reginald Maudling, were concerned that London would 'carry the can' for decisions made by the Unionist government in Belfast. This applied not just to the very sensitive area of security but also to the wider aspects of political reform in Northern Ireland. A few key civil servants had been dispatched from London to keep a watching brief on local matters. Attached to departments in Belfast, they established an alternative channel of advice for their ministers at Westminster. As the violent instability increased, the dangers of London working at one remove from policy-making on the ground became manifest. As British ministers really were held by public opinion to 'carry the can' for events in Northern Ireland, especially events like Bloody Sunday in January 1972, the conclusion was reached that Stormont would have to go. It was dispensable. On 24 March 1972, the Prime Minister Edward Heath told the House of Commons that there was no alternative to the British government assuming full responsibility for Northern Ireland's administration. Direct rule had begun.

This first phase of direct rule under the first Secretary of State for Northern Ireland, William Whitelaw, had as its objective the reconstruction of a new form of devolved government which would be widely acceptable. In other words, the objective of direct rule was to undo itself as efficiently and as swiftly as possible. The comprehensive solution fashioned by Whitelaw collapsed just as comprehensively in May 1974. Yet even the experiment of power-sharing revealed that the British government would be more involved in and responsible for administration in Northern Ireland than had been the case between 1921 and 1972. There would remain an important residual role for the Secretary of State.

A second phase of direct rule, this time with a longer perspective of its responsibilities, opened up with the end of the power-sharing Executive. In the late 1970s both the Labour government and the Conservative opposition appeared disposed to look favourably upon extending direct rule indefinitely while amending its mode of operation and increasing some of the responsibilities of local government. The faint prospect of re-establishing devolved government encouraged the favourable consideration of administrative integration. However, the Conservative government of Margaret Thatcher which took office in 1979 eventually moved towards a more radical course of action. The outcome of this new strategy was the Anglo-Irish Agreement of 1985. The signing of the Agreement may be said to have initiated a third phase of direct rule.

This third phase of direct rule has been called direct rule with a 'green tinge'. The institutions set up under the Agreement – the Anglo-Irish Conference and Secretariat – have provided the government of the Irish Republic with a consultative role in the affairs of Northern Ireland. Dublin can put forward views 'on proposals for major legislation and on major policy issues'. The Agreement specifies that 'determined efforts shall be made to resolve any differences' between the British and Irish governments on these matters. The Irish government can also put forward views and proposals on the role and composition of statutory boards. The Agreement involved, therefore, a significant change in the operation of direct rule. Because of the secrecy attaching to the work of the Conference and Secretariat it is impossible as yet to know the full extent of its administrative significance.

The structure of direct rule

The political direction of direct rule is provided by the Secretary of State for Northern Ireland who has a seat in Cabinet. The Secretary of State is responsible for the conduct of policy in Northern Ireland and for representing and defending the interests of Northern Ireland both at Westminster and, when necessary, on an international stage. In this formal manner Northern Ireland has attained the same status as Scotland and Wales within the British governmental structure. The Secretary of State has his own 'team' of ministers to whom are delegated responsibilities for the Northern Ireland departments. The first Secretary of State, William Whitelaw, was served by three ministers. Since 1974 there have been teams of either four or five ministers.

The time of the Secretary of State and his ministers is divided between their duties in Northern Ireland and their parliamentary and constituency commitments in Great Britain. Despite the twin problems of air travel and intense personal security, the practical burden on Northern Ireland ministers is no greater than that experienced by others in modern government. The day-to-day coordination of political business is usually conducted in what has become known as 'morning prayers'. This is the gathering of those ministers who happen to be in Belfast, senior civil servants and press officers which meets to discuss pressing issues and immediate business. In Tom King's period in office (1985–89) a video-conferencing link was established to allow participation by the Secretary of State when he happened to be in London.

There have been well-publicized differences of attitude on the part of Secretaries of State towards their office. James Prior, appointed by Mrs Thatcher in 1981 after disagreements on Conservative economic policy, clearly viewed his posting as a form of punishment and political exile. Sir Patrick Mayhew, on the other hand, clearly welcomed his appointment as an opportunity, perhaps even as a vocation. What has been common to all Secretaries of State, however, is the unusual willingness for politicians to set in train developments which would ultimately divest their office of many of its powers. For it has been held consistently to be the case that Secretaries of State for Northern Ireland possess unusually extensive powers of patronage, appointment and control in terms of traditional British practice. This has entailed seeking some devolved solution to the 'Northern Ireland problem', the central political task of the Secretary of State.

The 'Northern Ireland problem' involves political, constitutional, security, human rights and justice issues and these are the responsibility of the Northern Ireland Office (NIO), a new Department of State created in 1972 as a consequence of direct rule. The NIO is also responsible for all matters to do with the Anglo-Irish Secretariat and preparations for Anglo-Irish Intergovernmental Conferences. Headed by a Permanent Secretary from the Home civil service, the NIO's key senior officials are seconded from departments in Whitehall. The NIO has a staff of slightly under 5,000 of which about one-third are members of the Northern Ireland Civil Service (NICS). Many of their responsibilities are both extremely sensitive and contentious locally and considered to be of vital national importance. The NIO is organized into two divisions, one in Belfast and one in London. Senior officials based in Belfast are charged with advising the Secretary of State on these 'high' policy matters. They were intimately involved, for instance, in the negotiation of the Anglo-Irish Agreement and serviced the inter-party talks of 1991–92. They were instrumental in the drawing up of the Framework Documents. Those based in London have the task of liaising between government departments in Northern Ireland and the political and administrative structures in London. They facilitate the conduct of the details of all Northern Ireland business at Westminster.

When direct rule was introduced the Secretary of State not only took over responsibility for all matters previously transferred to the devolved Parliament in Belfast but also inherited that devolved system's separate civil service and its distinctive administrative structure. The NIO has always been separate from the NICS and from the provincial departments. The main contact citizens will have with government will most often be contact with members of the NICS in their various departmental roles.

The Northern Ireland departmental structure has undergone a number of administrative reorganizations since 1972, the most significant being that to facilitate the distribution of distinct responsibilities to members of the power-sharing Executive in 1974. Today there are six departments employing some 24,000 civil servants (Table 10.1).

Table 10.1 Northern Ireland departments and functions

Agriculture	Development of agriculture, forestry, fishing, animal health, education and advisory services and the administration of UK and Common Agricultural Policy support arrangements
Economic Development	Development of industry and commerce, employment and training, industrial relations and tourism
Education	All educational matters, sport and the arts. The major educational services are delivered by five education and library boards (the government proposes to reduce them to four)
Environment	Housing, planning, roads, transport management, water and sewerage. Many of these functions were formerly carried out by local authorities but have been centralized since direct rule. Housing services, for instance, are delivered by the Housing executive
Finance and Personnel	Control of public expenditure in Northern Ireland and liaison with the Treasury, management of NICS staffing
Health and Social Services	Health and personal social services, social security and child support. The department's health and social services are delivered by four health and social services boards

Each department has its own Permanent Secretary responsible for the conduct of its administration. Coordination of departmental strategies and inter-departmental business is conducted in the Policy Coordinating Committee (PCC) comprising departmental Permanent Secretaries and the head of the NICS. The PCC is frequently concerned with options for the allocation of public spending and in this regard the Department of Finance and Personnel plays a leading role.

The head of the NICS is in overall charge of the Northern Ireland departments and accountable to the Secretary of State. He is serviced directly by the Central Secretariat which has carried on many of the functions of the old Cabinet Office that formerly served ministers in the Stormont government. It is responsible, among other functions, for the operation of the Honours system in Northern Ireland. The head of the NICS is also Second Permanent Secretary at the NIO and as such the most senior Northern Ireland (official) advisor to the Secretary of State. There remains some doubt about the extent to which the head of the NICS is fully taken into the confidence of senior NIO officials or consulted on political manoeuvres by the Secretary of State. For instance, the former head of the NICS, Sir Kenneth Bloomfield, had only the vaguest of ideas about the nature and extent of the deliberations between the British and Irish governments in advance of the

Anglo-Irish Agreement. Only in the last few weeks before its signing were the contents fully divulged to him.

Procedure and scrutiny

The view that direct rule is an 'interim' or 'temporary' measure has had significant implications for the procedures and scrutiny of Northern Ireland business at Westminster. The commitment to re-establish a devolved assembly has made successive British governments reluctant to consider ways of reforming and improving the conduct of that business. Direct rule, for example, is subject to an annual renewal debate in the House of Commons. Albeit for very different reasons, the consensus of all political parties is that the present system is unsatisfactory. In short, it is felt that there exists an obvious 'democratic deficit' which renders government less accountable in Northern Ireland than elsewhere in the United Kingdom.

The present legislative basis for direct rule is the Northern Ireland Act of 1974. That Act, though, takes as its basis the provisions of the Northern Ireland Constitution Act of 1973 which was in turn the basis of the devolutionary experiment of the Assembly and power-sharing Executive. The 1973 Act (like the Government of Ireland Act of 1920) distinguished three types of legislation: excepted, reserved and transferred. Excepted matters involve exclusively national concerns such as international relations, the armed forces and the Crown, matters which would *always* be outside the competence of any devolved administration. These are the responsibility of the sovereign legislature at Westminster. Reserved matters involve responsibilities, such as policing and prisons, which would *normally* be outside the competence of an Assembly in Northern Ireland. These too would remain in the hands of Westminster. Transferred matters are those matters which are not excepted or reserved and capable of coming within the competence of an Assembly.

Under the terms of the 1974 Act, legislation on excepted matters was to continue to be dealt with by way of formal Act of Parliament and subject to the normal procedures of debate. All those matters which come under the categories of reserved and transferred were to be dealt with by way of Orders in Council. An Order in Council is a form of delegated legislation. This means that it cannot be amended. It can only be accepted or rejected. Delegated legislation usually involves modifications to existing legislation, the authority to do so having been incorporated into an original Act of Parliament. It does not require the usual procedures of scrutiny and debate since the principle of the legislation has already been duly accepted. In the case of Northern Ireland, however, it is *primary* legislation itself which is being made in this way. Proposals for draft Orders may be circulated in advance by the government to parties and interest groups. Suggestions for amendment at this stage may be canvassed. This method of procedure tends to displace representative politics by the representation of interest. Approval of Northern Ireland Orders usually takes place at a poorly attended House of Commons after 10 p.m. and following a brief and perfunctory debate.

This was an exceptional arrangement. It was accepted precisely because dealing with the bulk of Northern Ireland business at Westminster was assumed to be exceptional (and temporary). From the point of view of the government this is an efficient and effective manner of expediting Northern Ireland business *and* maintaining its distinctiveness from the normal work of Parliament. From the point of view of representative democracy it is highly unsatisfactory. And the unsatisfactory nature of Parliamentary discussion of Northern Ireland legislation has been compounded by the inadequacy of procedures at Westminster to scrutinize the activity of government in Northern Ireland.

Until 1979 – apart from periodic debate – the main form of Parliamentary scrutiny of all government activity was Question Time. Question Time allows MPs to raise a whole range of issues and to confront ministers on the floor of the House of Commons. Question Time occupies only between 40 and 55 minutes from Monday to Thursday. Departments such as the Northern Ireland Office appear on a rota basis, meaning that there will be a Northern Ireland Question Time about once every four weeks. However, oral questions are often of less value to the MP seeking precise information. Alternatively, members may table questions for written answer which are put on public record in Hansard. Northern Ireland MPs have been reasonably assiduous in the tabling of questions which can range from security policy to the dangers of glass-fronted fireplaces. Questions do provide, nonetheless, only a limited form of scrutiny, a fact which was acknowledged by the House of Commons itself in the late 1970s.

There is one respect in which the administration's accountability to Parliament seems to operate as effectively in Northern Ireland as in Great Britain. The Comptroller and Auditor General, who formerly reported to the Stormont Parliament, is, under direct rule, an Officer of the House of Commons. He publishes reports to the Public Accounts Committee in Westminster on a wide range of issues. The Committee summons the relevant Northern Ireland Accounting Officers to give public evidence on these reports (about four to six each year) and then publishes its own findings. These are taken very seriously. While there are no Northern Ireland MPs on the Public Accounts Committee, local issues receive a reasonable proportion of the Committee's time in relation to the expenditure involved.

Following the Conservative victory in the general election of 1979 a major reform of the powers of Parliamentary scrutiny was introduced. This was the establishment of departmental select committees. The function of these committees is to examine the expenditure, administration and policy of the principal government departments. They can appoint specialist advisers and have the power to send for 'persons, papers and records'. Select committees, which have control of their own agendas, have the potential to investigate thoroughly an area of policy, to examine witnesses and to make recommendations. Ministers and civil servants may be called before select committees to defend or to explain current policy. No select committee was set up to cover Northern Ireland affairs unlike, Scottish and Welsh affairs for which committees *were* established (the Scottish Affairs Committee was in abeyance in the 1987–92 Parliament). Consideration of issues relevant to Northern Ireland depended on the time devoted to it by other functional select committees such as Agriculture or Trade and Industry. Instead,

Northern Ireland witnessed another experiment with a local Assembly under the Northern Ireland Act of 1982. For a short period of its existence in the mid-eighties it was this body and its committees which had responsibility for scrutinizing and influencing the operation of direct rule.

In the 1990s, however, there have been a number of important changes in the way in which direct rule is conducted. On 9 March 1994 the House of Commons finally approved the creation of a Northern Ireland Affairs select committee. This had been a long-standing objective of the Ulster Unionist Party. Among the topics investigated by the committee so far have been the price of bread in Northern Ireland and the role of the International Fund for Ireland. Another change which has been effected by the persistent influence of Ulster Unionists has been the growing practice of including provision for Northern Ireland within general United Kingdom legislation. This allows amendments of a Bill to be tabled appropriate to the needs of citizens in Northern Ireland (which is not the case, as we have seen, with Orders in Council). In the 1993–94 session legislation such as the Criminal Justice and Public Order Bill, the Statutory Sick Pay Bill and the Education Bill contained such specific provision for Northern Ireland.

Conclusions

Direct rule has proved more durable and less temporary than most parties either expected or desired. In the absence of an agreed form of devolution for Northern Ireland, direct rule established a minimum level of stability and continuity in the very difficult conditions of political violence. Though it was no party's optimum arrangement it has provided some satisfaction to many. At the financial level, high degrees of public expenditure have been maintained. The planned total of expenditure for Northern Ireland in 1995–96 is £7,720 million, rising to £8,020 million in 1997–98. At the political level, Unionists had come to acknowledge its advantages, its lack of accountability notwithstanding, as confirming their place within the United Kingdom. After 1985 and the Anglo-Irish Agreement, Unionists experienced a crisis of confidence in the procedures of direct rule. Equally, constitutional Nationalists had come to acknowledge that direct rule fostered greater equality of opportunity and was certainly preferable to Unionist majority rule. After the Anglo-Irish Agreement, constitutional Nationalists felt that their position was greatly strengthened.

It remains the strategy of the British government to end direct rule and to devolve to Northern Ireland's politicians responsibility for most of the day-to-day business of politics. This is part of an ambitious programme which now embraces the various elements of what is known as the 'peace process'. At the same time, changes have been made in the way in which Northern Ireland business is conducted at Westminster to make it more democratically accountable. These two agendas are not necessarily incompatible.

Further reading

Bell, P., 'Direct rule in Northern Ireland', in R. Rose, (ed.), *Ministers and Ministries.* Oxford: Clarendon Press, 1987.

Bloomfield, K., *Stormont in Crisis.* Belfast: Blackstaff Press, 1994.

Connolly, M., *Politics and Policy-making in Northern Ireland.* Hemel Hempstead: Philip Allan, 1990.

Connolly, M. and Loughlin, S. (eds), *Public Policy in Northern Ireland: Adoption or Adaptation?* Belfast: Policy Research Institute, 1990.

Hadfield, B., *The Constitution of Northern Ireland.* Belfast: SLS Publications, 1989.

Hadfield, B. (ed.), *Northern Ireland: Politics and the Constitution.* Buckingham and Philadelphia: Open University Press, 1992.

O'Leary, C. *et al.*, *The Northern Ireland Assembly 1982–86.* London: Hurst, 1986.

Chapter 11

LOCAL GOVERNMENT
Arthur Aughey

Introduction

Local government has had a troublesome history in Northern Ireland. At the very beginning of the state 21 councils controlled by Nationalists refused to accept the authority of the Unionist government and their functions were carried out by appointed commissioners. In response to this challenge to its authority the government at Stormont passed the 1922 Local Government (NI) Act which abolished proportional representation for local elections. The major consequence of this Act, which also permitted the Unionist government to change electoral boundaries, was to consolidate Unionist power at the local level. In the 1960s most of the specific grievances of the Civil Rights movement focused on the conduct of local government. Complaints about housing allocation (discrimination), about the manipulation of ward boundaries (gerrymandering) and above all about the restriction of the franchise (one man, one vote) were local government issues which crystallised a general catholic discontent with Unionist administration. The symbolism of the undoubted abuse of Unionist control in the case of Londonderry had a potent impact on world opinion. Less attention was focused on employment discrimination in Nationalist-controlled Newry.

As one would expect, the crises of Northern Ireland society as a whole find their political expression in local government whether or not local government itself has any relevant statutory powers to address these crises (and it almost always does not).

Origins and structure

The origins of the present local government system are to be found in two distinct though historically related considerations. The first is administrative and concerned with the efficient delivery of public services. The second is political and concerned with avoiding the abuses which were manifest in the old system.

In the 1960s there was a general consensus of opinion amongst academics and administrators in the United Kingdom that the institutions of government needed to be reformed to cope with the demands of a rapidly changing society. Much of this reforming energy was directed at the practices of central government and parliament but such is the nature of power in British politics that the organisation of local government is amenable to change in a way that Westminster and Whitehall are not. Local government became the arena for testing theories of public service. The key idea of this era was that of 'planning'. It was considered appropriate that local government should be restructured in order to assist in the proper planning of welfare state provision. Behind the general idea of planning lay the key principles of contemporary public management – administrative rationality, organisational efficiency, bureaucratic expertise and impartiality. These principles informed the recommendations that were made for local government reorganisation in Great Britain, for instance the Redcliffe–Maud and Wheatley reports of 1969 and 1972 respectively.

Northern Ireland was not immune from this spirit of administrative reform. Nor was it indifferent to the prevailing ideas of planning and governmental efficiency. Indeed, these ideas seemed at one point to define the character of the government of Terence O'Neill after 1963. Before the outbreak of the Troubles the Northern Ireland government had been preparing proposals to reform local government. If the precise form of reorganisation might have been disputed, what was not at issue was the need to overhaul the cumbersome structure inherited from the 19th century which had been only slightly adapted in the early 20th century. Northern Ireland was 'over-governed'. Beneath the Stormont administration (which could itself be seen as a sort of regional council) was a complex two-tiered network of 16 borough and county councils and 56 urban and rural district councils. In addition to these authorities were the two all-purpose county boroughs of Belfast and Londonderry. And all of this for a population of about one and a half million people.

In 1966 there had been a White Paper suggesting the need to reduce the number of councils and in 1969 there had been consideration of a thorough transformation of responsibilities which would remove from local government direct responsibility for the provision of health and personal social services and education. These were radical and controversial proposals providing for an unprecedented form of provincial centralisation. Even these proposals were rapidly overtaken by events. The Civil Rights campaign was to have important consequences for the responsibilities which councils would exercise in the future.

Thus the recommendations of the Review Body of June 1970 which established the current local government system were a development of proposals which had emerged in the 1960s and of decisions already imposed on Stormont by the British government in response to the Civil Rights disturbances. The Macrory Report (named after its chairman Patrick Macrory) favoured a distinction between regional services, which should be under the direction of the Stormont ministries, and district services which should remain in the sphere of local councils. These recommendations were accepted and formed the basis of the Local Government (NI) Act of 1972 which came into effect in 1973. This Act entailed a drastic reduction in the statutory powers of local government.

If these changes could be justified according to the administrative priorities of the day they were also confirmed by the political priorities of the day. In contrast with the principles of modern public organisation – rationality, efficiency, expertise and impartiality – local politics in Northern Ireland presented itself as a site of sectarianism, discrimination, inefficiency and incompetence. However unjust this general perception may have been, it established an operative principle of policy. That principle proposed that de-politicising as far as possible the delivery of local services was the condition of good government in Northern Ireland. Control should be returned to politicians only insofar as they conformed to practices defined as appropriate to good government, namely power-sharing under the supervision of the Secretary of State for Northern Ireland. Following the prorogation of Stormont, power-sharing was envisaged to be the arrangement at regional rather than local level (in the first instance at any rate).

The old two-tier system of local government with its 73 elected local authorities was replaced by a single tier of 26 district councils founded on the main centres of activity, the district towns and the cities of Belfast and Londonderry. The smallest of these councils is Moyle on the North Antrim coast (with an electorate of 10,500) and the largest is Belfast (with an electorate of over 210,000). This structure, which has endured throughout the Troubles, has recently come under review in line with a general reconsideration of local government organisation throughout the United Kingdom which began in the spring of 1991. The preliminary recommendations of the boundary commissioner, Dr Maurice Hayes, that Moyle should be abolished and the number of councils reduced from 26 to 25, met with determined resistance. The final and revised recommendations confirmed the status quo. The Conservative government has favoured a single-tier system for the whole of the United Kingdom. While this might suggest some trend towards uniformity between Great Britain and Northern Ireland there is, of course, no equivalence between the powers and responsibility of elected councils in England, Scotland and Wales and those in Northern Ireland.

Functions

With the collapse of the power-sharing experiment in 1974 many of the assumptions about local democracy and accountability contained in the Macrory proposals also collapsed. The upshot has been that directly elected politicians in Northern Ireland have lost the ability to control those major services which Macrory had deemed regional. They remain responsible only for those minor services which were deemed appropriate for the district councils. Since 1974, therefore, the balance of local service provision has swung heavily in favour of the principles of administrative efficiency and bureaucratic expertise and against the principle of local democratic accountability. Most observers have detected here a 'democratic deficit'. This unforeseen development has become known as the 'Macrory gap' – that is, the gap being some devolved assembly, accountable to the electorate and responsible for the day-to-day administration of those (regional) services provided elsewhere in the United Kingdom by a county council. Under direct rule these services have remained the responsibility of the Secretary of State for Northern Ireland and his junior ministers at the Northern Ireland Office. This accountability gap or democratic deficit has been compounded by the lack of appropriate procedures to debate Northern Ireland business in the House of Commons. Scrutiny of local affairs therefore has tended to slip through the grid of democratic politics. Only recently has reform of the procedure of direct rule gone some way towards redressing this problem.

There is a perfect administrative logic to this division of powers. When responsibility for housing had been removed from local government in 1969 and vested in the newly centralised Housing Executive it also seemed wise to coordinate regionally those services which complemented housing provision, such as the planning of water, sewage and roads. These tasks were vested in the Department of the Environment. Once housing had been removed from local authority control it was not an unnatural step to consider the removal of other key welfare functions such as health and education. This was precisely the logic which we find in the Macrory Report. District councils then became 'residual' authorities. They became directly responsible for those limited community services 'left over' once the strategic services had been removed. Thus we have today the following division of functions.

The 26 district councils are charged with regulatory tasks such as the licensing of entertainment and with environmental health. They are also responsible for leisure provision, street cleaning, refuse collection and the maintenance of cemeteries. They register births, deaths and marriages. More recently, councils have been encouraged to promote community relations projects and are allowed minor scope to promote local economic development. The disparaging, though frequently used, definition of district council work is that it is about cleaning the streets, emptying the bins and burying the dead; disparaging, but with a strong element of truth. Under government legislation of 1988 which introduced compulsory competitive tendering, council workforces must now compete with other potential service providers in the open market.

The place of elected councils in the scheme of things can perhaps best be gauged by consideration of its share of overall public expenditure in Northern Ireland. In 1986/87 out of a total Northern Ireland budget of just over £4.5 billion district councils were responsible for spending £109 million, or about 2% of public expenditure. In 1993/94 the figures were roughly in proportion – £7 billion; £200 million; a little under 3%. This compares with an average local authority expenditure in Great Britain of about 30% of all public expenditure. The small sum expended by councils in Northern Ireland may help explain why they did not experience the turmoil of changes in local government financing which dogged centre–local relations in Great Britain under the Conservatives after 1979. The traditional property rate has remained the basis of council revenue. There was never any threat of a poll tax or of a council tax.

Regional services are provided through boards, agencies and departments. We have already mentioned the Housing Executive and Department of the Environment. Health and personal social services such as hospitals, general practitioner services and community care are the responsibility of four area boards. Education and library services are provided by five area boards. Forty per cent of the places on the education and library boards are reserved for representatives of the district councils; three out of the ten members of the board of the Housing Executive are also local councillors. Until recently, 30% of the places on the health and social services boards were held by local councillors. The participation of councillors on these boards fulfils two functions specified by Macrory, namely the function of representation and the function of consultation. Nevertheless, it remains the case that all district councillors on the boards are subject to confirmation by the relevant government minister at the Northern Ireland Office. The minister has the authority to reject some and to nominate others if it is felt that such action would provide a more accurate reflection of political opinion. Remaining places on the boards are held by members of professional bodies, trade unions, interest groups and members of the general public. They too are appointed by ministers. These appointments are designed in principle to represent a fair balance of local views as well as a selection of the 'brightest and the best'.

Despite the attempt to achieve a reasonably representative cross-section of appointments to the boards there has been pervasive criticism of the current system for being undemocratic. Both Nationalists and Unionists have argued from time to time that appointees are 'yes men' (or women) chosen specifically because of their amenability to the main principles of government policy. Latterly the accusation has been made that these appointees tend to be 'Alliance Party types'; in other words, middle-of-the road appointments who are unrepresentative of either community in Northern Ireland. These accusations have been vigorously rebutted by the government and by the boards. But they do illustrate a general perception by elected politicians that a new class of public figure has emerged over the last two decades to rival their own mandate, a new class which gains preferment not because of its standing with the electorate but precisely because of its immunity from popular pressure. Such a political class is less likely to strike up partisan positions which might frustrate the smooth implementation of public business.

This is a local aspect of a more general trend which has taken place in the delivery of public services throughout Great Britain. A system of appointed agencies is nothing new. National Health Service management is a case in point. However, since 1979 there has been a tendency, according to some academics, towards a 'new magistracy' in which the former functions of elected councillors are being put into the hands of government appointees in so-called quangos (quasi-autonomous non-governmental organisations). Indeed, it might be argued that the Northern Ireland model – with its priority of efficiency of service over local democratic control – is the sort of model which many of the Conservative reforms in Britain have been tending towards. Local government reform in Northern Ireland, instituted to adapt society to the needs of centralised planning, is now employed to adapt society to the needs of a competitive market.

Politics of local government

The first elections to the reorganised structure of local government in 1973 indicated an unprecedented level of party political competition for council seats. In the previous election to the old system the majority of seats had been uncontested and many of these seats had been held by independents. The number of seats had been cut from 1,300 under the old system to 526 under the new (since 1993 there have been 582). Nevertheless there were 1,222 candidates for these seats (in 1993 there were 933). One incentive for party competition was the introduction of proportional representation (single transferable vote) reversing the simple majority procedure enacted by Stormont in 1922. The other major political incentive was the opportunity to mobilise public opinion in the aftermath of the introduction of direct rule in 1972. It is interesting to note that the 1973 district council elections actually brought Northern Ireland into line with trends in local government politics which had been observable in the rest of the United Kingdom for years. The first of these trends was the growing domination of council business by explicit party organisation. The second was the transformation of local elections into an opinion poll on central government policy. Given the passionate intensity of politics in Northern Ireland it is not difficult to explain why, given the few responsibilities which district councils actually do exercise, local elections should be so fiercely contested. Indeed, electoral turnout at local elections in Northern Ireland (about 57%) has remained consistently higher than that in Great Britain (about 40%). District council elections have taken on this 'barometer of opinion' function in political speculation and the results are scrutinised by academics, journalists and officials to provide some indication of the balance between 'extremism' and 'moderation' in the public mood.

In the 1980s the council chambers became the focus of Unionist political disaffection brought about by two separate developments: firstly, the entry by Sinn Féin into local politics in the elections of May 1985, and secondly, the signing of the Anglo-Irish Agreement in November 1985. Both of these events made the four-year term 1985–89 one of particular friction and conflict which inflicted damage on the reputation of local politics and polarized further the local parties. Thus the Ulster Unionists and Democratic Unionists campaigned in the 1985 election on a platform of 'smash Sinn Féin'. Unionists were outraged that their representatives were expected to sit in the council chamber with, and conduct policy in the presence of, members of a party which supports the IRA and its 'armed struggle'. They felt this more keenly since British government ministers refused to meet with Sinn Féin councillors. The elections of 1985 saw Sinn Féin secure 59 seats on 17 district councils. Where possible, Unionist councillors saw it as their duty to deny Sinn Féin any legitimacy by using procedural rules to exclude them from normal council affairs. This involved tactics such as suspension of individual members; establishing special general purpose committees to conduct business without Sinn Féin participation; and adjournment of meetings. Craigavon Borough and Belfast City councils, both with Unionist majorities, were to take the lead in this exclusion strategy.

These practices were challenged in the courts and in almost every case the

99

judgement went against the Unionists. It was held that Unionist actions were unreasonable and beyond the powers of local councils to enforce. However, in response to one of the central grievances of Unionists – that Sinn Féin councillors could use their positions to advance the cause of political violence – the government introduced the Electoral Authorities (NI) Act of 1988 which required all candidates at local elections to make a declaration that they would not express support for or approval of violence for political ends. Since enforcement of that provision of the Act was to be a civil and not a criminal offence the onus was placed on individuals and not on the government, weakening the force of the legislation. Furthermore, the declaration proved to be one with which Sinn Féin candidates could live. These judicial decisions and government action could not, of course, remedy the poisonous spirit in which many councils operated and in some cases continue to operate.

Following the Anglo-Irish Agreement, and in particular following the dissolution of the Northern Ireland Assembly in June 1986, the councils were the site of Unionist protest. The two main tactics of protest in the 18 councils in which Unionists had overall control were to refuse to strike a domestic rate and to adjourn council business. Unionist councillors also boycotted government ministers. In November 1986 it was mooted that Unionists should resign their seats and withdraw from participation on the area boards. Many Unionists argued that the council disruption campaign was the only legitimate form of political protest open to them in their opposition to the Agreement. Others thought that the strategy was ultimately counterproductive. Far from deflecting the government from its intentions the only consequence seemed to be to threaten the interests of Unionist councillors and those of their own constituents.

In Belfast the Alliance Party brought a successful action in the High Court in February 1986 which ordered the resumption of normal business. The City Council only avoided a £25,000 fine in May 1986 by ending its suspension policy (though Unionists then adopted the policy of 'deferral'). Exactly one year later the fine was imposed and the Council also had to pay legal costs of £11,000. Again in February 1987 Castlereagh Council was fined £10,000 for defying a court order to conduct its business normally. By this time the government had appointed a commissioner to set rates in those districts where Unionists refused to do so. Faced with such measures the protest began to lose steam and most dissenting councils began slowly to resume business as usual.

If the years 1985–89 created the impression of chaos and disruption the years after 1989 proved that it was at least possible to establish some *modus vivendi*, though not perfect harmony, between the constitutional parties on most district councils. By 1994–95 16 councils operated 'power-sharing' arrangements for the top posts – chair or deputy chair, mayor or deputy mayor. Generally, council committee membership is allocated proportionately among the parties and there have been agreements to share out the posts of chair on committees and sub-committees. Critics have argued that much of this is merely symbolic. Rotating posts at the top does not necessarily constitute *effective* sharing of power nor involve *cross-community* cooperation. Moreover, district councils have little power to share. Those who defend this initiative argue that symbolism in Northern

Ireland is important. Indeed, it is the first step that counts. Once the symbolic barrier is broken then a more substantial form of power-sharing will be easier to implement.

Nevertheless, there remains a clear divide between the Unionists and the SDLP on policy towards local government. The Ulster Unionists in particular have long been advocates of a return of more extensive powers to local authorities as a first step towards restoring accountable government to Northern Ireland. They have argued that from such small beginnings a more stable and responsible political culture can be built within which the political parties may move on to a more comprehensive form of devolved administration. The SDLP have been opposed to such a move which, it believes, would be retrogressive and put power back into the hands of Unionist councillors who, they argue, abused that power in the past. The politics of local government, therefore, remains controversial.

Conclusions

Local government in Northern Ireland plays only a very minor role in the allocation of public resources. The present structure and functions of district councils were originally conceived to fit into a system of devolved government which would be accountable for the major services of the region. When that tier of democratic control ceased to exist after the demise of the Executive in 1974, the 'Macrory gap' or democratic deficit has distinguishing council politics for two decades. What has always been seen as a local anomaly – the management of major public services by appointed boards and quangos – no longer seems so peculiar in the light of changes which have taken place in the rest of the United Kingdom since 1979. There too, commentators have pointed to a trend towards non-elected local administration. Nonetheless, local government powers in Great Britain remain extensive compared with those in Northern Ireland.

This does not mean that district councils are without any significance. The absence of a devolved parliament in Northern Ireland has given them a symbolic importance far beyond the actual powers they command. How district councils operate and the image they project are vital ingredients of the political culture and provide a test for the principles of party co-operation.

Further reading

Birrell, D. and Murie, A., *Policy and Government in Northern Ireland: Lessons of Devolution* Dublin: Gill and Macmillan, 1980.

Connolly, M., *Politics and Policy-making in Northern Ireland.* Hemel Hempstead: Philip Allan, 1990.

Connolly, M., 'Learning from Northern Ireland: an acceptable model for regional and local government', *Public Policy and Administration*, 7(1) 1992.

Connolly, M. and Loughlin, S. (eds), *Public Policy in Northern Ireland: Adoption or Adaptation?* Belfast: Policy Research Institute, 1990.

Knox, C., 'Sinn Féin and local elections: the government's response in Northern Ireland', *Parliamentary Affairs* 43(4), 1990.

McKay, M. and Irwin, G., *Cooperation in Local Government: A Study of Local District Councils and Power-sharing in Northern Ireland*. Belfast: Institute of Irish Studies, 1995.

Wilson, D. and Game, C., *Local Government in the United Kingdom*. London: Macmillan, 1994.

Chapter 12

LAW AND ORDER
Paul Hainsworth

Introduction

Policing is a difficult practice in most, if not all, modern societies, but when the society in question is characterized by a high degree of polarization and the constitutional nature of the state is fundamentally questioned then problems of law and order are accentuated. These are central problems in Northern Ireland where communal and political divisions have promoted a crisis of legitimacy over policing and legal matters. While this crisis has been evident since the late 1960s, with the onset of 'the Troubles', the roots of the problem go back at least to the formation of Northern Ireland in the early 1920s.

History

Policing in Northern Ireland is primarily the responsibility of the Royal Ulster Constabulary (RUC). It was established in 1922 following the widespread unrest which resulted in the division of Ireland. In Northern Ireland the devolved government passed the 1922 Constabulary Act, a product of the new administration's very first report, which recommended a 3,000-strong force, with one-third of the places reserved for Catholics. The RUC was to be supported by a largely part-time reserve force, the Ulster Special Constabulary (USC), which came to be known as the 'B' Specials. From the outset, the police forces were allocated a dual role: responsibility for 'ordinary' crime and also for policing the new political settlement which meant protecting the border and confronting internal opponents.

However, at least three factors contributed to the lack of acceptability of the new police force. First, the boundaries of the state were contested by Irish Nationalists and therefore the police were seen as part and parcel of the unwanted Unionist state. Second, the one-third Catholic quota was never filled, falling from 21% in 1922 to less than 8% in the 1990s. Initially, Catholic recruits came from the old Royal Irish Constabulary (RIC) but Unionist hostility, Nationalist intimidation, the police's early links with the Orange Order and the effects of emergency legislation all contributed to make the RUC a mainly Protestant and

103

Unionist force. Moreover, the 'B' Specials drew heavily from the loyalist paramilitary Ulster Volunteer Force (UVF), thereby further shaping the Unionist composition of the police force. Third, emergency legislation provided potentially sweeping powers which, in practice, were used primarily to police Nationalist communities.

In particular, the 1922 Special Powers Act (SPA) furnished the Minister of Home Affairs with wide authority to intern and arrest without trial, interrogate, execute, flog, ban meetings, commandeer land and property, proscribe organizations, restrict publications and suspend coroners' inquests. Initially, the SPA was renewed annually, but in 1933 became permanent. Up to 1966, associations proscribed via the SPA were all pro-republican and the other provision of the Act – internment – was used almost exclusively against Nationalists. Unsurprisingly, then, in the mid-1930s a National Council for Civil Liberties' investigation criticized the nature of the emergency powers. Between 1922 and the late 1960s, the framework for law and order remained basically unchanged and the civil rights protests of 1969 focused upon policing/emergency legislation as a key area of concern. Moreover, in 1969 police reaction to the civil rights movement put policing at the centre of attention.

Policing and 'the Troubles'

Following serious clashes between civil rights demonstrators and the police, the 1969 Cameron Commission criticized the police's role, misconduct and ill-discipline while the subsequent Scarman Tribunal (1969) – dealing with the continued nature of the Troubles – endorsed this critique, simultaneously pointing to a lack of confidence in the police. One particular problem was the evidence of the involvement of off-duty 'B' Specials in attacks upon civil rights marchers. A third and influential official report in late 1969, the Hunt Report, dealt specifically with the issue of policing and the RUC's dual role, making various benchmark recommendations for reform in order to render the police more widely acceptable. These included the abolition of the 'B' Specials; the creation of a Police Authority; demilitarization and disarming of policing; repeal of emergency legislation; the introduction of an effective system for complaints against the police; and remodelling or civilianizing the RUC on UK police lines. By this time, the British Army had been brought into Northern Ireland and allocated prime responsibility for restoring law and order during a long, 'hot' summer which left 10 people dead, many injured and thousands homeless.

Parts of the Hunt Report were implemented although the continuing unrest in Northern Ireland prevented the disarming and civilianizing of the police. The 'B' Specials were disbanded almost immediately and replaced by the Ulster Defence Regiment (UDR), a new local force within the British Army, with a Catholic intake of 18% initially, falling to 3% in the 1990s. Also, the 1970 Police Act legislated for a Police Authority for Northern Ireland (PANI) whose function would be to secure the maintenance of an adequate and efficient police force accountable to the public through the Police Authority. PANI is part of a tripartite structure for policing which includes the Chief Constable and the Secretary of State for Northern Ireland. The responsibilities of PANI include the following: determining the size of the RUC; providing and maintaining buildings and resources; appointing chief officers and responding to any complaints against them; monitoring complaints against the police generally; and exercising financial and budgetary control over expenditure on policing. The Chief Constable (previously called the Inspector General) is responsible for operational matters and enforcing law and order while the Secretary of State for Northern Ireland has overall responsibility for security matters. In the 1970 Police Act, the size of the police was set at 3,500 but by the end of the 1970s, amid continuing violence and civil unrest, this figure had doubled. In the 1990s there were 8,489 regular full-time police, 3,202 full-time reservists (RUCR) and 1,765 part-time reservists. At the same time about 18,000 troops were stationed in Northern Ireland, although the peace process initiated in 1994 prompted some withdrawal.

Developments in the early 1970s ensured continuing attention on law and order matters. Internment without trial, which commenced in 1971, brought widespread criticism against the one-sided and badly informed application of the exercise, leading to further distancing of Nationalist communities from the police and army. Moreover, internment led to condemnation – *inter alia* from the European Court of Human Rights – of the security forces' interrogation techniques. Furthermore, emergency legislation was strengthened providing wider powers of arrest, detention, stop and search, the introduction of non-jury trials for scheduled (politically motivated) offences in so-called Diplock Courts and discretionary exclusion orders to restrict movement of individuals within the UK. The main acts providing for emergency legislation were the 1973 Northern Ireland (Emergency Provisions) Act – which superseded the 1922 SPA – and the 1974 Prevention of Terrorism (Temporary Provisions) Act, known simply as the PTA and applicable to the whole of the UK. Both these pieces of legislation have been revised and strengthened since 1973–74, with the current versions dating now from 1991 for the EPA and from 1989 for the PTA.

The initial resort to greater utilization of emergency legislation signified an official recognition that a military solution to terrorism would not suffice. Indeed, by the mid-1970s, the British government moved away from the policy of army supremacy on law and order. The police were now given primacy through an 'Ulsterization' process, with the UDR providing back-up for the RUC. As a consequence, the RUC was increased in size, re-equipped, modernized and retrained in public order and riot control techniques. Greater emphasis was placed upon anti-terrorist covert operations by the creation of SAS-style units – Special Support Units (SSUs) and Divisional Mobile Support Units (DMSUs) – while the use of informers was encouraged. In 1976 convicted terrorists were criminalized by withdrawing the special category status first granted in 1972.

The Chief Constable, Sir Kenneth Newman, favoured greater concentration upon a community relations strategy in order to challenge the Nationalist images of the RUC as the armed wing of Unionism. However, these aspirations were dented as allegations of ill treatment of detainees in police holding centres, particularly in Castlereagh (Belfast), increased alongside criticisms of the admissibility in court of confessions obtained under duress. In the late 1970s, investigation by Amnesty International, revelations by police doctors, critical international attention (American President, Jimmy Carter, vetoed a consignment of arms from USA exporters to the RUC) and the official Bennett Report collectively led to some reforms over detention practice, although accusations resurfaced in later years. Certainly, levels of violence and conflict remained high in this period with tensions further increased in the early 1980s with the deaths of republican hunger strikers at the Maze Prison, near Belfast.

Stalker, supergrasses, Stevens

The RUC suffered further damaging allegations over deaths caused by the lethal use of force in contested circumstances, prompting accusations that the police was operating a 'shoot-to-kill' policy against republican terrorist suspects. Fatalities in 1982, and subsequent revelations of a police cover-up, resulted in the Chief Constable (Sir John Hermon) agreeing to an inquiry, which the Deputy Chief Constable of Greater Manchester, John Stalker, was appointed to direct in 1984. However, the investigation was dogged by enormous controversy as the so-called 'Stalker affair' unravelled. Stalker's investigations quickly ran into difficulty, leaving him complaining of lack of cooperation from the RUC, including the Chief Constable. After delivering a weighty report in 1986 Stalker was taken off the case abruptly and suspended from office as unsubstantiated and patently contrived allegations against his own record in Greater Manchester were investigated. Stalker was soon exonerated and reinstated to full rank in Greater Manchester but was not reappointed in Northern Ireland. Stalker's own view – shared by many observers – was that he had probed too deeply on matters related to policing in Northern Ireland and therefore paid the penalty.

Among the key concerns raised by the Stalker affair were questions about the use of informers, the role of overlapping and rival intelligence agencies, the limitations of coroners' inquests and the efficacy of police procedures relating to accountability. There were some disciplinary actions against 20 officers, but no prosecutions, as a result of 'shoot-to-kill' investigation. In Westminster, the Attorney-General recognized that the RUC had tried to pervert the course of justice – thereby validating Stalker's and others' probing – but prosecutions were ruled out 'in the public interest'. Ultimately, the Stalker episode discredited the cause of law and order, raising several serious questions about the administration of justice in Northern Ireland. The 'shoot-to-kill' controversy overlapped with another contested policy innovation, the usage of the 'supergrass' system by which witnesses passed on information to the police and courts in exchange for police protection and financial reward. At its height between 1982 and 1984, the process led to hundreds of arrests on serious charges. However, the exercise eventually created a loss of confidence in the legal system despite providing some temporary respite from previous high levels of violence.

The Stalker and supergrass controversies were added to in the late 1980s by charges of police collusion with loyalist paramilitaries. Classified information from the RUC's Criminal Intelligence Unit found its way into the hands of loyalist paramilitary groups, with photographs of suspects ending up posted openly on street walls. As a result, John Stevens, Deputy Chief Constable of Cambridgeshire, was appointed to lead an official inquiry and his report blamed elements in the UDR for 'leakages'. The Stevens Report claimed that only a small number of offenders were implicated – 94 were arrested, 59 charged, none from the RUC – and that collusion was not a widespread practice. However, Stevens recommended greater accountability, monitoring and auditing of documents, and tighter recruitment procedures. The episode probably helped to accelerate reform of the UDR and, in July 1992, the force was merged with the British Army's Royal Irish Rangers to create the 6,000-strong (full and part-time) Royal Irish Regiment (RIR). Disbandment of the UDR had become an increasing demand of Nationalist critics as some members and ex-members were convicted of sectarian offences. However, on- and off-duty, serving and ex-UDR officers had been identified and killed by the Provisional IRA as 'legitimate targets', so the restructuring brought criticism from Unionist quarters. More serious Unionist disaffection with security policy emerged as a by-product of the Anglo-Irish Agreement.

Unionist problems

In the 1970s under Sir Kenneth Newman's leadership, the RUC made some conscious attempts to redress its image in Nationalist eyes as a predominately Unionist and Protestant force. For instance, policing of the 1977 United Unionist Action Council strike and prosecution of the hard-line loyalist Shankill Butchers' gang were seen as evidence of more even-handed policing. However, progress in this direction was nullified to a large extent by the simultaneous effect of some of the other developments discussed above – Castlereagh, the Hunger Strike, Stalker, Stevens. Nevertheless, increasing Anglo-Irish rapprochement in the 1980s brought the RUC more and more into the strictly political arena and led to serious confrontation between the police and Unionist activists. The Democratic Unionist Party leader, the Reverend Ian Paisley, attacked the Chief Constable, Hermon, as the puppet of the British government's Anglo-Irish policy and Unionist critics called for tougher security measures against republican terrorists.

The Anglo-Irish Agreement (1985) provided the Irish government with an advisory input on behalf of northern Catholics on legal, social and economic matters via a new Inter-Governmental Conference, serviced by a Secretariat at Maryfield (Belfast). Unionist demonstrators protested strongly against the growing Irish dimension, but confrontation with the RUC became particularly acute over the policing of parades and Orange marches. The town of Portadown experienced heated confrontation during the traditional marching seasons in 1985–86 as parades were rerouted away from Catholic and Nationalist areas. Unionist protests against meetings of the Anglo-Irish Conference and the Maryfield Secretariat led to violent clashes which severely tested the resources of the RUC. An unprecedented aspect of the Unionist-RUC confrontation was the wave of attacks and petrol bombings on police officers' houses, forcing over 100 to relocate. The Public Order (Northern Ireland) Order 1987 provided the police with a new instrument to monitor potentially inflamatory parades but in the 1990s the police had to face up to a further taxing development. Loyalist paramilitaries under new, younger leadership were responsible for more sectarian deaths than their republican counterparts, forcing some redeployment of police energies. However, in 1994, the paramilitary ceasefires and the peace initiatives which followed opened up a totally different situation for the RUC as well as producing a broad debate about the future of policing.

Policing the peace

A key issue to emerge in recent debate about the police in Northern Ireland is how to make the service broadly accountable to and representative of the community while recognizing past problems without losing sight of the sacrifices made by the RUC during the troubles – including nearly 300 officers killed and over 7,000 injured. Virtually all sectors of society acknowledge that change ought to accompany the peace and proposals for change have been widely canvassed. However, the various proposals reflect very different agendas.

Basically, there are three different formulas for the future of the police. One approach seeks to portray the police as part of the problem in Northern Ireland and consequently nothing short of disbandment will suffice. From this perspective, the RUC symbolizes the armed wing of Unionism. This is the view of militant Irish republicanism. A second, intermediary approach calls for significant reforms on issues such as accountability, complaints procedures and emergency legislation but recognizes the difficult role the police must play. A third perspective, more prevalent in Unionist thinking, favours the status quo while perhaps taking on board some reforms. The RUC would fall into the last category with the Chief Constable arguing for a government-led debate or even a government-appointed commission on policing, and initiating, therefore, a Policing Review Team in 1995. The government has expressed a commitment to some reform of policing, has set up its own review committee and does not rule out adjustments to emergency legislation. However, in June 1995, the PTA was renewed despite nine months of peace. Meanwhile, civil liberties groups – such as the Committee on the Administration of Justice (CAJ) – have suggested that adequate powers exist under the Police and Criminal Evidence (Northern Ireland) Order 1989, without recourse to excessive and counterproductive emergency law.

The government's pre-ceasefire discussion document, *Policing in the Community* (1994), recognized *inter alia* that the tripartite relationship for policing (see above) was in need of statutory clarification. It also promised greater police accountability. The Police Authority, too, has pushed for more power to act as a conduit between police and people. PANI wants to see convincing evidence that the views of local people are being taken into account by the RUC and, to this effect, launched a public consultation process in 1995, inviting submissions on the future of policing. The Police Authority, though, is caught between two stools:

republican/Nationalist critics boycott it as a tame, ineffectual body while the Chief Constable resists perceived encroachment upon his/her operational independence and policy-making. At stake here, for instance, are questions such as who should have responsibility for rerouting parades or authorizing the use of plastic bullets?

Agreement is widespread, however, that the police should be as widely acceptable as possible. The RUC queries accusations of biased policing, drawing encouragement from attitude surveys suggesting higher levels of endorsement of the RUC than might have been expected on the basis of religion alone. Young, lower income, Nationalist males, unsurprisingly, are the cohort least supportive of the RUC. Disfavoured by the Chief Constable are any substantial name change for the RUC or fundamental restructuring such as envisaged by the Social Democratic and Labour Party's call for a regionalist structure for a newly-entitled Northern Ireland Police Service. This has been criticized from various quarters as too complicated, divisive and prone to achieving differential policing standards or criteria. Other reformers would go further still down the decentralist road.

Conclusions

The notion of accountability remains crucial in the contemporary debate about policing. Undeniably, reforms have taken place in the past decade or so: an Independent Commission for Police Complaints (1988), lay visiting provisions for detainees (1991), Community and Police Liaison Committees (CPLCs) (1991), the RUC's (Citizens') Charter (1993), reports from HM Inspectorate of Constabulary, an Independent Commissioner for the Holding Centres (1992), the RUC's Professional Policing Ethics code (1993), RUC Annual Strategy Statements, and more community relations work. However, a persistent grievance is the lack of a genuine independent element in processing complaints against the police. Accountability, of course, can be enhanced at different levels – such as through a stronger, elected Police Authority, a wider scope for the Ombudsman/woman, revamped CPLCs, devolved government structures, monitoring via the Anglo-Irish process, extended lay visiting practices, a Bill of Rights, better training of recruits, utilization of audio and video facilities in detention centres, repeal of emergency legislation and amendments to the official instructions on the lethal use of force, reform of coroners' inquests and so on.

The peace process, therefore, has opened up the prospect of reform with the above issues as part of the agenda. Reduced violence levels also leave greater scope for the redeployment of personnel on other policing concerns such as drugs, domestic violence, traffic offences and child abuse. The RUC's own 'trade union', the Police Federation, has warned that the ceasefires have unleashed a premature debate on the role and nature of policing since consensus is lacking still on a political settlement or framework. Nevertheless, the new agenda has combined with the legacies of history to push the policing debate to the forefront in the search for a durable peace in Northern Ireland.

Further reading

Brewer, J. D., 'The public and the police', in P. Stringer and G. Robinson (eds), *Social Attitudes in Northern Ireland. 2, 1991–1992*. Belfast: Blackstaff Press, 1992.

Brewer, J. D. *et al*, *The Police, Public Order and the State*. Basingstoke: Macmillan, 1988.

Centre for Research and Documentation (CRD) Belfast Community Forum on Policing, *Policing in a New Society*. Belfast: CRD/BCFP, 1995.

Committee on the Administration of Justice (CAJ)/Hainsworth, P., *The Stalker Affair: More Questions than Answers* (2nd edition). Belfast: CAJ Pamphlet No. 10, 1988.

Dickson, B., 'The legal response to the Troubles in Northern Ireland', in P.J. Roche and B. Barton (eds), *The Northern Ireland Question: Myth and Reality*. Aldershot: Avebury, 1991.

Dickson, B. (ed.), *Civil Liberties in Northern Ireland* (The CAJ Handbook, 2nd edition). Belfast: Committee on the Administration of Justice, 1993.

Dickson, B., 'Criminal justice and emergency laws', in S. Dunn (ed.), *Facets of the Conflict in Northern Ireland*. Basingstoke: Macmillan, 1995.

Greer, S., *Supergrasses: A Study in Anti-terrorist Law Enforcement in Northern Ireland*. Oxford: Clarendon Press, 1995.

Guelke, A., 'Policing in Northern Ireland', in B. Hadfield (ed.), *Northern Ireland: Politics and the Constitution*. Buckingham and Philadelphia Open University Press, 1992.

Northern Ireland Office (NIO), *Policing in the Community: Policing Structures in Northern Ireland*. Belfast: HMSO, 1994.

Ryder, C., *The RUC: A Force Under Fire* (2nd edition). London: Mandarin, 1992.

Stalker, J., *Stalker*. London: Penguin, 1988.

Stringer, P. and Robinson, G. (eds), *Social Attitudes in Northern Ireland. 2, 1991–1992*. Belfast: Blackstaff Press, 1992.

Section Five

POLICY

Chapter 13

ANGLO-IRISH RELATIONS
Paul Arthur

When the historian A.J.P. Taylor wrote in 1965 that Lloyd George had conjured the Irish question out of existence in 1922 he was expressing a peculiarly Anglocentric opinion which was to be overtaken by events before the end of the decade. Taylor would have been more accurate had he stated that Lloyd George had quarantined the Irish question from British domestic politics. In that respect out of sight was out of mind. In fact what had been an Anglo-Irish problem simply changed its territorial base and became 'the Northern Ireland problem'. The fundamentals remained. The Anglo-Irish settlement of 1920–22 changed neither the number of actors nor their conceptual approaches, simply their status. Now there were two sovereign states, the Irish Free State and the United Kingdom of Great Britain and Northern Ireland, and a subordinate Parliament and Government in Northern Ireland. British governments adopted a philosophy of 'let sleeping dogs lie' in relation to Northern Ireland. So long as the Unionist government was able to hold the peace in that peripheral region of the United Kingdom no matter at what cost, government in London was not going to intervene. And so it was until the late 1960s.

If Belfast and London settled into an amicable relationship the same could not be said about Dublin and London. Dublin had objected to its 'mere' Dominion status which it considered to be quite alien to its sense of nationality. Over the years it was to strive after a recognition of that nationality; and in doing so it changed the name of the state from the Irish Free State (1922) to Éire (1937) and to the Republic of Ireland in 1949 when it finally left the Commonwealth. It made its presence felt in the international community through (a) advancing the principle of equality of status among British Commonwealth members; (b) playing a role in the League of Nations in an effort to distance itself from British influence; and (c) identifying with anti-imperialism and the quest for world peace in the United Nations. In short it was stressing its own sovereign status, culminating in its decision to remain neutral throughout World War Two. Its policy towards claiming the lost territory of Northern Ireland was to be found in 'the larger general play of English interest' to quote Éamon de Valera, the leader of Fianna Fáil, who was to become both Taoiseach and President. In other words, Dublin had to persuade London that it was in British interests to renounce its sovereignty in Northern Ireland and then to persuade Unionists that their best interests would be served through Irish unity.

One way in which they set about this was to use every opportunity at international forums to complain about the evil of partition. The policy had certain defects. The rest of the world did not see the Northern Ireland problem as a threat to peace; and the Irish did not have the resources to mount a serious diplomatic challenge. To make a rather obvious comparison: the British diplomatic service had over 6,000 officials and 131 accredited foreign missions in 1972 whereas the Republic of Ireland had 153 officials of foreign service or equivalent grades and 31 accredited foreign missions. One way in which it attempted to overcome this asymmetry was to use the Irish diaspora, especially in the United States, as leverage. Here again it suffered under an illusion.

In the years between partition and the imposition of direct rule in 1972 Irish–American political clout was non-existent. President Woodrow Wilson had objected to Irish interference in US domestic politics during and immediately after the Great War. The Roosevelt administration was hostile to Irish neutrality in the Second World War. In 1951 a (rare) motion before the House of Representatives seeking Congressional hearings on an anti-partition resolution was decisively defeated by a vote of 206 to 139. The United States placed much more emphasis on the Anglo-American 'special relationship' in which the Northern Ireland problem was seen within the British sphere of influence. In any case, successive Irish governments had reverted to using the problem simply as a rhetorical device. They invested in what became known as 'verbal republicanism' whereby they complained about the evils of partition but did very little to rectify the situation within Northern Ireland.

A sea-change occurred when Seán Lemass became Taoiseach in 1959. He extended the Taoiseach's role in the field of foreign affairs. Lemass expounded his philosophy of economic Nationalism in a Dáil statement on 3 June 1959 when he said that 'the historic task of this generation is to secure the economic foundation of independence'; and on 9 November 1960 that it was meant 'to confound those Northern defenders of partition who contend that in joining us in freedom would be an economic disadvantage to the north-eastern counties'. In place of rhetoric he sought functional cooperation. He brought the era of economic protectionism to a close with the signing of the Anglo-Irish Free Trade Agreement in 1965. In January of that year he went to Stormont to meet Terence O'Neill which symbolized the end of the 'cold war' in Ireland.

All of this was important in creating better Anglo-Irish relations but in spite of it all no one was prepared for the impact of the Troubles late in 1968. Policy was often conceived on the spot, reacting to the politics of the last atrocity and deeply ingrained historic animosities. The Irish Department of Foreign Affairs, for example, had had no officials specifically and exclusively assigned to Anglo-Irish relations before the conflict re-emerged. In addition, the Foreign and Commonwealth Offices were being merged in London just as Northern Ireland erupted. Until October 1968 the British Ambassador to Dublin was reporting to the Commonwealth Office, that is almost 20 years after Ireland had departed from the Commonwealth. The result was confusion and a fundamental lack of knowledge about the nature of the problem.

The Troubles

By August 1969, when the situation in Belfast was very serious, the Irish authorities insisted on referring to the 'Six Counties' of Northern Ireland to stress its diminutive status and appealed to the United Nations for the urgent despatch of a peace-keeping force. On 19 August the British government produced what became known as the (first) Downing Street Declaration which affirmed 'that responsibility for affairs in Northern Ireland is entirely a matter of domestic jurisdiction'. A day later Patrick Hillery, the Irish Minister for Foreign Affairs, requested by virtue of Article 35 of the UN Charter 'an urgent meeting of the Security Council' to consider the crisis. The general demeanour of Hillery and of Lord Caradon, the British representative, suggests that what mattered on this occasion was catharsis, and that the setting was being used as a form of 'sacred drama'. In practice the Irish had little choice and were reduced to pursuing a policy of 'quiet diplomacy and personal conversation' (the Taoiseach's address to the UN, 22 October 1970) and to acting as 'second guarantor' for the Catholic minority in Northern Ireland.

With the rise of the IRA and allegations of gun-running made against members of the Irish government (three Fianna Fáil ministers were cleared by the courts) a more sober relationship developed between Dublin and London. It was assisted by the return of a Conservative government led by Ted Heath in June 1970. Initially the Conservatives placed their faith in the government of Northern Ireland led by James Chichester-Clark (until March 1971) and by Brian Faulkner, and in a security response to the violence. That response had always been questioned vigorously by the Irish government and by the SDLP so that London's relations with constitutional Nationalism deteriorated.

The Irish dimension

Shortly thereafter, Anglo-Irish relations entered a brief fruitful phase in the period after the imposition of direct rule in March 1972. It ran until the collapse of power-sharing in May 1974. During this time the concept of the 'Irish dimension' was introduced into official documentation. It appeared first in a Discussion Paper of October 1972 and was reinforced in a White Paper – 'Northern Ireland Constitutional Proposals' [Cmd 5259] – which acknowledged in paragraph 110 that the United Kingdom 'favours and is prepared to facilitate the formation of a Council of Ireland'. Stripped of its rhetoric the Irish dimension accepted that a settlement must include a recognition of Northern Ireland's status and that that status would remain undiminished unless with the express consent of a majority; it recognized that there was and is an economic and security interdependence underlined by both states' accession to the EEC on 1 January 1973; and it assumed that the Republic would reciprocate in any arrangements.

The extent to which relations between Dublin and London improved (and those between the Conservatives and Unionists had frayed) was manifest in the introduction of the Irish dimension and of the decision that the Westminster model was unsuited for a deeply divided society like Northern Ireland – hence the decision to form a power-sharing Executive. Further, Dublin's input was such that when a new coalition government came into office on 14 March 1973 it was told that a final drafting of the White Paper [Cmd 5259] was underway but that Dublin's views were being sought. The new Minister for Foreign Affairs, Dr Garret FitzGerald, set to work immediately on a draft document which, he told the Dáil on 9 May, 'I understand, from my subsequent contacts, to be taken fully into consideration and to influence the shaping of the White Paper'. This new-found amity was repeated at the Civil Service College at Sunningdale on 6–9 December when the two governments negotiated with the Faulknerite Unionists, the SDLP and the Alliance Party the nature and scope of a power-sharing Executive which took office on 1 January 1974.

Sweetness and light did not extend much beyond the defeat of the Heath government following the general election of February 1974 and the collapse of power-sharing after the UWC strike in May. Labour had replaced the Conservatives and they did not have the same proprietorial claims on the Sunningdale settlement. When the loyalist working class rose against the settlement – 'Dublin is only a Sunningdale away' was the very effective slogan used by the anti-power-sharers in the February election – Harold Wilson's government decided it could not fight on two fronts, hence their reluctance to take on the loyalist strikers. This led to bitter recrimination between Dublin and London, all of which is evident in the memoirs of both Merlyn Rees, the then Secretary of State for Northern Ireland, and Garret FitzGerald. During the period of Labour rule between 1974 and 1979 Anglo-Irish relations entered a black hole. The Irish dimension had entered the realm of rhetoric; and as early as July 1974 the hard edges of power-sharing had been softened to an aspiration for a government of Northern Ireland which in the words of an official Paper [Cmd 5675] 'would be likely to command the most widespread acceptance throughout the community'. Mr Rees's successor, Roy Mason, tried to write it out of history when he told the Commons on 12 January 1978 that 'I have never used the expression "power sharing". I have always insisted that it should be a case of partnership and participation in the administration of Northern Ireland'. He described it as 'an emotive term'. One explanation for this about-turn lies in domestic politics. To remain in power Labour desperately needed the support of Unionist MPs at Westminster. Besides, both Merlyn Rees and Roy Mason seemed to possess some animus towards Irish Nationalism: Mr Mason's description of the SDLP as extremists and 'greens' did not exactly endear himself to them.

Between 1974 and 1979 Irish Nationalist strategy changed to 'internationalizing' the question. Bilateral relations with London were cool and infrequent. Contact with prominent Irish American politicians became crucial. The result was a shift in US policy from one of benign concern to that of incremental involvement, all of which was to be seen in the signing of the Anglo-Irish Agreement in November 1985 and in the Framework Documents of February 1995. Three explanations can be deduced: divisions in Irish America between supporters of the IRA and those in favour of constitutionalism; the nature of Congressional arithmetic; and a carefully devised policy led by John Hume of the SDLP and by Irish governments to lobby the administration.

Internationalizing the question

Irish-American divisions first surfaced in 1970 when the Irish North American Committee (better known as the Irish Northern Aid Committee, NORAID) was founded. It was perceived as being a fund-raising organization for the IRA. Establishment Irish America opposed it through the 'Four Horsemen' (Senators Kennedy and Moynihan, Speaker 'Tip' O'Neill and Governor Hugh Carey). This arrangement evolved into the 'Friends of Ireland' in 1981 embracing both Republican and Democratic members of Congress. The 'Friends of Ireland' had influence on the Carter Presidency because O'Neill was the third most senior member of the political establishment and Kennedy was seen as a potential rival of President Carter. Besides, although this group favoured Irish unity they were firm opponents of IRA violence and had consistently condemned it in their annual St Patrick's Day messages. The result was that the British Embassy publicly recognized their worth and President Carter adopted a more sympathetic policy towards Irish Nationalism.

One example of this more assertive, more moderate, voice of Irish America occurred during the 1979 general election when, in a visit to Britain and Ireland, Speaker O'Neill accused the former of treating Northern Ireland like a political football. He demanded positive action from the incoming government. His 'interference' was greeted with anger but, surprisingly, Mrs Thatcher's government was soon to change tack on Northern Ireland. The Prime Minister herself was seen as a firm supporter of the Union, and the Conservative manifesto had suggested a more integrationist and security-conscious policy. Within a year this policy had been turned round to seeking a devolutionist solution and improved Anglo-Irish relations, both of which were encouraged by the new Republican administration in Washington led by President Reagan. Mrs Thatcher was to find that it was easier to develop better relations with Dublin than to pursue a devolutionist course. The latter needed the whole-hearted consent of Northern Ireland's political parties and that was not forthcoming. The former could be pursued through diplomatic channels without interference from busybody politicians.

The formal Anglo-Irish process began at a summit in London in May 1980 when Mrs Thatcher and the Taoiseach, Charles Haughey, issued a joint communiqué which spoke of a unique relationship between the two islands. The Prime Minister had been pleasantly surprised that after Mr Haughey had become Taoiseach in December 1979 he had demonstrated his anti-terrorist prowess – Mr Haughey had been one of the Fianna Fáil ministers accused of gun-running in 1970. The May summit was followed by one on 8 December when Mrs Thatcher was accompanied by the most impressive British political delegation to visit Dublin since partition. Then they agreed that substantial progress had been made since May on matters of energy, transport, communication, cross-border economic development and security. All of these activities came under the rubric of what the communiqué called 'the totality of relationships within these islands'. Additionally, senior officials agreed on joint studies covering possible new institutional structures, citizenship rights, security matters, economic cooperation and measures to encourage mutual understanding. Between December 1980 and November 1985 (when the Anglo-Irish Agreement was signed) a series of summits took place. In November 1982 an Anglo-Irish Inter-Government Council was created.

All of this suggests that relations between both governments were harmonious and fruitful. In fact Anglo-Irish relations entered a sticky patch in 1981–82. There are four possible explanations. One concerns the use of that fateful phrase, 'the totality of relationships'. Mr Haughey interpreted it in a maximalist sense; in an address to the Dáil three days after the summit the Taoiseach said that it meant 'that the special consideration to which our next meeting will be devoted does not exclude *anything* that can contribute to achieve peace, reconciliation and stability and to the improvement of relationships within these islands' (emphasis added). The rhetoric of a Taoiseach besieged by a faltering economy inevitably raised the temperature in Northern Ireland just as the hunger strike campaign was beginning to wreak havoc and do serious damage to the political process. The second was centred around perceptions of how to deal with the hunger strike. The Irish government was not in favour of conceding the strikers' demand for political status but believed that compromise on humanitarian grounds was necessary to avoid total polarization within Northern Ireland. On the other hand Mrs Thatcher conducted the debate in terms of a battle between good and evil. The results were an increase in Irish-American funding for the IRA, the creation of a potentially explosive communal polarization, and a fatal ambivalence on the part of political leadership. Republicans moved centre-stage and Anglo-Irish relations deteriorated.

The Anglo-Irish Agreement

Hard on the hunger strikes came the Falklands War and Ireland's unilateral move to end EEC trade sanctions on Argentina after the sinking of the *Belgrano*. Mrs Thatcher interpreted this as treachery which only added to Anglo-Irish woes. The final explanation lay in yet another attempt to find an internal settlement to the Northern Ireland problem. This was to be a form of rolling devolution orchestrated by a new Secretary of State, James Prior (appointed in September 1981). The SDLP and the Irish government, both of them under pressure from a more confident Sinn Féin, saw it as a distraction from the real business of Anglo-Irish cooperation. The SDLP (and SF) contested the Assembly elections but refused to take their seats, arguing that there was no purely internal solution to the problem and that an Assembly would only perpetuate the problem. Without the SDLP's presence the Assembly became a charade and political attention shifted to Dublin where the constitutional Nationalist parties (Fianna Fáil, Fine Gael and Labour in the south, and the SDLP in the north) had constituted the New Ireland Forum. The Forum sat during 1983–84 re-examining Nationalism in the late twentieth century and producing a report (in May 1984) which showed some sensitivity towards Unionism and offered alternatives to old-fashioned Irish unity. The report contained enough to enable Dublin and London to kick-start the Anglo-Irish process with a summit in November 1984 followed by another a year later culminating in the signing of the Anglo-Irish Agreement.

The Agreement was significant at a number of levels. It was accepted as 'a formal and binding Agreement' which was registered under Article 102 at the UN. It had an international dimension in that Article 10(a) of the Agreement sought to regenerate a struggling economy by considering 'the possibility of securing international support for this work'. The US, Canada and New Zealand contributed to an International Fund for Ireland (IFI) established in September 1986 – the EC was to join later. The Agreement had a strong institutional framework. Article 2(a) established:

'an Intergovernmental Conference . . . concerned with Northern Ireland and with relations between the two parts of the island of Ireland, to deal, as set out in this Agreement, on a regular basis with:

(i) political matters;
(ii) security and related matters;
(iii) legal matters, including the administration of justice;
(iv) the promotion of cross border cooperation.'

The bulk of the Agreement outlined what was to be the role of the Conference with specific reference to these four matters. It was to be serviced by a Secretariat composed of senior officials from London and Dublin which was to act as a channel of communication between the governments but not as a decision-making body. In addition, a good degree of flexibility was built into the Agreement to ensure (a) that it was impervious to boycott and (b) that it held out some attractions to Unionists. In that respect the carrot of devolution was offered. The whole thrust of the Agreement gives some indication of the strides which had been made in improving Anglo-Irish relations. The two governments were now firmly in the driving seat as far the Northern Ireland problem was concerned. Despite its protestations, the UK government was accepting a Nationalist interpretation of the problem and had moved light-years away from the August 1969 declaration that the problem was purely one for domestic consideration. The downside was that the Agreement had alienated the Unionist community completely. Over the next five years it fought a bitter campaign to have the Agreement upended. Only when stalemate ensued did the Unionist parties return to the negotiating table. In January 1990 the Secretary of State, Peter Brooke, launched a tentative initiative to open up talks with the four main parties within Northern Ireland. After 14 months of tenacious and skilful bilateral meetings he secured the agreement of the UUP, DUP, APNI and SDLP to enter into structured discussions with both governments to discuss the three strands to the question: (a) relationships between the communities within Northern Ireland; (b) relationships between the people of Ireland, north and south; and (c) relationships between the peoples of Ireland and Britain. Added to this three-stranded approach was the principle that nothing is agreed until everything is agreed.

These talks moved forward at a snail-like pace and were complemented by (secret) talks taking place between the British government and SF and between the SDLP leader, John Hume, and SF President, Gerry Adams. The purpose of these latter talks was to persuade the IRA of the futility of their armed campaign and of their marginality in the search for a solution. When John Major and Taoiseach Albert Reynolds produced another Downing Street Declaration (on 15 December 1993) it appeared that all the bits were in place because that declaration was premised on the complete cessation of all violence. That was to follow when first the IRA (on 31 August 1994) and then the Combined Loyalist Military Command (on 13 October 1994) announced ceasefires. For the first time since the creation of Northern Ireland all parties to the problem were to become parties to a solution – a solution unveiled by both governments in February 1995 when they offered *Frameworks for the Future*.

Two features of this document are noteworthy. One is that it offers two papers, the first concerned with a framework for accountable government in Northern Ireland; and the second being a 'shared understanding between the British and Irish governments to assist discussion and negotiations involving the Northern Ireland parties'. In other words governments were being tentative and were pursuing a twin-track policy of devolution within the three-stranded approach. There is no guarantee that this will succeed but what it does show is the degree to which the motor of political change is being driven by an Anglo-Irish team assisted in the background by the Clinton administration in the United States.

Conclusions

If one cannot speak with absolute confidence about an outcome, this much can be stated. Relations between Dublin and London have never been more purposeful and more consistent than they have been for the past decade. They have recognized the parameters of the problem and they have introduced two new concepts to the political lexicon – 'inclusivity' and 'process'. Both are part of normal political dialogue but are novel in the Irish context. They work on the assumption that all parties who have any sort of veto must be part of the solution, and that we must not think of politics as a zero-sum game. Rather it has more to do with a state of permanent negotiation in which compromise and tolerance must be essential.

Further Reading

Arthur, P., 'Three years of the Anglo-Irish Agreement', *Irish Political Studies*, 1990.

Arthur, P., 'The Anglo-Irish Joint Declaration: towards a lasting peace' *Government and Opposition*, 29(2), Spring 1994.

Aughey, A., *Under Siege: Ulster Unionism and the Anglo-Irish Agreement*. Belfast: Blackstaff Press, 1989.

Hadden, T. and Boyle, K., *Anglo-Irish Agreement: Commentary, Text and Official Review*. London: Sweet and Maxwell, 1989.

O'Leary, B., *The Politics of Antagonism*. London: Athlone Press, 1993.

Owen, A.E., *The Anglo-Irish Agreement: The First Three Years*. Cardiff: University of Wales Press, 1995.

Chapter 14

NORTHERN IRELAND ECONOMY
Henry Patterson

The economy has played an important if often underestimated role in the politics of Northern Ireland. For Ulster Unionists, the emergence of Belfast as Ireland's only large industrial city in the nineteenth century was both a product of the Union and one of the foremost reasons for its maintenance. For Nationalists, partition prevented the harmonious development of a single natural economy on the island. Independently of conflicting ideological presentations, the shifts in the northern economy since partition form an essential backdrop for our understanding of political developments and possibilities.

Stormont's economic inheritance

The economic structure of the new state was dominated by industries which would experience severe problems in the inter-war decades – shipbuilding, linen and agriculture which together employed between 40 and 50 per cent of the working population. The Harland and Wolff shipbuilding complex had come to symbolize the modernity and strength of the north's economy and employed more than 30,000 people in 1920. It very soon faced major difficulties in a world market where there was over-capacity. With the rest of the British shipbuilding industry, it was subject to increased competition from countries like the United States and Scandinavia which had fostered their industries with subsidies during the war. Despite this, Northern Irish shipbuilding performed reasonably well until 1930. In 1929 both the largest tonnage in the world and the largest single ship, the *Britannic*, were launched in Belfast. The industry was hard hit by the world slump after 1929. By 1932–33 employment fell to only a tenth of the 1929–30 level and in 1935 the smaller of the two yards, Workman Clark, closed. Although shipbuilding recovered from the depths of the depression, its progress in Belfast was less than in other British yards largely because its past specialization in large liners and merchant vessels meant it received few Admiralty contracts.

The linen industry employed 76,000 in 1912 and the workforce expanded rapidly to 90,000 due to war-time demand for articles like tents and hospital equipment. However, after the First World War there was a sudden decline in demand. This was a product of a number of factors but most important were changes in female fashion and the increasing cost of linen in comparison with other textiles like cotton and new fibres like rayon.

Throughout the world economy in the inter-war period agriculture suffered from over-capacity and worsening terms of trade. The prices of agricultural goods compared to industrial goods fell in the 1920s and plummeted after 1929. Agriculture employed a quarter of the total labour force in Northern Ireland in 1926. It was dominated by small farms: 70% were under 30 acres, and output per head was low at only 46% of the British level in 1924. It was a low income–low wage sector and any improvements in efficiency and productivity resulted in less demand for labour.

Given the dependence on these industries it was not surprising that Northern Ireland had persistently high rates of unemployment: 19% of the insured labour force on average between 1923 and 1930 and 27% between 1931 and 1939. These rates were the worst of any UK region with the exception of Wales. Its peripheral location, insulation from the rest of the UK, and a small domestic market made Northern Ireland unattractive for any of the new industries which developed in the Midlands and south-east England in the 1930s: chemicals, electrical engineering and motor vehicles. The one new industry that did develop was the Short and Harland aircraft factory. Started in 1937 and employing 6,000 by 1939, it was a product of a unique set of circumstances, particularly the move to rearmament in the late 1930s.

The government did adopt a range of policies to mitigate the unemployment problem. The Ulster Unionist movement had always seen the overwhelmingly Protestant and Unionist shipyard labour force as a key group whose interests had to be catered for. This explains the introduction of the Loans Guarantee Act whereby the government guaranteed against default any loan to the shipyards made by banks and insurance companies. Without the support of the Midland Bank the Harland and Wolff yard might well have gone under in the 1930s. Likewise, the New Industries (Development) Acts of 1932 and 1937 which aimed to attract new firms to the province with financial inducements, although relatively unsuccessful, reflected a government concern to be seen by their working-class constituency to be doing something to tackle unemployment. However, given the predominantly *laissez-faire* attitude in UK government for much of the inter-war period, there were strict limits to what any regional government could achieve in the way of the attraction of new industry.

The struggle for parity

Perhaps the most significant political struggle for the Northern Irish government was the attempt to transform the financial provisions of the Government of Ireland Act to allow it to alleviate the widespread economic hardship in the province. The Act was introduced at a time when local industries were still flourishing from the war and post-war boom. It assumed that the devolved administration in Belfast would be able to support all its functions and the services it provided from the taxes levied in the province. It was also expected that the Northern Ireland exchequer would make an 'Imperial Contribution' to the cost of such 'reserved' services as the Army and Navy. When the boom collapsed in 1921 and the government faced a major unemployment problem it was obvious that the assumptions of the Act were no longer relevant. In response, successive governments argued for a financial relationship based on the concepts of 'parity' and 'leeway'.

Parity meant that as Northern Ireland taxpayers paid the same taxes as citizens in the rest of the UK (Westminster controlled the major forms of taxation) Northern Ireland should enjoy the same levels of social support in terms of unemployment and sickness benefits and old-age pensions. Leeway meant that the citizens of the province as members of the UK had a right to have their social standards brought up to the UK average. As the poorest region in the UK, Northern Ireland's standards of health, housing and education were far behind the national average.

An important step in the achievement of parity or 'step-by-step' was the agreement with the Treasury in 1925 that the payment of an Imperial Contribution would become a residual: it would be paid after Northern Ireland's services had made their claim on tax revenues. The Treasury also agreed in 1926 to help subsidize the north's Unemployment Insurance Fund in those years when, because of the large numbers out of work, it ran a deficit. Although some members of the Northern Ireland Cabinet and senior civil servants in Belfast shared the British Treasury's view that as far as possible Northern Ireland should live within its own resources, the dominant attitude of successive Unionist administrations was that as citizens of the UK they were entitled to British standards even if this meant a subvention from the Treasury.

The arguments on parity and leeway were not decisively won until after World War Two. Despite the reservations of a large section of the Unionist Party, the leadership embraced the welfare state, convinced that it would deepen the gulf between north and south and win back the support of those sections of the Protestant working class which had started to vote for the Northern Ireland Labour Party during the UK-wide shift to the left after 1940. In a series of agreements with the Treasury from 1946 onwards the extension of the welfare state to the province was financially underwritten and the Treasury permitted the northern Ministry of Finance to divert revenue from the Imperial Contribution to a special fund for industrial development and other projects. But if the principles of parity and leeway were finally conceded after 1945, the north still lagged behind most parts of the UK in many of its services and public expenditure per head of the population was still less than that in England, Scotland and Wales.

The economy in the 1950s and 1960s

After the end of the post-war boom in 1951 the old problems of the north's staple industries re-emerged. Shipbuilding and linen faced increased international competition and while the Harland and Wolff yard was still employing 20,000 in

1960 its workforce would be cut by over 11,000 in the next four years. The linen industry had to modernize and rationalize production in the face of intense competition from artificial fibres and as a result reduced its workforce significantly.

Agriculture, which still employed a sixth of the workforce in 1950 saw an intensification of a process of amalgamation of holdings and mechanization which resulted in a decline by a third in its labour force between 1950 and 1960. The post-war extension of the welfare state and the making up of leeway allowed a compensating increase in service employment in the areas of education and health. However, the contraction of the staples and a relatively high birth rate entailed a substantial employment shortfall. Throughout the 1950s unemployment averaged 7.4%. Although far removed from the figures of the 1930s (or 1980s) it existed in a broader British context of full employment – it was four times the national average – and a better performance in other regions facing similar problems.

The Northern Ireland government had decided as early as 1944 that the inevitable post-war problems of the staple industries could only be tackled by a diversification of the industrial structure through the attraction of investment from outside the province. The Industries Development Act provided a range of incentives to attract new firms to Northern Ireland: investment grants, tax concessions and new factories at low rents. By 1963 some 50,000 jobs had been created in government-assisted undertakings since 1945, the majority in plants set up by external investment. The process of attracting external investment accelerated in the 1960s as the Unionist government of Terence O'Neill put major emphasis on modernizing the infrastructure of the province with new motorways, a new university and an ill-fated new city project at Craigavon. Between 1958 and 1973 employment in foreign-owned companies increased from 4,515 to 26,141 – the largest employment growth in foreign enterprises of any UK region. In the 1960s manufacturing production rose much faster in Northern Ireland than in the UK as a whole with growth totalling 60% over the decade. By the early 1970s the foreign-controlled manufacturing sector had become the dynamic force in the province's economy.

However, there was little evidence that the local manufacturing sector had been able to improve its competitive position, and the optimism of the 1960s would soon give way to profound pessimism as the end of the post-war boom in the world economy revealed the fragility of a development strategy so dependent on inward investment.

Towards a 'workhouse economy'

The world slump after 1973 radically reduced the amount of internationally mobile. investment at the same time as some of the longer-established multinationals withdrew from Northern Ireland. This was most graphically the case in the area of textiles where most of the 'flagship' companies attracted in the late fifties and sixties pulled out in the seventies. These had been producers of synthetic fibres and faced a combination of world recession and competition from cheaper imports. The spiralling political violence also acted as an added disincentive to external investment. Local industry suffered from the recessions after 1973 and even more radically after 1979. The result was a 40% drop in manufacturing employment between 1974 and 1985. Unemployment which had averaged 7% in the 1950s had reached an all-time low of 5.2% in 1973/74. Already by 1976 a report on economic and industrial strategy in the province (The Quigley Report) noted that 'The Northern Ireland economy is in serious difficulty and if no serious measures are taken, the outlook is grim.' At that time the unemployment rate was 10%; by 1983 it had risen to 15.5% and by 1986, at the peak effect of Thatcherism on local industry, to 17.25%. By then the shake-out of local industry had largely been completed. By the early 1990s there were signs of growth and even relative success in some sectors. However, unemployment remained stubbornly high at between 13 and 14% in the early 1990s – the highest rate in any UK region.

If a major decline of the manufacturing sector was a central characteristic of economic change under direct rule, another feature much commented upon was the growing predominance of the services sector in the economy.

Throughout the 1970s the decline in industrial employment was offset by a rapid growth in the service sector. There were a number of factors at work. Under direct rule there was a massive expansion in government services. In the case of the social services like health and education there was a general expansion throughout the UK at the time, but in Northern Ireland there was a much faster increase than the national average. This reflected the fact that despite substantial improvements since the war the north's standards were still inferior to those of the rest of the UK; the traditional argument for making up leeway still applied. The violence itself encouraged British governments under direct rule to be generous to the province as it was generally believed that there was a relation between social deprivation and political unrest. For a period in the 1970s under the Labour Secretary of State, Roy Mason, economic development was seen as an alternative to what was regarded as the futile and thankless task of getting the political parties to agree to a political settlement.

However, it was not difficult to see the dangers of the development of an economy so dependent on the public sector, particularly where, as some economists pointed out, the 'real' economy, especially the manufacturing sector, was weak. By the end of the 1980s over 40% of the workforce was directly employed in the public sector. Another substantial sector was employed in firms that were heavily dependent on subsidies or public contracts. In 1986/87, according to figures from the Department of Economic Development, the manufacturing sector in the province was heavily subsidized: the scale was equivalent to £39 per manufacturing employee per week. It was only the peculiar political situation that allowed the Harland and Wolff shipyard to survive the heyday of Thatcherism with a subsidy of around £8,000 per worker in the mid-1980s. It would be privatized along with Shorts Aircraft factory at the end of the decade.

In fact, Northern Ireland was insulated from the full effects of the Thatcherite economic revolution. It was disparagingly referred to as the 'Keynesian republic' by some of the more ardent of her supporters. However, the Thatcher years did see a cap on the seventies' rapid growth of the public sector. Outside the area of security force employment, growth in the public services was halted and in some areas reversed. Nevertheless, the continuing weakness of the private sector and the very substantial job losses in manufacturing in the early Thatcher years did little to reduce the preponderant significance of the public sector in the economy. Public expenditure amounted to 65% of regional GDP at the end of the eighties. One economist, Bob Rowthorne, went so far as to label Northern Ireland a 'workhouse economy' where most of the population is involved in servicing and controlling each other, taking imports from the outside world and exporting little in return. While a rather extreme description it does highlight some of the main economic policy dilemmas.

One in particular has increasingly figured in both economic and political debate: the increasing size of the yearly subvention from the Treasury which supports the very large public sector. While in the 1960s the subvention came to only about 5–10% of total expenditure by the Northern Ireland government, by the end of the 1980s it had increased to about a third. There were persistent criticisms over the years from a few politicians and commentators about the burden of this expenditure. The British subvention had risen from £313 million in 1973/74 to £3.5 billion in 1994/95.

Nevertheless, such complaints and associated claims that the whole principle of parity should be re-examined came to nothing against the continuing pressure to use public expenditure as a fire-damper on a politically polarized and violent society. The scale of the subvention had ambiguous political effects. On the one hand, for some commentators from a republican perspective it demonstrated the bankruptcy of the northern 'statelet'. On the other hand, it was the strongest Unionist argument against constitutional change. No Dublin government would be willing to take over such a burden. Without the subvention, living standards of everybody in the north would drop catastrophically. The major reason for the subvention is the fact that Northern Ireland remains the poorest region of the United Kingdom with very concentrated pockets of mass unemployment and poverty: in this way it resembles substantial areas in the UK where the national exchequer 'subsidizes' those parts of the state which suffer from deindustrialization and all the social and economic problems associated with it.

There are, of course, problems with an economy so dependent on a large subsidized public sector. One response has been to argue for a shift in economic development strategy away from its focus on attracting inward investment projects, the path followed by the province's Industrial Development Board in the 1970s and first half of the 1980s. In 1987 the Department of Economic Development set out a new strategy in its Pathfinder document which proposed a shift from the inward investment policy option towards a model of self-reliant economic growth. The document outlined the economic problems that needed to be tackled: lack of an entrepreneurial culture as businesses were more oriented to extracting grants from the state than increasing their market share; a small manufacturing sector alongside a large service sector; overdependence on external funds; and the peripheral location of the province.

Some doubted whether it would be possible to achieve the spectacular increase in industrial output and productivity which the Pathfinder objective of an adaptable self-reliant economy would entail. Nevertheless by the beginning of the 1990s there was a growing consensus that Northern Ireland's dependence on such a massive public sector was not a sustainable option in the long term. Northern Ireland had a 'dual economy' where those employed in the public sector on nationally negotiated salaries and wages had relatively comfortable lives while those who were unemployed or in low-paid or part-time employment were ill-served by the existing economic system. While the large public sector was seen as a major obstacle to the long-term economic health of the province, it had to be acknowledged that in a context of little external investment and with a weak private sector, any reduction in the role of the public sector would have extremely harmful social effects. Northern Ireland's economy appeared to be in a double-bind.

Conclusions

A durable peace would certainly remove one of the major constraining factors in the attraction of foreign investment and there was some evidence by the summer of 1995 that this was occurring. However, in a bitterly competitive world economy, it is most unlikely that Northern Ireland could achieve again the record levels of external investment of the 1960s. The possibilities of a 'peace dividend' are more talked about by politicians than by economists. Political stability should create a better climate for investment and some economists have argued that increased cooperation between industrial development authorities in Northern Ireland and the Republic could, along with other forms of cross-border economic cooperation, produce real and significant economic gains. But peace will also mean reductions in the size of Northern Ireland's security apparatus, meaning fewer jobs and big drops in income for certain groups. It will remove the 'special case' argument that successive Secretaries of State have used to protect high levels of public expenditure from too close Treasury scrutiny. Any lasting political peace will bring as many problems as opportunities for what remains an economy with profound structural problems.

Further reading

Bew, P. and Patterson, H., *The British State and the Ulster Crisis*. London: Verso, 1985.

Bew, P., Gibbon, P. and Patterson, H., *Northern Ireland 1921–1994: Political Forces and Social Classes*. London: Serif, 1995.

Coopers and Lybrand, *Northern Ireland Economy Review and Prospects*. Belfast, 1994.

Johnson, D., 'The Northern Ireland economy, 1914–39', in L. Kennedy and P. Ollernshaw, (eds), *An Economic History of Ulster 1820–1939*. Manchester: Manchester University Press, 1985.

Rowthorn, B., 'Northern Ireland: an economy in crisis', in P. Teague (ed.), *Beyond the Rhetoric: Politics, the Economy and Social Policy in Northern Ireland*. London: Lawrence and Wishart, 1987.

Rowthorn, B. and Wayne, N., *Northern Ireland: The Political Economy of Conflict*. Oxford: Polity Press, 1988.

Smyth, M. and McCullough, W.A., 'Northern Ireland: a case study in the economics of survival', *Studies*, 80, Summer 1991.

Teague, P., 'Multinational companies in the Northern Ireland economy', in P. Teague, (ed.), *Beyond the Rhetoric: Politics, the Economy and Social Policy in Northern Ireland*. London: Lawrence and Wishart, 1987.

Tomlinson, M., *Twenty Five Years On: The Costs of War and the Dividends of Peace*. Belfast: West Belfast Economic Forum, 1994.

Whyte, J., *Interpreting Northern Ireland*. Oxford: Clarendon Press, 1990.

Wilson, T., *Ulster: Conflict and Consent*. Oxford: Oxford University Press, 1989.

Chapter 15

NORTHERN IRELAND AND THE EUROPEAN UNION
Paul Hainsworth

European Community membership

As part of the United Kingdom (UK), Northern Ireland joined the European Community (EC) in 1973, following votes in the Houses of Parliament to ratify this step. From this time a new dimension was introduced into the socio-economic and political context of Northern Ireland, and virtually all sectors of the state and civil society – such as policy-makers, political parties, pressure groups, various élites and the electors – had to come to terms with membership of the EC.

Looking back to entry into the EC, one factor stands out: Northern Ireland joined the Community at a time of immense political and civil unrest in the province. From the late 1960s, 'the Troubles' tended inevitably to preoccupy attention while developments in the 1970s, such as direct rule, power-sharing, internment and the 1974 Ulster Workers' Council strike, effectively relegated debate about the EC to a sideshow. Nevertheless, for Edward Heath's Conservative government (1970–74), European integration was a key policy area and one destined to play an increasing role in the years ahead. Gradually, therefore, socio-economic and political forces in Northern Ireland proceeded to map out their perspectives in response to membership.

Before 1973, discussion and speculation had concentrated on the likely effects of EC membership upon jobs, agriculture, trade, sovereignty and the Irish border. After 1973, an important landmark in taking stock of Europe was the 1975 referendum on membership. Again, local unrest and lack of familiarity with, or interest in, the EC combined to keep the electoral turnout down in Northern Ireland – 47% as opposed to 65% across the UK – but the occasion did provide political parties in the province with an obvious opportunity to set out their policies on the EC. Inevitably, the latter were bound up with respective viewpoints on political and constitutional matters pertaining to Northern Ireland. Thus, debate about Europe overlapped and interacted heavily with controversy about the status of Northern Ireland as an entity and, from the outset, this has been a notable feature of membership.

The referendum resulted in a marginal majority (52%) in Northern Ireland for continued membership and the pro-EC forces could claim a victory of sorts alongside the more resounding 'Yes' vote (64%) in the UK overall. Parties supporting the EC included the Social Democratic and Labour Party (SDLP), the Alliance Party and the Unionist Party of Northern Ireland (UPNI) – the latter now defunct – while those against included the Democratic Unionist Party (DUP), Sinn Féin (SF) and, to a lesser extent, the Ulster Unionist Party (UUP).

Political parties

The SDLP is, arguably, the most steadfast – and certainly the most significant – supporter of European integration. Under John Hume's leadership the SDLP draws lessons from the whole post-war process of European integration and applies these to Northern Ireland. The resolving of differences between European states – historically at war with one another – is seen as an example of good practice for the island of Ireland. Equally, West European political practices such as proportional representation in voting, power-sharing and compromise are viewed by the SDLP as worthwhile concepts for Northern Ireland. Moreover, Hume articulates a declared 'post-Nationalist' politics in which gradually nation-states, such as the UK and Ireland, will exercise less power and sovereignty as supranational (the EU) and regional levels will play a greater role. Unionist and other critics of the SDLP, however, do not accept this interpretation and perceive the SDLP's agenda to be a Nationalist (all-Ireland) one, drawing upon the language of European integration and post-Nationalism for its legitimacy. Nevertheless, the European arena has been fruitful for the SDLP in that Hume has built up support within the institutions of the EU, notably in the European Parliament (EP), where – as one of Northern Ireland's three Members of the European Parliament (MEPs) – he sits within the largest political grouping, the Confederation of European Socialists. Since the first direct elections to the EP in 1979, Hume has enjoyed re-election to Strasbourg and, in 1994, his 28.93% represented the SDLP's highest share of the poll in any major election.

The DUP party leader, the Reverend Ian Paisley – like Hume – has enjoyed four successive elections to the EP, each time topping the poll impressively with between 29% and 33%. Paisley is a long-standing critic of European integration, interpreting it as the creation of Catholic-inspired, Christian Democratic parties. The process – not least the Maastricht Treaty – is seen by the DUP as a threat to national sovereignty and a back-door means to undermine the Irish border and, therefore, the constitutional basis of Northern Ireland. Within the EP, Paisley sits as an independent, offering 'a free and fearless loyalist and Protestant voice', unfettered by any restrictive transnational party membership. Paisley's aim in Europe is to defend the union with Great Britain and fight off Irish republican and Nationalist forces. Although withdrawal from the EU has been a much-supported option inside the DUP, Paisley is quite prepared to work within the existing framework to secure aid for Northern Ireland and this approach was very evident throughout 1994/95, for instance, as all three local MEPs joined together to secure EU monies to underwrite current peace initiatives.

The Ulster Unionist Party shares many of the DUP's reservations about the

European Union but is less strident in its opposition. The UUP, which provided no concrete advice to its voters in the 1975 referendum, is more prepared than the DUP to accept the reality of the EU and work constructively within it. The less strident and often nuanced UUP stance on Europe is perhaps explained by reference to party supporters such as the Ulster farmers enjoying the benefits of the Common Agricultural Policy (CAP) and business interests anxious to compete in and exploit the Single European Market. The party's current MEP, Jim Nicholson, is a member of the pro-integrationist European Peoples' Party (EPP) at Strasbourg, despite the UUP's reservations about the EU. The party's 1994 Euro-election manifesto confirmed the sympathy for a Thatcherite Europe of nation-states with national sovereignties firmly intact. Also, a strong majority of UUP Members of Parliament voted initially against membership of the EC in the 1971 Westminster (free) vote on entry. More recently, the UUP has opposed in principle the Maastricht Treaty – except where tactical considerations dictated otherwise.

Like the DUP, the UUP denies to the EU any role in the political and constitutional affairs of Northern Ireland. However, one significant aspect of European elections in Northern Ireland is the inability of the UUP (normally the largest party in Westminster and local elections) to displace Ian Paisley as the leading Euro-candidate – although the gap between the two parties closed considerably in the 1994 Euro-election.

The Alliance Party is a member of the European Liberal, Democratic and Reformist (ELDR) grouping in the EU and, thereby, is strongly pro-EU. Consequently, most pro-integrationist measures – the Single European Market, federalism, Maastricht, the social dimension, economic and monetary union and so on – are supported by Alliance. In contrast, SF has been a longstanding critic of European integration, equating the process with loss of (Irish) sovereignty, a threat to traditional Irish neutrality and an ultra-capitalist-cum-imperialist vehicle. In the 1990s, though, SF has demonstrated greater recognition of the EU as a reality and attempted increasingly to project the Irish problem in a European context. In European elections, however, neither Alliance nor SF are able to compete with the attraction of the candidates from the major parties. In fact, only four individuals have represented Northern Ireland in the EP since 1979 – Paisley, Hume, Nicholson and, from 1979 to 1989, John Taylor (UUP) – and always they have come from the same main parties.

Representing Northern Ireland in Europe

The three MEPs are part of the structure of representation for Northern Ireland in the EU. The province is represented formally on the powerful Council of Ministers (i.e. representatives from national governments) by the UK government's ministers. This may mean an active and prominent role for the Northern Ireland Secretary of State when matters pertaining to the province are – albeit rarely – at the top of the agenda. Mostly, though, the Secretary of State for Northern Ireland, plus his ministers, serve as the official link between Northern Ireland and EC policy committees in London and Brussels. Occasionally, Northern Ireland matters take up a more central role in EC/EU affairs – notably in the early 1980s with EC support for urban renewal in Belfast and again in the mid-1990s with deliberations over the EU's contribution to the emergent peace process in Northern Ireland.

Representing Northern Ireland in Europe is, therefore, the remit of the Northern Ireland Office (NIO). The NIO's task is to ensure that the relevant government departments in Northern Ireland receive the appropriate EC/EU papers and documentation. Moreover, the NIO and NICS in turn try to ensure that government ministers, European Commission officials and other relevant parties are made aware of Northern Ireland's concerns in Europe and vice versa. The lead departments on European matters within the Northern Ireland Civil Service apparatus are the Department of Agriculture (DANI), the Department of Economic Development (DED) and the Department of Finance and Personnel (DFP), all of which have direct contacts with Brussels. Local structures such as the Industrial Development Board (IDB) and the Local Enterprise Development Unit (LEDU) are part of this structure. The Central Secretariat at Stormont Castle has also acted as the coordinator and facilitator on Europe within Northern Ireland departments and enjoys contacts with the European Commission via the United Kingdom Permanent Representation (UKREP). Attempts to encourage the Commission or the EU to play a wider *political* role in Northern Ireland have tended to fail. While there is an undisguised wish to bolster peace and reconciliation in Northern Ireland, this does not extend to a willingness to adopt a more active role in political and constitutional matters. Repeatedly, European Commissioners – usually at the time of visits to Northern Ireland – have ruled out this option, equating it with unwarranted and unauthorized interference in the domestic affairs of member states. The Council of Ministers, too, despite the expressions of goodwill towards Anglo-Irish rapprochement, has steered clear of adopting positions which might be construed as undue political interference. In the EP, however, there has been less hesitancy to take up Northern Ireland business and certain reports have addressed various matters, while debates too have covered controversial issues relating to the UK's internal security matters. Since the EP has lacked effective power, the UK government has not recognized the legitimacy of the EP's decisions in this respect.

Westminster, though, including the committee structures, provides a further and generally more coveted parliamentary level at which Northern Ireland's 17 Members of Parliament (and others) can question ministers and debate European matters. Since MEPs from Northern Ireland have doubled up, for the most part, as MPs throughout the past two decades, a useful linkage has been created between Westminster and Strasbourg – although critics point to the constraints of the so-called 'dual mandate'. Westminster, however, functions as an important representative layer, not only because of parliamentary sovereignty, but also because of the democratic deficit in Northern Ireland. Local government powers are weak, Stormont has been suspended and non-elected non-governmental organizations proliferate. Hitherto, devolution had provided opportunities to debate Europe and, via committees, question European policy makers. Nevertheless, despite lack of powers, district councils do interface with European policy-making, particularly over discussions on European funding, and councillors are regular visitors to Brussels.

A feature of recent years has been the growth of regional offices in Brussels, to lobby for the interests of sub-national entities within the EU. However, Northern Ireland has no specific, official, parallel body at the heart of Europe. To some extent, the Northern Ireland European Commission Office, based in Belfast, performs a useful role in articulating local concerns in Brussels and vice versa – providing advice, information and funding opportunities. Also, a fairly recent development has been the setting up of an independent, non-governmental Northern Ireland Centre in Europe (NICE). Based in Brussels, very near to the European Commission, the office serves as a listening post and lobby channel on business, community, social, legal, local government and other matters which have implications for Northern Ireland in Europe. Employer organizations, chambers of commerce and trades unions are in any case well integrated into the structures of European lobbying, but the launch of this office testified to the growing awareness locally of the importance of Europe, especially in the light of the emergent Single European Market.

Funding

Within the EU, Northern Ireland has special status as an Objective One region. This means that the region enjoys considerable financial support from the EU's structural funds, notably the European Regional Development Fund (ERDF) and the European Social Fund (ESF). Following reforms, monies are attracted now on the basis of multi-annual regional plans submitted to the European Commission by the relevant authorities (in this case the NIO/NICS) in the context of Community Support Frameworks (CSFs). For example, the plan submitted for 1994–99 is due to attract the commitment of approximately £940m from the ERDF and ESF (compared with £550m for 1989–93) and this will be supplemented by other sources such as the special peace dividend of £240m confirmed in Belfast by European Commission President, Jacques Santer, in March 1995. The main beneficiaries of ERDF support have been infrastructures including roads, bridges, harbours, airports and other buildings. Funds from the ESF have been targeted at the unemployed, especially in government-inspired training and education schemes such as the Youth Training Programme (YTP). Young people under 25 and the long-term unemployed are the recipients of the ESF, which co-finances schemes also drawing upon public monies. Over 150,000 people in Northern Ireland have enjoyed ESF-backed training between 1989 and 1992. Recent initiatives, too, have focused on the effects of the Single Market (EUROFORM), training and employment of women (NOW) and the needs of disabled people in less developed EU regions (HORIZON).

Northern Ireland qualifies for money from the structural funds since the province meets the criteria laid down by the EU – notably structural adjustment, long-term unemployment, industrial decline and conversion, agricultural adjustment and integration of youth. Objective One status is not strictly due to the economic problems of the Northern Ireland 'region' but is also given because of the delicate political situation. In short, the EU tries to look kindly upon the region's claims for support on account of 'the Troubles' – even though the 1980s EC enlargement brought in poorer Mediterranean areas. However, the latter – in Spain, Greece and Portugal – draw support from the Cohesion Fund, another Maastricht innovation, which is unavailable to the UK (including Northern Ireland).

Perhaps unsurprisingly, there have been calls from within Northern Ireland for inclusion in the group of recipients of the Cohesion Fund but, since criteria for funding is set at a national level, the UK does not qualify. More controversially, though, the UK government often stands accused by a variety of critics – including MEPs and others in Northern Ireland – of not adequately representing or 'pushing' Northern Ireland's cause in Europe. In this respect, failure to match or secure European funding is a familiar cry. Sometimes, comparisons are made with the situation in the Republic of Ireland, although difficulties arise in comparing like with like. The additionality question, however, is a further and well-aired bone of contention. Here, the British government stands accused of not transferring to Northern Ireland the full value of Euro-funds allocated. This issue has dogged discussion about European funds virtually from the outset of membership. The UK government maintains that public expenditure planning takes into account anticipated revenues from Europe and the latter enable spending to be at a higher level than otherwise. The European Commission, local interests and supporters of European integration are not entirely satisfied with this assurance. Suspicions are further aroused when the government does admit that certain European funds – notably the 1995 'peace dividend' – will be genuinely additional, suggesting therefore an exception rather than the rule.

Since Jacques Delors' forceful leadership, the European Commission has been lobbying increasingly for genuine additionality, as well as for genuine partnership with local players – such as local councils, voluntary bodies and 'the social partners' – and for maximum subsidiarity (meaning decision-making as close to the people as possible). Certainly, in Northern Ireland, there have been many complaints to the effect that consultation and partnership have been deficient in the drawing-up of regional plans to present to Brussels. However, improvements too have been noted and the 1994–99 CSF enjoyed a wider consultative process than its predecessors. Moreover, the Commission has encouraged the EC/EU to adopt coherent and less compartmentalized policy-making. The result has been a development from an emphasis upon projects to integrated operations through to programmes or CSFs. The rationale, of course, is to ensure that European monies to Northern Ireland (and elsewhere) are maximized in their effects. To this end, the Commission also set up a special task force in 1994 to support and coordinate mechanisms by which the EU might support peace and reconciliation in Northern Ireland. The Commission therefore emerges as a player of some significance in discussion about public expenditure in Northern Ireland, although it should be noted that monies from the UK government far outweigh the contributions – about 3–5% of total expenditure – from Europe.

Northern Ireland has also benefited from representation on the consultative Economic and Social Committee (ESC) and recently was allocated, by the British government, two of the UK's 24 seats on the new, consultative Committee of the Regions, itself a product of the Maastricht Treaty, aimed at giving sub-national entities a louder voice in European integration.

Agriculture

Pressure groups and civil society are also part of the picture of Northern Ireland/EU relations. For instance, the Ulster Farmers' Union is part of the main farming lobby – known as COPA – in Brussels. Membership of the EC/EU has meant that important decisions affecting agriculture – including farm product prices and grants for improvements – are now taken at European level. Farmers in Northern Ireland have enjoyed the benefits of the Common Agricultural Policy (CAP) through a period when agriculture monopolized two-thirds of the EC budget, and this has had an important direct effect within the province. Through the guarantee section of the European Agricultural Guarantee and Guidance Fund (EAGGF), Northern Ireland beef and dairy farmers, in particular, have enjoyed considerable support. Between 1973 and 1989 almost £800m in EC receipts supported agriculture in Northern Ireland, with about an eighth of this figure serving as farm modernization and improvement grants via the guidance section of the EAGGF, which has also co-financed the local fishing industry. The EAGGF, in fact, has provided almost half of total EC grants and subsidies in Northern Ireland. About three-quarters of farmland in Northern Ireland is designated as hill farming areas and enjoys EC 'less favoured area' status which again attracts special grants and concessions as a result.

While the local farm population has declined somewhat over recent decades, employment in this sector still accounts for about 4.5% of employees (that is, twice as many proportionally as in the rest of the UK) and, as a percentage of GDP, agricultural output is two to three times more important than in the rest of the UK. Significantly, in recent years the trend has been towards controlling the excesses and surpluses of the CAP and, therefore, farmers in Northern Ireland (as elsewhere) have experienced a less supportive regime, a period of adjustment, more restrictive pricing and quota limitations. However, reform of the CAP has been coupled with an EU concern to promote rural development more generally – notably via the LEADER initiative – and this may yield further benefits in Northern Ireland.

Overall, studies point to the benefits of the CAP to Northern Ireland but reservations certainly exist now in view of pressures for change. One key problem, too, is that the British government's ongoing campaign to reform the CAP and the EC/EU budget often has not been welcomed by farming interests in Northern Ireland.

Trade and the Single Market

While European funding and agriculture are key facets of Northern Ireland's membership of the EU, trade within the developing Single European Market is obviously of fundamental importance. Entry into the EC coincided with the energy crisis and world recession – as well as with 'the Troubles' and their economic consequences. Within the EC, Northern Ireland has been one of the most peripheral and socio-economically disadvantaged regions – although, as already intimated, the 1980s Mediterranean enlargement significantly altered the picture. Northern Ireland's standing, as regards EC regional disparities, has not improved since entry, but how much this is due to membership is debatable.

Recent developments have included the Single Market or 1992 process, and the Northern Ireland business environment has experienced the effects of greater competition and the provision of wider opportunities within an open, expanding market of some 350 million people. The 1992 process may be seen as the EC's quest to realize the free trade ideals of the founding Treaty of Rome. Although economic growth via increased trade promises to create more jobs, some restructuring will take place as the least competitive, least prepared and most protected sectors of the economy are confronted with stiffer competition in a Europe 'open for business'. In short, the gains and losses of intensified economic competition will be spread unevenly. To offset the effects of economic liberalism, the European Commission has promoted a social dimension to the 1992 process including the doubling of the structural funds and greater emphasis on the notion of economic and social cohesion. While these aspects have been welcomed by trade unions and voluntary agencies in Northern Ireland, it is not expected that they will have too great an impact in the province. Moreover, the trade union movement – as represented by the Northern Ireland Committee of the Irish Congress of Trades Unions – has expressed fears about the capacity of a small, open, peripheral regional market, such as Northern Ireland's, to withstand accelerated economic integration. The voluntary sector's concerns are articulated particularly by the Northern Ireland Council for Voluntary Action (NICVA), whose expanded European Unit provides training, coordination, documentation, expertise and advice, notably on funding applications. An increasingly active European Women's Forum, too, lobbies to push women's issues higher on the agenda while a whole range of private and public sector institutions – including the professions, the universities and private business – operate increasingly at a European level.

A further EU scheme (INTERREG) brings the Republic of Ireland and Northern Ireland together since it is concerned with the special problems of border areas. The EU's peace dividend places emphasis on cross-border measures taking in trade, infrastructure, agricultural cooperation and other issues. Recent years, too, have witnessed an upsurge in cross-border linkage focusing upon the impact of European integration and involving employers' organizations and the voluntary sector. Some voices argue for greater North–South economic cooperation and trade in the context of the Single Market while others see political rapprochement going hand-in-hand with functional exchange. The improved political climate following the 1994 paramilitary ceasefires provides an added boost to cooperation prospects.

Conclusions

The European Community/Union has become a significant and increasingly recognizable actor in Northern Ireland. European integration has become also part of the debate about the democratic deficit and any future devolved assembly in Northern Ireland will want to exercise some monitoring role in EU matters – possibly under the rubric of a 'Europe for the regions' or a 'people's Europe'. Meanwhile, popular opinion can be measured to some extent through the polls on Europe.

Public opinion polls have revealed a growing support for membership of the European Community. The European Commission's Eurobarometer surveys adopt a country-by-country format, but in the 1990s a breakdown of figures for Northern Ireland became available. Although the sample was small (thereby increasing the margin of error), returns indicated a steep upward trend since 1980 on the question of whether membership of the EC was 'a good thing'. In 1980, less than 20% of respondents were supportive of this opinion, while by 1990 the figures had moved to over 50%. Comparisons also revealed that Northern Ireland is marginally more pro-European than Great Britain.

These trends were confirmed in subsequent Eurobarometer surveys and in more recent statistics in the Fourth Report on Social Attitudes in Northern Ireland. Disillusionment in Great Britain in the 1990s over the course of European integration is not reproduced to the same extent in Northern Ireland, which exhibits appreciably more support for greater European union including a single currency. Youth, educational attainment and higher social class status variables all tend to point to a more pro-European perspective with these factors even helping to transcend traditional political divisions. Only 7% of respondents favour withdrawal from the EU, suggesting that the debate about membership is now over.

Nevertheless, there are anxieties evident within Northern Ireland on EU matters. While the political situation and the peace process may produce economic dividends the prospect of greater stability may threaten the region's Objective One status for attaining structural fund support. Also threatening, or at least double edged, is the future enlargement of the EU to Eastern Europe, bringing in poorer countries and very needy applicants for finite European funds. Anglo-Irish rapprochement, too, and the 1995 Framework Documents raise the possibilities (unwelcome for some) of cross-border institutions playing a wider role in the EC/EU policy hitherto determined at member state level. Sovereignty remains a cherished concept for many in Northern Ireland, despite the opinion poll indications of less anxiety than in Great Britain on this particular issue.

Further reading

Aughey, A., Hainsworth, P. and Trimble, M. J., *Northern Ireland in the European Community: An Economic and Political Analysis.* Belfast: Policy Research Institute, 1989.

Connolly, M. and Loughlin, S. (eds), *Public Policy in Northern Ireland: Adoption or Adaptation?* Belfast: Policy Research Institute, 1990.

Hainsworth, P., 'The European Election in Northern Ireland', *Irish Political Studies*, 10, 1995.

Moxon-Browne, E., 'The impact of the European Community', in B. Hadfield (ed.), *Northern Ireland: Politics and the Constitution*. Buckingham and Philadelphia: Open University Press, 1992.

Northern Ireland Economic Council, *European Community Structural Funds in Northern Ireland. Report 94*. Belfast: Northern Ireland Economic Development Office, 1992.

Simpson, J. V. (ed.), *Northern Ireland and the European Community: An Economic Assessment*. Belfast: Commission of the European Communities, 1988.

Simpson, J. V., *Northern Ireland: A Region of the European Union*. European Commission in the United Kingdom. London: HMSO, 1994.

Skar, O. and Lydersen, B., *Northern Ireland: A Crucial Test for a Europe of Peaceful Regions?* Oslo: Norwegian Institute of International Affairs, 1993.

Teague, P. (ed.), *The Economy of Northern Ireland: Perspectives for Structural Change*. London: Lawrence and Wishart, 1993.

Chapter 16

EQUAL OPPORTUNITIES FOR WOMEN
Carmel Roulston

For at least 20 years, the socio-economic status of women in Northern Ireland has attracted the attention of a small, but growing, group of researchers, most of whom would describe themselves as feminists. A common theme found in the majority of discussions is that of the 'marginalization', the 'invisibility', and the 'exclusion' of women and women's issues from the policy-making processes. This peripheral status is also assumed to extend to the world of work. A composite picture of Northern Irish women emerges from the literature: more disadvantaged than women elsewhere in the United Kingdom or Europe, burdened with responsibilities for family and community life but with few opportunities to articulate their own needs or desires. The explanation for the particularly disadvantaged position of Northern Irish women appears relatively easy to locate. In a conflictual society in which national identities and religious affiliations occupy the centre of the political stage, inequalities based on gender will have at best a very low priority. Thus, the Nationalist/Unionist divide may lead to the reinforcement of inequalities between men and women, with traditional gender roles reinforced in the name of community solidarity. In Northern Ireland, the nature of the conflict has led to an overlapping of religious and national identities and has enhanced the influence of institutions, such as the Churches, which promote conservative ideologies about the appropriate roles and forms of behaviour for women. In particular, conformity in matters relating to the family and sexual morality has become important in the defence of the idea of the 'community'.

The evidence to support this picture of women's lives is strong, as we shall see. Less well supported are a number of other stereotypical views of women, their concerns and attitudes. These views involve the following assumptions. Traditional gender roles are strong, with women prevailing in the domestic sphere. It is common to assume that the conflict has been 'a men's war', contrasting 'the women of peace' to 'the men of violence'. Women are concerned with 'bread and butter' issues, on which Catholic and Protestant women, particularly those from working-class communities, can agree. It is assumed that women are in some sense 'above' the narrow and absurd polarities which characterize mainstream Northern Irish politics. The inclusion of women into mainstream politics could result in greater conciliation. The obstacles in the way of such inclusion have, from this perspective, seemed formidable, since it would challenge not only male but also sectarian vested interests.

In fact, the experience of feminist and other women's activism tends to indicate that the relationships between gender-based conflicts and those deriving from national identity are somewhat more complex than this. Women's issues have not been entirely excluded from the policy-making agenda but in many circumstances they have a lower priority for both women and men than the conflict over the constitutional future of Northern Ireland. It is also by no means easy to assume that any likely resolution of the violent conflict in Northern Ireland would result in a transformation of the political scene to allow women's issues a higher priority.

Women in work

Although there is overwhelming evidence of gender inequality in Northern Ireland, the situation has not remained static. Women are far from confined to the domestic sphere, but have been entering the world of paid work in ever-increasing numbers. In 1961, less than 30% of married women were in employment; by the 1990s, this had risen to 60%. In 1959, only 12% of mothers with pre-school age children were in the workforce; by 1990, 43% of this group had taken up jobs outside the home. While this is a much lower figure than the UK average (53%), this disparity may be due to the absence of opportunities for part-time work in Northern Ireland, rather than a result of 'traditional' or 'conservative' attitudes or ideologies. The evidence shows that a higher proportion of mothers of school-age children in Northern Ireland are in full-time employment compared with the average for the UK. In other respects, patterns of male and female engagement in paid employment and domestic labour appear to be emerging that are similar to those elsewhere in the UK. Women aspire to continue to work outside the home whether or not they have children. They hope to improve their conditions at work and to be promoted but tend to be hindered in their careers by factors such as the poverty trap and the lack of affordable childcare. This is not meant to suggest that life is problem-free for working women in Northern Ireland; on the contrary, there is a sexual division of employment opportunities which results in women being concentrated in a small number of – usually – low-paid occupations. Women's earnings have risen relative to men's, but, even excluding the effects of overtime, women in Northern Ireland still earn considerably less than men. Again, this pattern of inequality is similar to that prevailing in the rest of the UK and elsewhere.

Discrimination and unequal treatment are not accepted with resignation by women, however. The number of complaints about pay and discrimination at work has risen steadily over the past 10 years and there are indications of a gradual, if rather slow, improvement. There are also indications that men's involvement in domestic labour, if still unacceptably low, has increased in recent years at a rate similar to the rest of the UK. The state of Northern Ireland's economy creates problems for working women which are greater than those experienced elsewhere. The combination of a benefits system based on the idea of a male breadwinner and the fact that women's jobs are low-paid means that wives of unemployed men are less likely to take up work. Given the high rates of male unemployment, it is clear that a significant proportion of women in Northern Ireland who would like to work outside the home will be unable to do so.

Women in politics

If women in Northern Ireland have become a significant presence in the workforce, the same cannot be said for the arena of politics. In this area, comparisons with the UK and the Republic of Ireland are less comforting. Northern Ireland now returns 17 members of Parliament to Westminster; none of these are women, nor are there any women candidates likely to be selected for safe seats in the next general election by any of the major parties. By European standards, the UK Parliament elects relatively few women. Constituencies in Great Britain in the last election, however, did manage to return 57 women out of 634 seats. In the Irish Republic, 13% of those elected to the Dáil at the last election were women. Most strikingly, in 1992 voters in the Irish Republic, chose a feminist, social-democratic lawyer, Mary Robinson, as President. She was not only the first woman to hold that office but the first candidate to triumph over the Fianna Fáil party's presidential candidate. In the most recent European elections, the Republic of Ireland returned four women Members of the European Parliament out of a total of 15 representatives, while British constituencies returned 17 women out of a total of 84 MEPs. In Northern Ireland, three MEPs are returned, elected by proportional representation for a single constituency. None of these has ever been a woman, nor is it likely that a woman will be selected as a candidate by any of the three major parties next time. In the 1994 election, there were four women candidates, including Mary Clark-Glass, a former Chair of the Equal Opportunities Commission for Northern Ireland (EOCNI), who stood for the Alliance Party. Her share of the vote was 4.1%, representing a small decline compared with previous Alliance performances. In local government, the situation is somewhat better. Although district councils in Northern Ireland have few powers, they do have influence over issues of concern to women, including environmental issues and provision of parks, playgrounds and leisure services. Of the 26 local district councils, three have no women members, nine have only one woman member and overall, 12% of Councillors are women. These figures represent a very slight improvement on previous years.

Since the introduction of direct rule, of course, a great deal of policy-making in Northern Ireland has been in the hands of public bodies supervised by various Departments of the Northern Ireland Office (NIO). In these non-elected bodies the representation of women is higher than in elected institutions, and, thanks to the efforts of the EOCNI, it is growing. In 1978, 15% of those appointed were women, while in 1993, the percentage of women appointed had reached over 27%. There are still 20 bodies with no women members. Women are more likely to be appointed to public bodies dealing with issues traditionally seen as female concerns and women are under-represented among the chairs of public bodies. Women are more likely to serve as unpaid members, or to be paid less for their service than men. It is difficult to draw conclusions about the significance of the higher representation of women on these non-elected bodies. To some extent, the NIO and ministers are responding to pressure from the EOCNI and other groups to increase the numbers of women serving on public bodies. It appears that, as in other areas of socio-economic life, direct rule has brought about progressive change which would not have been achieved through elected institutions in Northern Ireland. On the other hand, doubts have been expressed about the benefits of a system of appointments which is based upon informal and somewhat inscrutable selection processes, with suspicions that 'token' women may be chosen who are unable to raise the issues relevant to the majority of women.

Given that women from Northern Ireland have kept pace with women elsewhere in Europe in claiming a place in the world of work and in redefining the domestic sphere, why has politics continued to be a male-dominated arena? Women are far from apolitical, being visible in numerous campaigns and pressure groups attempting to influence policy-making on a wide spectrum of issues. This community activism and campaigning has not, up to the present, led to women becoming career politicians or political leaders. A number of factors seem to combine to perpetuate the absence of women from the key, leadership sectors of Northern Ireland politics. One problem is that Northern Ireland is a small community, with a correspondingly small political élite. It is therefore more difficult for women to get the support needed to make the breakthrough into positions of influence. In addition, being a political representative or leader is not just a job like any other. There are practical and procedural obstacles to attaining such leadership positions which are not easily dealt with. For one thing, there is a limited turnover of openings for new entrants to the political élite, and access to it is not based exclusively on merit. While women are very slowly moving into other élite positions – for example, in the legal profession or the Civil Service – becoming an elected representative requires not only the possession of skills and qualifications but also a whole range of other resources, material and non-material, which women find it more difficult to acquire. The centrality of the national conflict in Northern Ireland both reduces the turnover of places in the élite and makes it unlikely that women will be viewed as having the appropriate strengths to deal with 'the other side'. Involvement in community groups, particularly those with a 'cross-community' or 'reconciliatory' focus, may help to reproduce an image of women having the wrong sorts of qualities for the business of politics. If a new regional tier of government is created in the near future, we can expect that there will be women members at least in proportion to the numbers of women in local government. Whether this will represent the 'critical mass' necessary to allow representation of all the issues which women consider important seems much less likely.

Campaigning for women's rights*

The fact is that, although there are problems and policies which unite women across religious, national or even class divisions, there are also quite profound differences. The relative lack of interest in the Euro-election candidacy of Mary

Clark-Glass would seem to indicate that women in Northern Ireland will not abandon their allegiance to their preferred political party in order to support a rival party's woman candidate, even one with a record of commitment to promoting women's rights. The experience of feminist organizations supports the view that gender is not the primary basis for political identification for a significant number of women in Northern Ireland. This is not to imply that feminist or women's activism has been futile or unsuccessful. On the contrary, since the early 1970s, groups campaigning on women's issues have had a considerable impact on policy and consciousness. Nonetheless, even among that minority who consider gender inequalities to be of fundamental importance, disagreements about the national question have surfaced.

Since the early 1970s there have been three principal types of women's groups in Northern Ireland: feminist movement, single-issue and community groups. Influenced by the experience of the Northern Ireland Civil Rights Association (NICRA), in which many women had been active, and by the 'second wave' of feminism which was flourishing elsewhere in Europe, women's liberation and consciousness-raising groups appeared among students, academics and left-wing circles from 1973 onwards. To mark the opening of the United Nations Decade for Women in 1975, an attempt was made to create a broad, inclusive movement with a coherent set of demands which would both increase awareness of women's oppression and lead to changes which would benefit women.

One of the aims of the Northern Ireland Women's Rights Movement, which had a socialist orientation, was to appeal to the majority of women, particularly from working-class communities. Following a tradition established in the trade union movement, this aim of unity was to be achieved by avoiding discussion of 'the national question'. This self-denying ordinance soon led to splits, as some feminists saw this as *de facto* a Unionist position. For some groups, women's liberation required national liberation and vice versa. These groups set themselves the impossible task of maintaining an autonomous feminist organization while also advocating support for broadly republican goals, though not necessarily for republican tactics. Eventually, the remaining adherents of this version of feminism became incorporated into Sinn Féin, advocating sensitivity to women's issues and challenging that Party's adherence to traditional Irish Catholic values in its policies on sexual morality and reproductive rights. Relationships between republican-oriented feminists and the Northern Ireland Women's Rights Movement became very fraught during the campaign by republican prisoners for political status, a campaign which involved women prisoners. Attempting to avoid taking sides, the Women's Rights Movement tried to shift the focus by developing general policies on the human rights of women prisoners. To republican feminists, this seemed like a betrayal. On some issues, all feminist groups could unite, but from the 1980s unity became more difficult to achieve. Nevertheless, from all sides the desire for unity was a recurrent theme, most strongly expressed in a conference organized by the Workers' Educational Association (WEA) in 1990. Attended by 350 women, all the difficult issues were discussed, but no solution was forthcoming to the problem of creating a movement which could speak for all women while acknowledging their profound differences.

It would be misleading to suggest that feminists turned to single-issue campaigns in frustration at the divisions within the broader women's movement. For many, this was a result of decisions about priorities, or of assessments of likely effectiveness. Indeed, many of these campaigns have been very effective. The Northern Ireland Women's Aid Federation has changed public awareness of domestic violence and influenced police methods, court procedures and housing policies as well as providing practical short- and long-term help to women who have been subjected to violent abuse by husbands or partners. This has been accompanied by a commitment to working in a non-hierarchical style, designed to avoid labelling women as victims who must be rescued by others. This commitment to 'empowerment' is a feature of other groups, such as the Rape Crisis Centre and the Women's Education Group, both of which have been influential in spite of limited resources and initial lack of interest from policy-makers and public alike. Single-issue campaigns have not always been immune to the divisions over national identity. In particular, the Northern Ireland Abortion Law Reform Association (NIALRA) has been criticized for making its focus the extension of the 1967 Abortion Act to Northern Ireland, on the grounds that this means accepting the legitimacy of Westminster.

Women and community groups

Community-based women's groups have also had considerable success throughout Northern Ireland. Such groups have remained autonomous from women's liberation groups, accepting some aspects of feminism but on the whole remaining sceptical of the value of feminist politics. For many of those active in such groups, feminism appears to be a concern of middle-class women. Feminists are often viewed as just another set of career women, who have educational and financial advantages which set them apart from the majority. The formidable issue which absorbs the energies of these groups is poverty. They exist to support women in dealing with the consequences for their families of Northern Ireland's economic difficulties. Managing the limited budget of low-income families has been identified as the responsibility of women in many countries. In Northern Ireland, one of the tasks which falls on the shoulders of women is negotiating with housing and benefit agencies in an effort to increase family income or offset the effects of loss of income.

A network of community-based groups has been created to share information and experience and to lobby for policies to improve the situation of those living on low pay or benefits. At this level of activism, there is a high degree of cooperation across the religious/political divide. The numbers of these groups have increased steadily over the past 10 years, extending throughout Northern Ireland and, most recently, beginning to represent the particular problems of women in rural communities. As these groups have become more numerous and assertive, there has been a corresponding growth of interest in women's issues in both voluntary agencies and in the community-development sectors of district councils. There are, therefore, opportunities for women to speak for themselves on issues which they have defined as important. The present political arrangements, with their mix of the elected and the bureaucratic, allow for some aspects of gender inequality and some women's interests to be dealt with in the policy-making process. While this is not altogether satisfactory, there are reasons to be concerned that the political institutions being constructed in the aftermath of the ceasefire will not be sensitive to the need for the representation of women.

Conclusion

Throughout the years of the conflict in Northern Ireland, women have been appealed to as 'peacemakers'. A high profile has been allowed, by the mass media and the NIO, to successive campaigns initiated by women, appealing for 'peace'. The most notable of these was the Peace People movement, launched and maintained by two 'ordinary women'. Women have also been represented by all sides as the stoic and suffering victims of the conflict, and have been the mainstay of non-violent movements of community solidarity and resistance, particularly in relation to prisoners' rights. In spite of this recruitment of women to 'worthy causes', with a few exceptions women are not participating in the process of constructing a political future for Northern Ireland and it is hard to avoid the impression that an opportunity is being missed. There are two factors which have led to this state of affairs.

One is the assumption, common to many liberal democracies, that on all but a specific set of 'women's issues', women can quite satisfactorily be represented by men. So, women can be assumed to be included when constitutional arrangements which affect the whole community are being made. The other factor is that the arrangements are being discussed in a series of bilateral and multilateral meetings involving the political parties in Northern Ireland and representatives of the British and Irish governments. There are few women in the leadership structures of the larger parties. Sinn Féin has made efforts to include women, as have some of the smaller loyalist parties. The Alliance Party has included women in the process, but neither of the two major Unionist parties appears to make the inclusion of women a priority. The SDLP has agreed to guarantee women a representation of 40% on its executive committee and has now set up a women's section. Whether this will result in the reflection of women's interests in the present political process is difficult to estimate.

At a series of conferences and meetings in 1995 some community groups and feminists attempted to argue that an awareness of gender inequalities must be built into the 'peace process'. There is a particular concern that any new political structures are created with the need to increase the representation of women in mind, so that women can have their say on all matters which they consider of importance. The EOCNI has recently called for targets for women's participation to be set for all political institutions, including political parties. Other groups have proposed the creation of a body equivalent to the Irish Republic's Council for the Status of Women, which has a consultative role in policy-making. The absence of women makes a difference; for example, one of the few issues on which all the

Northern Ireland parties at Westminster are united is in their opposition to abortion law reform. Marjorie Mowlam, Shadow Northern Ireland Secretary, recently stated that women had a vital role to play in the evolving peace process, but needed an entry to the political system. The demand for this entry appears likely to bring about a revival of the women's movement in Northern Ireland.

Further reading

Davies, C. and McLaughlin, E. (eds), *Women, Employment and Social Policy in Northern Ireland: A Problem Postponed?* Belfast: EOCNI, 1993.

Equal Opportunities Commission, *A Matter of Small Importance? Catholic and Protestant Women in the Northern Ireland Labour Market.* Belfast: EOCNI, 1995.

Hughes, E. (ed.), *Culture and Politics in Northern Ireland.* Milton Keynes: Open University Press, 1990.

Kramer, J. and Montgomery, P. (eds), *Women's Working Lives.* Belfast: EOCNI, 1993.

Loughran, C., 'Armagh and feminist strategy: campaign around republican women prisoners in Armagh Jail', *Feminist Review,* 23, 1986.

O'Connor, F., *In Search of a State: Catholics in Northern Ireland.* Belfast: Blackstaff Press, 1993.

Pollak, A., (ed.), *A Citizens' Inquiry: The Opsahl Report on Northern Ireland.* Dublin: Lilliput Press, 1993.

Roulston, C., 'Women on the margin: the Women's Movement in Northern Ireland 1973–1988', *Science and Society,* 53, 1989.

Chapter 17

FILLING THE GAP:
POLICY AND PRESSURE UNDER DIRECT RULE
Duncan Morrow

Policy-making networks

In all modern democratic societies many people, groups and organizations both outside and within government play a part in formulating and developing policy: politicians, civil servants, local councillors, political parties, business leaders and companies, public bodies, pressure groups, mass media, trade unions and so on. Policy-making is thus a complex, and often contentious, process of negotiation.

It is usually difficult to be certain which aspect of the process, if any, is decisive in the final formulation of policy in modern states. The interrelationships between different groups and the relative importance of any one influence on policy obviously changes according to the policy in question. In his book *Beyond Westminster and Whitehall* (1988), Rod Rhodes has described the policy-making process as a network of interlinked and interlinking agencies of different influence and power. While some writers would go as far as suggesting that all groups in society, including government and civil service, can best be understood as pressure groups, it is clear that the particular functions of government in the state give it a pre-eminent role in all public-policy decision-making.

In representative democracies this ultimate authority of government comes from its central and unique relationship with the electorate to which it is finally and regularly responsible and accountable. Under direct rule, Northern Irish political parties have not participated in government in the province, undermining their very *raison d'être*. This weakness of political representation has raised the profile of community and pressure groups organized around specific issues or working in restricted geographical areas. In the absence of local representative democracy or full political integration into either the United Kingdom or the Republic of Ireland, the importance of community and pressure groups has been correspondingly heightened.

Policy-making in Northern Ireland

The very unusual relationship of government to society in Northern Ireland has created unusual and distinct policy-making networks. In the first place, the abolition of the Stormont Parliament in 1972 and the subsequent failure to establish any broadly acceptable form of devolved government ended the power of local Northern Irish politicians to decide policy. The different party-political structure of Northern Ireland from that of England, Scotland and Wales means that no major Northern Irish party has a direct link to UK government. Thus the central plank of political representation in liberal democratic societies, the vote, has had little direct influence on the policy content of government in the province.

The problem for the government under direct rule remained the same central dispute about the legitimacy of the state to govern at all which made devolved administration unworkable. Indeed, this issue has continued to constrain all UK government policy and made the emergence of a single consistent approach very difficult.

The central dilemma for governments has been whether to treat Northern Ireland as integral to the UK or as 'a place apart'. The advent of direct rule brought the interests and concerns of central UK government much closer to the forefront of local policy-making. At the same time, one of those very concerns was to contain the civil unrest within the geographical and political community of Northern Ireland. The result was a rather *ad hoc* mix of policy. In some areas, such as health, social security and even economic policy, Northern Ireland has increasingly been treated as an integral part of the UK, while in other areas, such as Fair Employment legislation, the exceptional and non-transferable nature of policy in Northern Ireland has been emphasized.

The primary outcome of this division for the UK government is that it has to live with chronic and deep suspicion of its motives in relation to the constitutional future of Northern Ireland from both Unionists and Nationalists. As a result, policy decisions about issues which, on the surface at least, are only marginally related to the question of the border, are interpreted in the light of these fears. Thus the decision in 1989 to privatize the two largest local engineering firms (Harland and Wolff Shipbuilders and Short Brothers Aircraft and Missile Manufacturers) was regarded by some Unionists as evidence of a phased economic withdrawal from the province. Likewise, the increasing similarity of policy between Northern Ireland and the rest of the UK in other areas is regarded as evidence of strengthening the Union by Nationalists.

The third distinct difference distinguishing the policy-making network is the extreme weakness of local government in Northern Ireland. The Local Government (Northern Ireland) Act 1972 was designed to remove deep-rooted sectarian bias at local level by reducing the powers of local authorities in housing, personal social services, health, education and planning and replacing them with non-elected agencies made up of nominees from various quarters. The act nevertheless assumed some form of devolved Northern Ireland administration. The absence of this administration has had the effect of making local councils a focus of sectarian symbolic politics and at the same time keeping them powerless.

The very weakness of local government has increased the importance of nominated boards, agencies and departments of the Northern Ireland Office (NIO). Furthermore, the emphasis on administration as opposed to representation has increased the scope for civil service influence over policy. Given the small size of Northern Ireland, the result has been a tight and intimate policy network dominated by administrative interests. The inability of local political parties to influence policy has not, however, abolished the need of the government to stay in contact with the governed. As a result, the civil service has increasingly developed its own extensive and direct relationship with numerous groups and agencies.

A shattered mould: pressure and policy before and after civil rights

Before the 1960s, there were very few groups outside government and political parties which had significant influence on policy-making in Northern Ireland. There were several reasons for this. Representational organization in Northern Ireland was traditionally shaped by the constitutional divide between Unionists and Nationalists. Both groups put a premium on internal unity and shared an abhorrence of public division. There was considerable internal pressure to channel disquiet and discontent through traditional organizations. Secondly, the fact that Northern Ireland was a provincial government rather than a fully-fledged state further reduced the number of areas where pressure group politics might act. After 1945, most of the reforms of the welfare state were adopted without alteration from Westminster. Furthermore, the rural influence on Northern Ireland remains strong even today while much group organization and militant action were rooted in towns and cities. As a result, local pressure politics was largely channelled through a small number of key institutions, in particular the churches and related politico-religious bodies such as the Orange Order and economic interests such as employer, trade union and farmers' organizations.

The Orange Order was particularly significant within Unionist politics. Often regarded as the key lynchpin of Protestant Unionism linking different churches, working class and upper class as well as rural and urban lodges, the Order had direct formal links with the ruling Unionist Party. Before 1971, up to two-thirds of the adult Protestant male population of Northern Ireland belonged to the Order. The explicit link between the Bible and the Crown within the Order served also to cement the Protestant foundations of the Northern Ireland state. Partly through this association with Orangeism, too, came the generally assumed association of the Protestant churches with the Unionist Party and the state.

While the Ancient Order of Hibernians (AOH) flourished among certain sections of the Nationalist population and retained close informal links with the opposition Nationalist Party, its inability to deliver any particular policy made it, generally, a pale imitation of its Orange counterpart. Instead, the most prominent pressure group with a strong base within the Nationalist community was consistently the Roman Catholic Church. Together with the Protestant churches, the Catholic Church was particularly active in the sphere of schools and education policy where they were largely successful in establishing a separate Catholic school system.

The rural bias of Northern Ireland reduced the authority of traditional trade unions. Furthermore, sectarian divisions in the workplace meant that class loyalties were always threatened by Nationalist/Unionist divisions. Thus while some trade unions were organized on an all-Ireland basis (for example the Irish National Teachers' Organization, INTO) and others on a Northern Ireland basis (Ulster Teachers' Union, UTU), the majority were branches of British unions. Partition in 1921 resulted in the creation of a special Northern Ireland Committee of the Irish Congress of Trade Unions (NIC-ICTU). The all-Ireland dimension, however, led to an effective boycott of this main union umbrella group by the Unionist Party. Many Protestant industrial workers channelled their frustrations through individual workplace unions, the Orange Order and the Unionist Party or else remained largely passive. Only in the 1960s did O'Neill finally recognize NIC-ICTU and co-opt them into consultative structures.

Locally resident employers in Northern Ireland were often integrally part of the Unionist system. With the opening up of the international economy after 1945 and the establishment of the Confederation of British Industry (CBI), most large-scale employers became members. The combined economic power of CBI members has made them an important influence over economic policy, although much of CBI policy in Northern Ireland is determined in London rather than Belfast.

Farming has always been organized separately. As elsewhere in the UK and Ireland, the Ulster Farmers' Union developed a close relationship with the Ministry of Agriculture and other marketing and price-fixing institutions. In Northern Ireland, the close personal nature of rural relationships has made this network even more intimate than elsewhere.

A number of crucial developments radically altered this tightly ordered pattern. Firstly, the establishment of the welfare state gave rise to numerous pressure groups which desired to improve, extend or defend particular aspects of the new system. The switch in policy emphasis from direct provision of social services by the state and the introduction of the internal market within the National Health Service (NHS) in the 1990s has multiplied rather than reduced the number of agencies and groups in negotiation with the government.

Related to this, the growing importance of government within the economy made direct contact between numerous interest groups and the government inevitable. Even in Northern Ireland, the central importance of agriculture as an employer was in decline. Mass unemployment returned to Northern Ireland in the 1970s and subsequent attempts to revive and sustain the economy have relied heavily on public finance, intensifying the public–private relationship.

Most dramatically, the events of 1968–72 radically altered the organizational form, if not the underlying polarities, of public life in Northern Ireland. The emergence of the Northern Ireland Civil Rights Association (NICRA), which campaigned initially on issues of economic and social inequality, especially in the sphere of housing, voting and employment, represented the first serious and sustained mass-protest movement in Northern Ireland since 1921. Already during the 1960s, discontent with the Unionist Party among many working-class Protestants had led to some successes for the Northern Ireland Labour Party (NILP). In response to the rise of NICRA, the Protestant Unionist Party under the leadership of Ian Paisley emerged. All of this signalled the ending of the old monolithic system. The eruption of physical violence on the streets after 1969, the mass flight of many threatened families into ghettos between 1970 and 1972 and the aftermath of the introduction of internment without trial in 1971 all created a radically different political climate.

The establishment of the Community Relations Commission by the Stormont government in 1970 and its deliberate policy of establishing local community development groups gave a boost to the growth of local community associations. New agencies, such as the Northern Ireland Housing Executive (NIHE), encouraged the spread of tenants' action groups. Furthermore, the emergence of terrorist and paramilitary organizations in both Catholic and Protestant parts of Northern Ireland gave rise to numerous new sub-groups and organizations, all of which now sought to influence aspects of public policy.

By 1974, in place of the old monoliths there were now five local parties who were broadly supportive of the Union, a new Nationalist party, numerous new terrorist and paramilitary groups and hundreds of community groups. The presence of the Army on the streets made security a constant source of policy pressure. Furthermore, the explosion of violence led to vastly increased media interest in Northern Ireland, a necessarily central place for Northern Irish affairs on the agenda of British and Irish governments and considerable international interest. International pressure groups such as Amnesty International and Irish emigrant interests started to challenge aspects of government policy in Northern Ireland through both domestic and international channels.

Small groups and public policy

As a result of ongoing and still unresolved political upheaval, central government, the Civil Service, various non-governmental organizations (NGOs) and the myriad of local community groups emerged as stronger influences within the policy network than elsewhere, whereas political parties, local government and classical economic interests, particularly trade unions, were notably weaker. The emergence of local alternatives to classical representative politics was one of the most dynamic features of Northern Irish public life, particularly as these groups often developed direct links with government bodies and NGOs, bypassing elected representatives.

The rise of community and pressure groups reflected in part a widespread disillusionment with the electoral system in Northern Ireland. The problem had both chronic and acute dimensions. Following the abolition of Stormont and the failure of successive attempts to relaunch reformed versions of local democracy, the UK government, and increasingly also the Irish government, sought to create a constituency of support beyond the confines of traditional political parties and structures which were seen to have failed. Community groups appeared to represent one possibility of altering or changing the climate in such a way as to redefine traditional politics over the longer run. More immediately, the inability of political parties to agree on sustainable structures beyond Unionism and Nationalism and the record of discrimination associated with local government left the UK government with few formal channels of communication between the government and the governed. The development of direct channels of communication between the administration (usually civil servants or NGO employees) and directly funded community groups has partly filled this gap. Furthermore, the economic decline of Northern Ireland meant that short-term employment opportunities were not available in manufacturing or service industry. As a result, the government turned to community groups to administer and develop employment and training programmes.

By 1989, there were over 800 active local and community groups in Northern Ireland, or approximately one group per 2,000 people, many of whom were in direct contact with government agencies. Many of these groups were themselves ambivalent about their relations with government, caught between (supposed) principled objection to Britishness, existing authority in general or a combination of both and a pragmatic need to find financial resources both to maintain their existence and to undertake specific practical projects. Thus many community groups found themselves trying to reconcile the role of pressure group and local demands for militant activism with that of provider of services and watchdog. The result is an increasingly complex network of roles and relationships within the policy process.

Policy and pressures

A number of policy initiatives in the 1980s and 1990s illustrate the ambiguous outcome of these developments. By the early 1980s, the need to provide training and job opportunities for the long-term unemployed had become critical. As a result, the government, backed by money from the European Social Fund, introduced the Action for Community Employment (ACE) scheme. By 1990, nearly 11,000 people (Department of Economic Development (DED) figures) were employed in over 300 different community schemes, the majority employing between 10 and 100 employees each. The various employers illustrate the range of groups co-opted into this scheme: YMCA, Coleraine and District Churches, Dungannon Development Association, The Ulster Society, Cathedral Community Enterprises and so on. Many organizations and districts became dependent on the continued flow of ACE employees. In effect these groups, sometimes with roots in oppositional activism, became key service-providers of government social and economic policy.

The row over 'political vetting' of ACE schemes which emerged in the mid-1980s illustrated the serious problems of building a coherent policy network on supposedly independent groups who depend on state funding for their existence. Furthermore, in the context of sectarianism, the government felt itself obliged to invoke their power inherent in this dependent relationship to ensure other policy goals, thus making clear the ultimately unequal relationship.

In 1984, the government came under pressure from Unionist MPs to stop ACE funding to a number of community groups on the basis that the money was being used to shore up the political respectability of Sinn Féin and might find its way into IRA funds. ACE funding was duly removed from a number of groups, such as Twinbrook Tenants' Association and Conway Mill on the Falls Road, on the grounds of close links to paramilitary organizations, although the government produced no concrete evidence. At the same time, the number of posts in other schemes, particularly those run by the Catholic Church, was increased. This gave rise to considerable anger, particularly in West Belfast, and encouraged a conflict which was widely interpreted along traditional lines as a conflict between innocent community and heavy-handed British authority. The situation was not resolved when funding was restored in some cases, such as for example, the Irish language group, Glór na nGael, after appeal. The row highlighted all of the weaknesses of the pragmatic networks which have emerged in Northern Ireland: the absolute dependence on central government funding of key elements of the policy process, the absence of elected scrutiny both of government and of funding provision, and the difficulty, some would argue the impossibility, of circumventing the sectarian division by administrative means.

All of these issues re-emerged in the programme announced for Belfast in 1988, 'Making Belfast Work' (MBW). Aimed primarily at reducing unemployment and social deprivation in the city, finance was allocated specifically to projects in the spheres of economic and employment regeneration, environment, education, health and social services. This sought to link ministries within the Northern Ireland Office with numerous NGOs and community agencies and groups. One of the most innovative projects has been the setting up of locally based 'Belfast Action Teams' (BATs) composed of seconded civil and public servants each with their own budget. Their task is to liaise directly with the local community, assessing projects and committing short-term funds to groups within the limits of the goals of Making Belfast Work.

BAT teams thus represent the most systematic direct linkage of the civil service and local community groups, without specific reference to locally elected councillors. Throughout deprived areas of Belfast, civil servants made direct personal and financial relationships with numerous local groups. Inevitably this gave rise again to renewed accusations of favouritism and political vetting. Furthermore, the dependence of local groups on central finance was not subject to the direct scrutiny of any local politician. At the same time, the BAT system provided the civil service with direct local knowledge and insight and established flexible mechanisms of working in the absence of a functioning regional parliament.

Conclusions

Direct rule has seen the transformation of the old Northern Irish policy-making process. With hindsight, the roots of the dissolution of the old monolithic structures were visible in the 1960s, but the extent of the reshaping could hardly have been predicted.

Having responsibility for the administration of Northern Ireland, Westminster governments have still failed to achieve the necessary consensus to re-establish stable regional government. However, this has not removed the need to maintain working institutional relationships in whole areas of policy. In the absence of acceptable locally elected representatives, the role of the public and civil services has grown. This has necessitated finding partners through which policy could be implemented, demands could be articulated and change could be sought. In general this gap has been filled by local community groups which did not exist prior to 1972.

As a result, a whole new class of leadership has emerged which has no direct electoral mandate but has sufficient local legitimacy to carry out specific appointed tasks. Furthermore, it appears that much of the leadership talent of Northern Ireland has been channelled into these organizations and groups rather than into formal political parties which aspire to take power and full responsibility.

The primary advantage of these policy networks is that they have provided a means of sustaining basic services and local consultation processes in the midst of constitutional crisis. Furthermore, they have enabled the development and application of new policy areas without the direct involvement of local government.

At the same time, this has led to an unusual reliance on small groups who often seek this independence to represent local feeling at the same time as relying entirely on public funding for their existence. This has sometimes created unsustainable pressures. It has also established an extensive pressure group system which is not scrutinized by any clear democratic mechanism, creating in effect small local agencies and élites which rival, and often outperform, elected officials in their ability to deliver services. This very fact has made groups vulnerable to takeover by paramilitary or party interests. In response, the government has sometimes been seen to choose between different local élites and has found itself embroiled once more in party political or sectarian controversy. By working through community groups the government has not yet fundamentally altered the division between Nationalist and Unionist. Indeed, by working through often parochial groups, who operate within sectarian demography and geography, they may reinforce the divisions of Northern Ireland society.

The emergence of small local pressure groups and the decline of political parties is part of a wider trend in western society. The particular political circumstances of Northern Ireland have exaggerated these effects to an unusual extent. Like direct rule itself, this *ad hoc* system of administration and policy formation which has now grown up exists less because of its intrinsic desirability than because of the fact that it seems to be least defective of the real possibilities available.

Perhaps more than any other area, policy-making networks will be altered by agreement on representative government for Northern Ireland. Any elected forum will wish to reclaim many of the decision-making and monitoring functions which have been distributed under direct rule between the civil service, NGOs and community groups, such as Health, Social Services and Education. It should not be forgotten, however, that the rise of NGOs and community politics was itself based on the inability of Northern Irish electoral politics to escape sectarian demands and pressures. The most potent example of this phenomenon is probably the Northern Ireland Housing Executive (NIHE) set up in 1970 in the wake of persistent evidence that the allocation of public housing was based on sectarian political considerations. Like direct rule itself, the central importance of NGOs, administrators and community groups, no matter how short of democratic legitimacy, may therefore remain in operation as the 'least defective' option until there are specific and clear guarantees preventing any future elected body from returning to overtly sectarian practices.

Further reading

Community Development Review Group, *Community Development in Northern Ireland: Perspectives for the Future.* Belfast: WEA, 1991.

Connolly, M., *Politics and Policy-making in Northern Ireland.* Hemel Hempstead: Philip Allan, 1990.

Connolly, M. and Loughlin, S. (eds), *Public Policy in Northern Ireland: Adoption or Adaptation?* Belfast: Policy Research Institute, 1990.

Darby, J. and Williamson, A., *Violence and the Social Services in Northern Ireland.* London: Heinemann Educational, 1978.

Lyons, F.S.L., *Ireland since the Famine.* London: Fontana, 1973.

Pollak, A. (ed.), *A Citizens' Inquiry: The Opsahl Report on Northern Ireland.* Dublin: Lilliput Press, 1993.

Rhodes, R., *Beyond Westminster and Whitehall.* London: Unwin Hyman, 1988.

Williamson, A. and Acheson, N. (eds), *The Voluntary Sector in Northern Ireland.* Basingstoke: Avebury, 1995.

ASPECTS OF SOCIETY

Chapter 18

PARAMILITARISM
Alan Bairner

Introduction

The relationship between politics and violence is always problematic. While there is widespread agreement that legitimate governments should have the right to use force in particular circumstances, this raises questions about what constitutes political legitimacy. For their part, ordinary citizens are normally denied the right to resort to violence for political purposes, whether in opposition to the state or in its defence, if it can be shown that there exist sufficient alternative channels for the expression of their demands. This again raises questions about political legitimacy. Who decides whether or not existing political mechanisms are adequate? Who, ultimately, decides if certain violent acts can be described as political rather than as merely criminal? What, in any case, is the relationship between political and criminal violence? Nowhere in the western world in recent times have such questions figured so prominently in political debate as in Northern Ireland.

Between 1969 and 1994, paramilitary organizations, engaged in what they would have described as political violence, were responsible for the overwhelming majority of the deaths which were the direct consequence of the political crisis. Whether their violence was political or merely criminal was a constant question informing discussion about how paramilitaries ought to be dealt with. Although no agreement was ever likely to be reached on that particular matter, there was general recognition, in Northern Ireland and beyond, that the paramilitary groups had the weaponry, the organization and the will to continue their violent activities for an unlimited period of time. It is scarcely surprising, therefore, that the ceasefires called by the paramilitaries during the second half of 1994 were greeted with a considerable sense of relief not only in Northern Ireland itself but also in the rest of the United Kingdom, the Republic of Ireland and even parts of mainland Europe, all of which had witnessed violence perpetrated by these groups. That the paramilitaries had become such a prominent part of the fabric of society in Northern Ireland, however, meant that few people were ready to believe that violence had come to an end once and for all.

A major reason for the scepticism which cast a shadow over even the most optimistic responses to the ceasefires was the fact that violence had been a feature

159

of political life in Ireland for centuries and had not simply emerged in the late 1960s. Indeed, for some people, particularly those who do not live on the island of Ireland, the paramilitary violence associated with the modern Troubles was merely the most recent manifestation of the Irish propensity for violence. More sophisticated analyses, while rebuking those who regard the Irish, both Catholic and Protestant, as intrinsically violent, nevertheless argued that because of political circumstances, the acting out of ancient rivalries through violence had become part and parcel of the Irish way of life. As a result, the violence of 1969–94, while by no means indicative of the behaviour of an entire people (or of entire peoples), was manifestly the product of ancient impulses serving deeply felt needs. Ironically, analysis of this sort has been endorsed to some extent by the paramilitaries themselves who have made every effort to establish their historic credentials by claiming links between their organizations and earlier groups which adopted violent methods for political purposes. Claims of historical continuity, however, whatever their sources, offer only partial insights.

Paramilitarism has certainly been a long-standing feature of Irish politics. One can argue, for example, that the Royal Ulster Constabulary (RUC), particularly the 'B' Specials, together with the Ulster Defence Regiment, later the Royal Irish Regiment, have fulfilled roles similar to those assigned to paramilitary sections of the security forces in other western societies. This made the tradition in Northern Ireland rather different from the British norm of 'civilian' policing. Moreover, organizations committed to the use of violence and outside the state's control have been a more or less permanent feature. However, the fact that there has been a lot of violence associated with the history of Ireland, north and south, is insufficient cause to suggest that violence is an inevitable element in Irish political life. Equally, the fact that people have used violence in the past offers no immanent justification for its continued use. To explain the violence of the recent troubles, therefore, it is necessary to examine the activities and philosophies of the organizations directly involved. Such an examination reveals not only undeniable links with the past, but also the extent to which these paramilitary groups were products of a particular set of circumstances.

Legitimation of violence

Although numerous separate organizations were responsible for paramilitary violence during the Troubles, all of them can be categorized as either republican or loyalist. The republican groups used violence to promote the cause of Irish unity; loyalist violence, on the other hand, was intended to defend the Union. At various times, all of the paramilitary factions have been proscribed by the British government which has sought repeatedly to criminalize the paramilitaries, to portray them simply as terrorists and, thus, to show that their actions could not be dignified by the title of 'political activity'. For the paramilitaries themselves, however, their recourse to violence was not merely politically inspired but also necessary and legitimate.

According to republicans, their violence derived its legitimacy from the fact that it served a goal which was shared by constitutional Nationalists and which was enshrined in the constitution of the Irish Republic, the very existence of which owed much to earlier phases of republican violence. Loyalists sought to legitimize their violence by arguing that their objectives were shared by constitutional Unionism and, it was their hope, by the British government. The Union had to be defended and, if the coercive agencies of the state were unable to deal fully with the threat posed by republican violence, it was deemed necessary by loyalist paramilitaries to act outside the law in order to bring republicans to justice. Because they regarded their actions as being supportive of the constitutional authorities, therefore, they rejected the idea that their violence was criminal.

Despite their protestations, however, a majority of those engaged in paramilitary activity during 1969–94 were also involved in criminal behaviour, with armed robberies and various forms of racketeering being used, primarily but by no means exclusively, to fund military operations. Nevertheless, psychologists have argued that their studies of paramilitary prisoners did not indicate psychotic personalities. During the Troubles, Northern Ireland acquired a young and relatively well-educated prison population, most of whose members were in prison because of political circumstances and their own, arguably misguided, responses to them. This is not to deny that some psychopaths were only too willing to masquerade under the rival flags of convenience or that some members of the paramilitary organizations came to regard making money by criminal methods as an end in itself rather than as a means to more noble ends. There is sufficient evidence to suggest, however, that the violence of the paramilitaries was never simply ordinary criminal violence as defined by the British government itself. In any event, regardless of how it was defined by the authorities, this violence was consistently seen in an altogether different light not just by its protagonists but more importantly by sections of the wider community. The support of the latter helped the paramilitaries to continue to regard themselves as members of legitimate organizations even after the status of prisoners of war was denied to their imprisoned comrades.

In the quest for legitimacy, a curious relationship between the rival paramilitary groups was established. Not only did they feed off one another, using the violence of their rivals to help justify their own activities, but they also shared a need to be treated with respect. To what extent they deserved any respect and how they managed to sustain their murderous campaigns for 25 years can only be answered by examining the organizations themselves.

Republican paramilitarism

On the republican side, the dominant paramilitary organization during the period of the troubles was the Provisional Irish Republican Army (PIRA), formed in 1969–70 as a breakaway from the Irish Republican Army (IRA) which was largely dormant at the time of the outbreak of civil unrest in the cities of Belfast and Derry in 1969. The IRA had belonged to a tradition of physical force Irish Nationalism which can be traced back to Wolfe Tone's revolutionary movement of

1798 and the Irish Republican Brotherhood (IRB), a secret body established in 1858. With the IRB continuing to operate covertly, an openly Nationalist paramilitary body, the Irish Volunteers, was formed in 1913 to promote the cause of Home Rule and to confront the anti-Home Rule Ulster Volunteers. The IRB acquired control over the Irish Volunteers, resulting in the formation of the IRA which, in 1916, was responsible for proclaiming an Irish provisional government, from which the PIRA was to take its name.

The PIRAs emergence was the consequence of related ideological and strategic disagreements within the IRA. The immediate catalyst was a split on the matter of whether or not republican paramilitaries should recognize the British and Irish governments. But there were also important differences of opinion on internal discipline and military policy. Despite its history of political violence, the IRA had become less and less committed to armed struggle since its unsuccessful campaign during 1950–62 and its gradual adoption of Marxist politics. Indeed, although it continued to engage in sporadic violent activities after the formation of the PIRA, not least against its former members, the IRA effectively disbanded itself in May 1972. Regarding themselves as the true heirs of the men of 1916, on the other hand, the leaders of the PIRA were concerned with the continuation of armed struggle aimed at fulfilling what they regarded as the main objectives of a republican organization, namely the removal of the British presence from Ireland and the political unification of the whole island. The other significant republican paramilitary group to emerge during the 1969–94 period was the Irish National Liberation Army (INLA), formed by the Irish Republican Socialist Party, a Marxist and militarist splinter group of the IRA. Although never enjoying the level of support afforded to the PIRA and with only a handful of members, the INLA was responsible for many atrocities as was the Irish People's Liberation Organization (IPLO) with which it shared common roots.

In addition to fighting among themselves and bringing their own form of justice to ordinary criminals in working-class Nationalist areas from where they drew the bulk of their support, each of these groups directed its violence at a range of targets, the precise character of which varied from one day to the next depending upon considerations of tactical expediency and of the prevailing political situation. All of them sought similar justification for their violence.

They claimed to be defending Nationalist communities from attacks by loyalist death squads and the British security forces, often asserted to be acting in concert. They also claimed to have become the *de facto* police force in these areas in which the RUC was not trusted to perform policing duties adequately or fairly. Above all, their violence was justified by their involvement in a war of national liberation which had achieved only partial success with the establishment of a 26-county Irish Free State and which would not be completed until there was a 32-county Irish Republic. In a variety of ways, therefore, republicans sought to legitimize their violence. Furthermore, by linking their struggle to those of the Palestine Liberation Organization (PLO) and the African National Congress (ANC), republicans endeavoured to show that their violence was rooted not only in Ireland's history but in an international movement for civil liberties.

In the early years of the 1970s, the PIRA and other republican paramilitary groups went about their violent business with little or no reference to the political process. Since they did not support the political system on either side of the border, it was unthinkable that they should put up electoral candidates. In any case, because they claimed to be conducting a campaign on behalf of the Irish people, albeit as an abstract construction, it was considered unnecessary to seek electoral approval from individual Irish men and women. Furthermore, their continued capacity to pursue the armed struggle suggested that they already enjoyed adequate real support, rendering a broader political mandate unnecessary. The PIRA's negative attitude towards politics was to undergo fundamental change by the beginning of the 1980s.

The turning-point in the history of modern republican paramilitarism had its origins in protests by prisoners in the Maze Prison which began in the late 1970s and culminated in the republican hunger strikes of 1981. Having previously enjoyed special category status as 'prisoners of war', both republican and loyalist inmates were naturally angered by the decision, taken in 1976 by the British government, to withdraw this status as part of the attempt to criminalize paramilitary activity. The protest tactics used by republican prisoners, particularly the hunger strikes which resulted in 10 deaths, attracted sympathy from throughout the Nationalist community, most of whose members had consistently repudiated republican violence. Their sympathy for the prisoners did not mean that they had become convinced that the paramilitaries' activities were justified. However, they certainly regarded the prisoners as the victims in this particular episode and, as public sympathy grew, the leaders of the PIRA and its political wing, Sinn Féin, came to recognize that electoral politics might be a useful accompaniment, although never an alternative, to armed struggle. The first of those who were to die on hunger strike, Bobby Sands, was put forward as a candidate for a parliamentary by-election in Fermanagh and South Tyrone on 9 April 1981 and his victory revealed the degree to which even constitutional Nationalists could be persuaded to support the men of violence in certain circumstances.

Although Sinn Féin candidates were never subsequently able to achieve the scale of support given to Bobby Sands, the fact that they could acquire an electoral mandate at all was to send shock waves through the British political establishment as well as through constitutional Nationalist circles. Indeed, as Sinn Féin continued to fight elections during the 1980s with some notable successes, it began to seem as if most of the political initiatives of the British and Irish governments and also of John Hume, as leader of the Social Democratic and Labour Party, the main constitutional Nationalist party in Northern Ireland, were aimed at undermining the electoral support for republican violence. Despite these efforts, however, Sinn Féin received assistance from an unlikely source, namely loyalist paramilitarism. So often was the violence of the latter even less clearly directed and more overtly sectarian than that perpetrated by republican groups that it was always possible for the PIRA and others to convince relatively large numbers of people in Nationalist areas that they were defenders of ordinary Catholics and thus entitled to political support. The image of the loyalist paramilitaries as crude, sectarian killers was, of course, far removed from how they saw themselves and how they wanted to be seen by their fellow supporters of the Union, many of whom, however, were as repelled as Nationalists by the depravity of loyalist paramilitary violence.

Loyalist paramilitarism

The main loyalist paramilitary organizations during the 1969–94 period were the Ulster Defence Association (UDA) and the Ulster Volunteer Force (UVF). Other groups appeared from time to time, some of them, like the Red Hand Commando, having a more or less separate existence, but most being *noms de guerre* used by the main paramilitary bodies. Thus, the Ulster Freedom Fighters (UFF) operated from within the UDA; while the Protestant Action Force (PAF) was the name assumed by certain UVF members on active service. In addition, both the UDA and the UVF became linked to political parties, the former to the Ulster Democratic Party, the latter to the Progressive Unionist Party, each of which was to play a highly visible role in negotiations following the 1994 ceasefires.

Of the two main organizations, the UVF claims the older ancestry. Although a totally separate body, it shares its name with the force which was formed in 1912 by Edward Carson to oppose the Third Home Rule Bill, and which in 1914 was transformed into the larger 36th (Ulster) Division of the British Army. Many in the original UVF fought in the First World War and suffered heavy losses at the Battle of the Somme in 1916. Despite having no direct link with the earlier paramilitary body, the new UVF sought to gain legitimacy and public sympathy from the fact that it shared its name with a force which had played a respected role in Ulster history. In terms of membership, however, the UDA, established in 1971 as an umbrella organization uniting a number of defence associations set up in Protestant communities for the purpose of protecting the local population, was by far the larger of the two modern organizations. At its peak, in the early 1970s, the UDA claimed to have around 30,000 active members, considerably more than any other paramilitary organization in Northern Ireland. Indeed, the sheer size of the UDA was an important factor in the British governments refusal to proscribe the organization, as it had other paramilitary groups, until as recently as 1992.

Like their republican counterparts, the loyalist paramilitaries constantly tried to legitimize their violent activities and once again the parasitical relationship between the paramilitary adversaries was apparent, with the need for defence being an important weapon in the loyalist theoretical armoury just as it was for republicans. Loyalist paramilitaries also reserved the right to punish criminals operating in their areas. Finally, in broader political terms, the loyalist paramilitaries sought to legitimize their violence by arguing that their objectives were the same as those of the British security forces, or would be if the British government could be trusted as a true defender of the Union. Because the police and army were subject to constraints in their battle with republican terrorists, the 'pro-state' violence of loyalists was held to be justified. Above all, however, they felt justified in doing whatever was necessary to defend the Union even if this meant opposing the security forces and the policies of the British government.

If the hunger strikes represented the most significant episode in the recent history of Irish republican paramilitarism, the epoch-making event in contemporary loyalist paramilitary history was the Ulster Workers' Council strike of 1974. Leading members of the loyalist paramilitary organizations helped to plan a province-wide strike aimed at preventing the implementation of the Sunningdale Agreement which advocated not only power-sharing arrangements in Northern Ireland but also a Council of Ireland which would have permitted a limited role for politicians from the Irish Republic in the affairs of the province. Aided considerably by loyalist paramilitary muscle, the strikers succeeded after 14 days in having the proposals scrapped. This achievement was a coming-of-age for the loyalist paramilitaries but, to pursue the analogy, their adult years were to be dominated by the fantasies of childhood, particularly the belief that the spirit of the 1974 strike could be invoked at any later moment when the Union was perceived by the UDA and the UVF to be in jeopardy. That this was largely wishful thinking was to be demonstrated in 1977 with the failure of another loyalist 'constitutional stoppage'. It was shown further in 1985 following the signing of the Anglo-Irish Agreement. In 1985 action was again demanded by the loyalist paramilitaries and Northern Ireland held its collective breath in anticipation of a repeat of the events of 1974. But little happened. The main reason for this, aside from the fact that on this occasion there was scarcely anything to be brought down, was that the loyalist paramilitary groups were smaller and less influential than they had been in the 1970s and lacked the levels of public support which they had formerly enjoyed. Many factors were involved in the demise of the loyalist paramilitaries, but two were of vital importance. First, many people in Protestant areas had become increasingly offended by the non-political, criminal activities of the paramilitary organizations, in particular the UDA. Second, the paramilitaries had been implicated in such horrendous sectarian murders, for which political motivation was claimed, that it was difficult even for the most resolute constitutional defenders of the Union to have any sympathy for them. Therefore whereas the stock of the PIRA actually rose in some Nationalist areas during the course of the Troubles, the image of the loyalist paramilitaries in Unionist Ulster was irredeemably tarnished.

Perhaps it was inevitable that the perpetrators of pro-state violence in Northern Ireland would have more problems than their republican adversaries. Most Unionists remained of the opinion that if one wanted to participate in the armed defence of the Union, the proper course of action was to join the security forces. The republican paramilitaries were able to argue that, while many shared their long-term objectives, they alone were prepared to use force to realize these. The loyalist paramilitaries, on the other hand, were confronted continuously by the presence of armed men doing the same work which they felt called upon to perform, and even if the security forces were not doing this work to the satisfaction of the loyalist gunmen they continued to enjoy the support of an overwhelming majority of Unionists. As a result, there was never any likelihood that the political wings of the UDA and the UVF could have achieved even the limited degree of electoral support won by Sinn Féin. Furthermore, because of their intrinsic weaknesses, it was inevitable that when the PIRA declared a ceasefire in 1994, the loyalist paramilitary groups would be obliged to do likewise. By that time, and indeed for many years earlier, the only *raison d'être* for loyalist violence which made any sense to Unionists was the need to defend Protestant communities from republican attacks. The fact that even this had been used to justify the random killing of Catholics had long since weakened the morality of loyalist paramilitarism. Despite the growing sophistication and ferocity of loyalist attacks in the 1990s (by 1992 they were killing more people than PIRA), this lack of moral legitimacy was virtually acknowledged by Gusty Spence when he announced the loyalist ceasefire on behalf of the Combined Loyalist Military Command.

This is not to suggest, however, that the role of the loyalist paramilitaries has been totally negative. Indeed, some of the more imaginative proposals from Unionists about possible ways forward have emanated not from the major constitutional parties, but from members of the political wings of the UDA and the UVF. This is a long way from suggesting, however, that any of the paramilitary violence, whether loyalist or republican, was ever justifiable or politically constructive.

Conclusions

To assess the respective roles played by republican and loyalist paramilitary organizations in Northern Ireland during 1969–94 is to enter into the grey area between ordinary criminal violence and the real world of politics. Supporters of the PIRA, both in Northern Ireland and beyond, likened the struggle of republican paramilitaries to those of other liberation movements. The fact is, however, that unlike the PLO, the ANC and others, which were obliged to operate in contexts in which they were denied access to constitutional mechanisms for the pursuit of their objectives, republicans in Northern Ireland possessed constitutional rights, a fact which their increasing involvement in electoral politics actually highlighted. Furthermore, constitutional Nationalists in Northern Ireland together with the government of the Irish Republic were committed to similar objectives as those sought by the PIRA and other republican paramilitary groups. This was, however, a mixed blessing for armed republicans. On the one hand, it provided them with a sense of being involved in a legitimate struggle. On the other hand, it meant that their activities were regarded by many as neither necessary nor justifiable since constitutional Nationalists on both sides of the border were pursuing these objectives with far greater public support and a considerable degree of optimism that their aims could be realized. Despite the not inconsiderable support received in the north by Sinn Féin, therefore, the legitimacy of the armed struggle was always difficult to establish.

Almost identical problems were faced by the loyalist paramilitaries who moreover lacked any useful contemporary parallels with which to compare their struggle. Regardless of how distrustful they were at times of British politicians and even of some constitutional Unionists in Northern Ireland, most Protestants recognized the seriousness with which the security forces were seeking to defend their interests. Indeed, there was no escaping from the irony that the work of the police and army would have been made considerably easier had they not been obliged to deal with paramilitary violence carried out by men describing themselves as the Union's true defenders. In these circumstances, the continued legitimacy of loyalist paramilitary violence was difficult to maintain.

In the final analysis, therefore, both sets of paramilitaries were guilty of unjustifiable terrorism. This is not to say that their membership consisted of psychopaths. Indeed, it is undeniable that a majority of the combatants were no more intrinsically violent than members of legal armies and police forces or even certain members of the general public. As a result of personal as well as socio-political factors, however, they became involved in violent acts which were for some an end in themselves and for most the means to certain ends, only some of which were actually political. Violence itself became a way of life. The status accorded to a member of a paramilitary organization in certain areas was a powerful drug. The money which could be made through criminal rackets planned and organized by the paramilitary groups was welcomed by those for whom unemployment and life on the poverty line were often the likeliest alternatives. The fact that the men and women of violence were able to claim some linkage with Ireland's troubled past was a valuable embellishment.

It will be argued by some that without paramilitarism, the possibility of new and lasting constitutional arrangements for Northern Ireland would never have come about. Conversely, many may feel that without the paramilitaries, new arrangements would have been unnecessary. On the republican side, there is a strong belief that the Northern Ireland state could never have been reformed but only republican violence has ensured that it cannot now be reconstituted. The overthrow of the old Northern Ireland political system, however, was only one element of the republican agenda. The creation of a 32-county Irish Republic was the other key component and loyalist paramilitaries will argue, without convincing the majority even of Unionists, that their violence has helped to make that objective unrealizable.

In sum, the paramilitaries had a major and often traumatic impact on society in Northern Ireland during 1969–94. It remains to be seen whether they and their supporters can now play a constructive role in the future.

Further reading

Alexander, Y. and O'Day, A. (eds), *Terrorism in Ireland*. London: Croom Helm, 1984.

Bairner, A., 'The battlefield of ideas: the legitimation of political violence in Northern Ireland', *European Journal of Political Research*, 14, 1986.

Bishop, P. and Mailie, E., *The Provisional IRA*. London: Corgi, 1988.

Bruce, S., *The Red Hand. Protestant Paramilitaries in Northern Ireland*. Oxford: Oxford University Press, 1992.

Holland, J. and McDonald, H., *INLA Deadly Divisions*. Dublin: Torc, 1994.

Nelson, S., *Ulster's Uncertain Defenders. Protestant Paramilitary and Community Groups and the Northern Ireland Conflict*. Belfast: Appletree Press, 1984.

O'Day, A. and Alexander, Y. (eds), *Ireland's Terrorist Trauma. Interdisciplinary Perspectives.* Hemel Hempstead: Harvester Wheatsheaf, 1989.

Townshend, C., 'The process of terror in Irish politics', in N. O'Sullivan (ed.), *Terrorism, Ideology, and Revolution.* Brighton: Wheatsheaf, 1986.

Appendix 18.1 Number of deaths due to security situation, 1969–95

	RUC	RUC 'R'	Army	UDR/ RIR[a]	Civilians	Total
1969	1	–	–	–	12	13
1970	2	–	–	–	23	25
1971	11	–	43	5	115	174
1972	14	3	103	26	321	467
1973	10	3	58	8	171	250
1974	12	3	28	7	166	216
1975	7	4	14	6	216	247
1976	13	10	14	15	245	297
1977	8	6	15	14	69	112
1978	4	6	14	7	50	81
1979	9	5	38	10	51	113
1980	3	6	8	9	50	76
1981	13	8	10	13	57	101
1982	8	4	21	7	57	97
1983	9	9	5	10	44	77
1984	7	2	9	10	36	64
1985	14	9	2	4	25	54
1986	10	2	4	8	37	61
1987	9	7	3	8	66	93
1988	4	2	21	12	54	93
1989	7	2	12	2	39	62
1990	7	5	7	8	49	76
1991	5	1	5	8	75	94
1992	2	1	4	2	76	85
1993	3	3	6	2	70	84
1994	3	–	1	2	54	60
1995 to 28 Feb	–	–	–	–	–	–
Total	195	101	445	203	2,228	3,172

[a] Figures include Royal Irish Regiment (Home Service Battalions).

Appendix 18.2 Injuries as a result of security situation, 1968–95

	RUC	Army	UDR/RIR[a]	Civilians	Total
1968	379	–	–	–	379
1969	711	54	–	–	765
1970	191	620	–	–	811
1971	315	381	9	1,887	2,592
1972	485	542	36	3,813	4,876
1973	291	525	23	1,812	2,651
1974	235	453	30	1,680	2,398
1975	263	151	16	2,044	2,474
1976	303	242	22	2,162	2,729
1977	183	172	15	1,017	1,387
1978	302	127	8	548	985
1979	165	132	21	557	875
1980	194	53	24	530	801
1981	332	112	28	878	1,350
1982	99	80	18	328	525
1983	142	66	22	280	510
1984	267	64	22	513	866
1985	415	20	13	468	916
1986	622	45	10	773	1,450
1987	246	92	12	780	1,130
1988	218	211	18	600	1,047
1989	163	175	15	606	959
1990	214	190	24	478	906
1991	139	197	56	570	962
1992	148	302	18	598	1,066
1993	147	146	27	504	824
1994	170	120	6	529	825
1995 to 28 Feb	16	2	–	69	87
Total	7,355	5,274	493	24,024	37,146

[a] Figures include Royal Irish Regiment (Home Services Battalions).

Appendix 18.3 Security situation statistics, 1969–95

Year	Shootings	Devices used (Explosions and Defusings)	Armed Robberies
1969	73	10	–
1970	213	170	–
1971	1,756	1,515	489
1972	10,628	1,853	1,931
1973	5,018	1,520	1,317
1974	3,206	1,113	1,353
1975	1,803	635	1,325
1976	1,908	1,192	889
1977	1,081	535	676
1978	755	633	493
1979	728	564	504
1980	642	400	467
1981	1,142	529	689
1982	547	332	693
1983	424	367	718
1984	334	248	710
1985	237	215	542
1986	392	254	839
1987	674	384	955
1988	537	458	742
1989	566	420	604
1990	559	287	492
1991	499	367	607
1992	506	371	739
1993	476	289	643
1994	348	222	555
1995 to 28 Feb	7	1	60
Total	35,059	14,884	19,032

Appendix 18.4 Number of persons
charged with terrorist offences,
1972–95

1972 from 31 July	531
1973	1,418
1974	1,374
1975	1,197
1976	1,276
1977	1,308
1978	843
1979	670
1980	550
1981	918
1982	686
1983	613
1984	528
1985	522
1986	655
1987	468
1988	439
1989	433
1990	380
1991	397
1992	410
1993	372
1994	349
1995 to 28 Feb	28
Total	16,365

Appendix 18.5 Firearms and explosives finds, 1969–95

Year	Firearms	Explosives (kilograms)
1969	14	102
1970	324	305
1971	716	1,246
1972	1,259	18,819
1973	1,313	17,426
1974	1,236	11,848
1975	820	4,996
1976	736	9,849
1977	563	1,728
1978	393	956
1979	300	905
1980	203	821
1981	357	3,419
1982	288	2,298
1983	166	1,706
1984	187	3,871
1985	173	3,344
1986	174	2,443
1987	206	5,885
1988	489	4,728
1989	246	1,377
1990	179	1,969
1991	164	4,167
1992	194	2,167
1993	196	3,944
1994	178	1,285
1995 to 28 Feb.	8	–
Total	11,082	111,604

Chapter 19

THE MEDIA
Alan Bairner

Analysis of the role of the media in the recent history of Northern Ireland has tended to focus on two different but related issues. First, considerable attention has been paid to the degree of support which the British, Irish and international media, whether willingly, unconsciously or under duress, have given to particular political actors, such as the British government or the IRA. Among those who believe that media coverage from outside Northern Ireland has been influential during the course of the Troubles, there are two rival schools of thought. The first of these has concentrated on what is regarded as the manipulation of the media by successive British and, to a lesser extent, Irish governments. It is argued that the propagandist activities of the British government in particular have been important, and unacceptable, factors in the persistence of political crisis. The second, rival, school of thought has emphasized the use made of the media by the perpetrators and supporters of paramilitary violence. According to this per-spective, the real propaganda victories have been won, not by the democratically elected governments, but by the terrorists. Despite the obvious differences between these two approaches, both share the view that media coverage of the politics of Northern Ireland has actually contributed to the problem.

Another alternative view of the role of the media in Northern Ireland argues that media coverage from outside in fact has had little impact on the political situation. It is argued that the integrity of the local quarrel rises above media manipulation. Instead, it is suggested that the local media in Northern Ireland have played a significant part in supporting the rival perspectives around which the politics of division have been centred.

Whichever of these general approaches one favours, there can be no denying the extent of media coverage of Northern Ireland or the amount of access to the media which the people of the province enjoy. It is doubtful if any other part of the world has attracted as much sustained media attention as Northern Ireland has done since the late 1960s. Although the number of broadcasters and journalists actually based in the province declined as the Troubles persisted, particular moments of crisis and high drama continued to be accompanied by increased media attention. Certainly the people of Northern Ireland could have no grounds for complaint about the levels of interest shown by the international media,

173

although they were frequently uneasy about the quality of the analysis which resulted from that media interest.

In addition to having the experience of the media coming to them, Northern Irish people also had access throughout the Troubles to a wide range of media output. In terms of quantity, the province has been, and remains, exceptionally well served by the various branches of the media. Three local daily newspapers, the *News Letter*, the *Irish News* and the *Belfast Telegraph*, can be said to have a quasi-national status in that they are read throughout Northern Ireland, as is the locally produced *Sunday Life*. There is also a plethora of more genuinely local papers which serve smaller communities. In addition, all of the English national papers are widely available as are their counterparts from the Irish Republic and the Glasgow-based *Daily Record*. As for television, satellite channels are increasingly popular and viewers throughout Northern Ireland are provided for by the British Broadcasting Corporation's (BBC) Northern Ireland service as well as the Independent Television Authority's Ulster Television (UTV). With special aerials, viewers are also able to watch the two channels produced by the Irish Republic's Radio Telefís Éireann (RTE) and in a few eastern locations, Scottish television programmes can be seen. Similar patterns occur in the availability of radio programmes, with local and national (both British and Irish programmes), from both the public and private sectors, being widely available. Local radio stations include those of BBC Northern Ireland, Belfast Community Radio, Cool FM, Downtown Radio and the Irish language Radio na Gaeltachta. Overall, therefore, it is no exaggeration to suggest that the people of Northern Ireland have greater access to media output, in all its forms, than any other group of people in either mainland Britain or the Republic of Ireland.

The problems of broadcasting

It should also be noted that throughout the 25 years of the Troubles, the people of Northern Ireland were particularly news conscious. This is scarcely surprising given that they were living in a part of the world whose problems generated so much worldwide media attention. Inevitably, the local population were eager to watch, read and listen to the various ways in which their problems were being assessed by the representatives of the media, both local and international. To some extent, therefore, interest in media output was part of a wider desire to engage in debate about the political situation. At a more mundane, but no less serious, level people also turned to the media to hear about ways in which their day-to-day routine might be adversely affected by the Troubles. For example, they would listen to radio news reports for information about bomb scares and traffic disruption or about what was happening in another part of their city or town or even at the other end of their street.

It would be naive in the extreme, however, to imagine that during the Troubles the media simply acted as objective communicators of information. In fact, many of those who have studied the media's involvement in Northern Ireland have argued that journalists and broadcasters have been themselves political actors rather than detached observers. On the one hand, there are those who suggest that sections of the media have served the interests of the British state by acting as channels for the dissemination of government propaganda. It is generally accepted that this has not necessarily been the result of conscious decisions made by media executives. Rather, it is claimed, pressure has been put on the media to ensure their support for government policy. According to this view, the media have been restricted in what they have been able to say by a number of factors. These include the economic context of media production, indirect censorship through intimidation and the threat of legal sanctions, direct censorship and, finally, self-censorship especially at the senior management level of certain media agencies.

In general, it has been argued that there has been a concerted effort on the part of the British state to incorporate the media into its national security strategy and specifically its fight against terrorism. Consequences of this policy have included the banning, censorship and delays in showing of over 100 television programmes about Northern Ireland between 1969 and 1993 and, it is claimed, the loss of British broadcasting's reputation for independence and fairness. In addition, it is said that the British state has also been guilty of using the Northern Ireland Information Service to misrepresent the facts of the political situation under the spurious pretext of protecting human lives and the national interest. This strategy, however, has not been without its ambiguities, since governments have sought to combine an interest in highlighting the significance of terrorist violence in the creation of Northern Ireland's economic problems with a desire to convince the outside world of the relative normality of life in the province.

It is ironic that the most blatant attempts by the British and Irish governments to interfere with the work of the media were a response to the view that the real winners in terms of propaganda were the paramilitaries, particularly the Provisional Irish Republican Army, and not the governments themselves. According to this alternative perspective, while there is no denying the importance of the media in the conflict, the oxygen of publicity which sustained terrorism was far more significant than any amount of media manipulation by successive governments. Responding to that challenge, both Irish and British governments adopted policies of direct censorship.

RTE, the Irish national broadcasting service, was set up as a public authority under the Broadcasting Act of 1960. Section 31 of the Act allowed Ministers responsible for communications to prevent the broadcasting of material which would be likely to promote or incite crime or would tend to undermine the State's authority. In 1972, the political implications of Section 31 were made more explicit with the introduction of a ban on broadcast interviews with representatives of Sinn Féin and of any organizations proscribed in Northern Ireland. One obvious difficulty with this ban lay in the fact that viewers and listeners in the Irish Republic continued to receive programmes broadcast from the United Kingdom where such interviews were still permitted. This anomaly was removed, however, on 19 October 1988, when the British government imposed a similar ban to that operating in the Republic. This broadcasting ban was empowered by the terms of the 1981 Broadcasting Act and, therefore, required no parliamentary debate for it to become operative. The Northern Ireland Notice, issued by the then Home

Secretary, Douglas Hurd, outlawed the broadcasting of speeches by and interviews with representatives and supporters of proscribed organizations. This was intended to be enforced even if the individuals in question were addressing issues not directly related to violence. Some qualifications were made to the ruling. For example, special dispensations were made for the purpose of election campaigns. In general, however, the net result was the increasingly bizarre sight of representatives of Sinn Féin and other organizations appearing on television with their words being spoken by actors.

At the beginning of 1994, the Irish Republic's government lifted its ban and the old anomaly was reversed with viewers and listeners in Northern Ireland now able to hear the voices of members of proscribed organizations so long as they had access to RTE productions. The lifting of the ban in the Irish Republic was viewed with suspicion by Unionists and even by members of the British government who may have felt that their Irish counterparts were pushing ahead too quickly with plans to bring Sinn Féin into the political fold. The problem was, however, that the British were now seen in the eyes of the rest of the world, and especially by the government of the United States, as being engaged in a policy of censorship which changes in the Irish Republic appeared to indicate was neither necessary nor desirable. Moreover, the increasingly cunning ploys by the broadcast media to circumvent the ban in Britain were creating a farcical situation. In response to these considerations, and more significantly to the PIRA ceasefire of 31 August 1994, the British government lifted its ban on 16 September 1994.

Although they welcomed this policy development, many broadcasters in Britain as well as many media analysts believed that the British state would continue to interfere with programme making and reporting of the situation in Northern Ireland, albeit with less recourse to direct censorship. Other restrictions on media freedom, it was argued, were still in place although the political context had changed so dramatically after the paramilitary ceasefires that it became less likely that the British government would continue to regard media coverage of Northern Ireland as constituting a potential security threat.

It is undeniable that the British and Irish governments have both interfered, directly and indirectly, with media coverage of Northern Ireland. Whether this was absolutely necessary is another matter. While media spokespeople may have exaggerated their own capacity to provide fair and objective analysis, the politicians may well have overestimated the power of the media to influence public opinion. There is little evidence, for example, that British or, indeed, international coverage of the Troubles had a significant impact on the views of people in Northern Ireland itself. Most Northern Irish people formulate political views on the basis of numerous factors and their reaction to media output, regardless of its aim, is more or less predetermined. What remains to be discussed, however, is whether or not locally produced media output is one of the factors which contribute to the formation of political opinions.

Given the range of media output available in Northern Ireland, it is inevitable that some people will have been influenced by views expressed in programmes and newspapers produced outside the province. For example, some people may not even read local newspapers or watch locally produced television programmes. The overwhelming majority of people in Northern Ireland, however, are likely to read at least one local paper and watch news programmes produced by Ulster Television or BBC Northern Ireland. To what extent, then, have the local media played a role in the political conflict?

In fact, both television companies have acquired a substantial reputation for impartial reporting of events in Northern Ireland. Given that they aim to appeal to members of both of the major communities, this is perhaps scarcely surprising. For whatever reason, however, these companies cannot be said to have fuelled the divisions in Northern Ireland, although of course they have been forced to operate under the same conditions which, some have argued, have restricted the role of the British media in general. Whether locally produced newspapers in Northern Ireland deserve a similar reputation for relatively objective news coverage is another matter.

The press in Northern Ireland

Northern Ireland's local press can be divided into two separate categories – the quasi-national dailies together with the *Sunday Life* on one hand and, on the other, the more truly local papers available widely only in the districts, towns and communities which they are intended to serve.

Only the quasi-national publications are available throughout Northern Ireland. Given the problematic political status of the province, to describe these papers as national is inevitably contentious. In the context of the United Kingdom as a whole, the papers might be regarded as provincial. However, if one accepts that Northern Ireland is a distinct geopolitical entity, then these papers clearly serve a quasi-national as well as a provincial role. This description applies notwithstanding the fact that the papers themselves are not read by all or even by a majority of people in Northern Ireland. The fact is that although the *Belfast Telegraph* and the *Sunday Life* are read widely by members of both communities, the *Irish News* and the *News Letter* are important elements in nationalist and unionist civil societies respectively. This situation has been transformed to some extent with the appearance of a free edition of the *News Letter* delivered to many homes throughout the greater Belfast area, including those of Catholics. It remains true, however, that the *News Letter* is bought almost exclusively by Protestants and the *Irish News* by Catholics.

The *News Letter* was founded in 1737 and is the United Kingdom's oldest surviving newspaper. Although published in Belfast, it is sold throughout Northern Ireland and even in other parts of the historic province of Ulster. The religious or political identity of the readership can be discerned from various elements of the paper's content. For example, announcements of births, deaths and marriages which are printed in the *News Letter* mainly concern members of the Protestant population. The activities of the Protestant churches are commonly reported. The paper pays considerable attention to news items which confirm the difference between Northern Ireland and the rest of the island of Ireland. Thus, stories about Ulster traditions, the development of Orangeism and life in Northern

Ireland during the Second World War are common. The *News Letter*'s coverage of sport concentrates on those activities which are dominated by Protestants although not necessarily exclusive to them. Gaelic games, played almost exclusively by Catholics, receive little or no attention, a situation which has remained unchanged despite the fact that the paper's free edition now finds its way into Catholic homes. Finally, the editorial policy of the *News Letter*, while by no means uncritical of Unionist politics, has consistently espoused the Unionist cause. In a variety of ways, therefore, the paper has played its part in confirming Unionist attitudes and values.

The *Irish News* was first published in 1855. Like the *News Letter*, it is produced in Belfast but sold throughout the nine counties of Ulster. Although the paper has endeavoured in recent years to broaden its appeal, the main emphasis is still on those aspects of life which highlight the presence of a distinctive Catholic and Nationalist community in Northern Ireland. Personal announcements concern Catholics. Sports coverage, although extensive and relatively varied, pays special attention to Gaelic games and even when the focus shifts to non-Gaelic sport, a Nationalist perspective is still apparent. For example, coverage of Scottish association football tends to be concentrated on the activities of Celtic Football Club, founded by Irish Catholics in Glasgow and drawing the bulk of its support to this day from Scots with Irish roots. The *Irish News* also pays a great deal of attention to Irish culture and to events associated with the Catholic Church. Not surprisingly, its editorial policy, although consistently opposed to republican violence, has always supported constitutional Nationalist aspirations. In a variety of ways, therefore, the paper gives important support to an Irish Nationalist view of the world and, specifically, of the political situation in Northern Ireland.

The character of the other quasi-national daily paper, and also of its sister publication, the *Sunday Life*, differs markedly from that of the *News Letter* and the *Irish News*. The *Belfast Telegraph* was established as a Unionist newspaper in 1870. Its political origins are still testified to by the fact that far more Protestants than Catholics would insert items in the paper's personal announcements columns. In terms of readership, however, the *Telegraph* has been increasingly successful in making an appeal to members of both communities. This has been achieved by way of a combination of a moderate editorial policy and widespread coverage of relatively non-controversial news stories. In fact, the paper devotes more space to entertainment guides and general advertising than to potentially divisive issues. Even the *Telegraph*'s coverage of sport has been expanded over the years to take account of the interest of many of its readers in Gaelic games. This is accompanied, however, by extensive news about rugby, cricket, association football and so on. Far more than the other dailies, the *Belfast Telegraph*, and also the *Sunday Life*, would appear to be primarily concerned with financial success which means doing nothing which might alienate potential advertisers and readers from either community. Its owners clearly believe that the paper's economic future is best secured by a continued widespread appeal. As a result, the *Telegraph*'s editorial policy is directed towards the middle ground of politics in Northern Ireland and seeks to exclude neither community from its concerns.

In addition to the quasi-national Northern Irish press, the local newspapers which many people read are intended to serve much smaller areas. There are around 50 such local papers in Northern Ireland. Most localities are served by at least one of them and, in areas where both traditions are well represented, it is likely that there will be a paper which caters for members of each. Furthermore, if one community is clearly in a minority, thus making a separate paper an unviable commercial proposition, a paper intended primarily to serve a neighbouring area will carry material which is relevant to that minority. The overall effect ensures that even people sharing the same geographical space are kept apart in terms of local newspaper preference. Local news printed in the papers will either be of relevance only to members of one community or will be presented in such a way as to make the coverage acceptable to them. As a result, a sense of group identity is strengthened by these local papers.

Conclusion

It would be preposterous to suggest that the owners and editors of Northern Ireland's local newspapers are responsible for the divisions in their society. It is undeniable, however, that their papers, through the choice of stories which are published and even the use of language to tell these stories, give voice to the rival perspectives of the two communities and, as a consequence, give added strength to these perspectives in the eyes of those who hold them. Therefore, local papers as well as the *News Letter* and the *Irish News* have helped to reproduce sectarian attitudes and in so doing they have become complicit in the maintenance of the politics of division.

The role of the media in the recent history of Northern Ireland raises numerous questions. How one views the debate on censorship, the concept of the oxygen of publicity and various related issues will ultimately depend on how one views the political problems of the province. Of course, opinions on these problems can be influenced by the media themselves. But the extent to which any branch of the media can actually alter people's beliefs is greatly limited by other factors, including the existing views of the audience. Paradoxically, however, the local media, particularly the press, have played an important role in helping to form these beliefs and, thus, in the creation of formidable obstacles to other propagandist strategies. As long as Protestants and Catholics in Northern Ireland continue to support the existence of separate newspapers for their respective communities and these papers continue to reinforce radically different attitudes, deep divisions in society are likely to persist regardless of how much the wider media seek to influence the situation and governments endeavour to manipulate the media.

Further reading

Arthur, P., 'The media and politics in Northern Ireland', in J. Seaton and B. Pimlott (eds), *The Media in British Politics*. Aldershot: Gower, 1987.

Butler, D., *The Trouble with Reporting Northern Ireland. The British State, the Broadcast Media and Nonfictional Representation of the Conflict.* Aldershot: Avebury, 1995.

Curtis, L., *Ireland: The Propaganda War, the British Media and the Battle for Hearts and Minds.* London: Pluto Press, 1984.

Miller, D., *Don't Mention the War. Northern Ireland, Propaganda and the Media.* London: Pluto Press, 1994.

Rolston, B., (ed.), *The Media and Northern Ireland, Covering the Troubles.* Basingstoke: Macmillan, 1991.

Schlesinger, P., *Media, State and Nation. Political Violence and Collective Identities.* London: Sage, 1991

Chapter 20

THE ARTS AND SPORT
Alan Bairner

It would be absurd to suggest that life in Northern Ireland during the course of the Troubles was normal, regardless of one's conception of normality. Nevertheless, most people were able to take part in a range of normal activities. From time to time, these were hampered or even brought to a temporary halt by the conflict. For the most part, however, despite or arguably in defiance of civil unrest, they flourished, particularly as political violence became more clearly focused and, thus, less random in its effects. New shopping developments were built. Restaurants and bars did increasingly brisk business. The Grand Opera House was eventually restored to its former glory despite being a regular target of the bombers. The Queen's Arts Festival, first held in February 1964, grew during 'the Troubles' to become the second largest event of its kind in the United Kingdom after the Edinburgh International Festival. At the same time, Northern Ireland's reputation for producing writers and artists of various types remained high with, to name but a few, Seamus Heaney in poetry, Kenneth Branagh in theatre and James Galway in music. In the world of sport too, not only were large numbers of people in Northern Ireland directly involved, some of them were also to go on to make international reputations for themselves. One thinks of George Best in football, Denis Taylor and Alex Higgins in snooker, Mary Peters in athletics and Barry McGuigan, the former world flyweight boxing champion who, while born outside Northern Ireland in County Monaghan, was adopted as a sporting hero by the overwhelming majority of people in the province.

It would be easy to regard the worlds of entertainment, the arts and sport as having provided a useful escape from the Troubles for many of Northern Ireland's citizens and it is true that this has been one of their achievements. On the other hand, there are strong grounds for arguing that, in certain respects, many of the cultural pursuits engaged in by the people of the province not only reflected the deep divisions within society, but may even have contributed to their longevity. Youth trends such as punk or the rave scene may have succeeded partially in transcending inter-community division. But many forms of cultural expression, especially at the level of popular culture, have followed the contours of the sectarian divide and may have helped to inscribe them more deeply on Northern Ireland's political map. The annual Twelfth of July celebrations may represent an

181

extreme case of this phenomenon but in numerous, more discrete, ways culture has become interwoven with the politics of division.

None of this is to deny the capacity of some cultural activities to transcend divisions. It is merely to point out that culture has played a dual role in terms of the political crisis. On one hand, it has helped to give credence to claims that life in Northern Ireland has remained relatively normal and, indeed, rather pleasant for a majority of the province's inhabitants. By offering sanctuary from the Troubles, amateur operatic groups, literary societies, libraries, museums and sports clubs have made a positive contribution, making life tolerable despite the horrendous events which punctuated the political conflict. On the other hand, by helping from time to time, in different ways and to varying degrees, to consolidate those divisions around which the conflict centred, many cultural activities were implicated in the persistence of violence.

Because of their dual character, cultural activities have been recognized as significant by a succession of British governments, which have presided over them directly through the Department of Education for Northern Ireland (DENI) and indirectly through bodies such as the Arts Council of Northern Ireland and the Sports Council for Northern Ireland, with a view to supporting those activities which clearly have a positive contribution to make. Simultaneously a watchful eye was kept on those cultural enterprises which, although clearly preferable to the operations of paramilitary organizations, were regarded nevertheless as making some contribution to the construction of an environment in which the terrorists were able to flourish. Although the debate on the precise nature of the contribution made by culture, in its varied forms, to the politics of Northern Ireland is at the heart of the discussion which follows, an attempt will be made to offer a brief account of some of the main cultural activities, from the arts to sport and leisure.

The arts

Artistic pursuits in Northern Ireland, as in most societies, assume a variety of forms, by no means all of which are readily accessible to every member of the population. One's receptiveness to culture is strongly influenced by such factors as social class, educational background, ethnicity and gender. In Northern Ireland, it is also influenced heavily by one's national identity. Thus, the Arts Council of Northern Ireland promotes a wide range of cultural activities, both high and also popular in character, even when these are largely supported by certain sections of society rather than by the population as a whole. Nevertheless, its stated aim is to develop the arts in Northern Ireland so that as many people as possible can enjoy as many forms of culture as possible to as high a standard as can be achieved. It wishes to promote excellence but not élitism. It endeavours to support artists of various types within Northern Ireland itself and to allow them to display their talents not only in the province but further afield. To this end, the Arts Council works closely with other bodies involved in the promotion of cultural activity, including the media, educational institutions, the Arts Councils in the rest of the

United Kingdom and their counterpart in the Irish Republic, An Chomhairle Ealaíon. Most important of all perhaps is the fact that the Arts Council is responsible for the management of public funds placed at its disposal, which amounted to £6.1 million in 1993/94, and Northern Ireland's share of that portion of the National Lottery proceeds allocated to the arts.

According to Arts Council members, the main political issue which they must address constantly is that of public expenditure on the arts. They argue, for example, that *per capita* spending in Northern Ireland is far lower than in other parts of the United Kingdom, particularly Scotland and Wales. The result is the lack of an adequate infrastructure to support cultural activity in the province to the extent that the Arts Council would wish. Without denying that public expenditure is an issue, however, critics of the Arts Council and of the general direction of cultural policy in Northern Ireland raise two other important concerns. First, despite its protests to the contrary, the Arts Council is accused of élitism. Second, it is argued that there has been no coherent strategy by the Arts Council or indeed by government departments regarding the relationship between culture and the political conflict.

On the question of élitism, it is pointed out that the largest expenditure on any form of the arts in Northern Ireland is allocated to music and opera (£1.6 million between 1 April 1992 and 31 March 1993). A large part of this budget goes to the Ulster Orchestra, formed in 1981, and Opera Northern Ireland, formed in 1984. Despite conscious attempts at populism, neither of these bodies attracts regular interest from the bulk of the population. It is true that all kinds of other musical endeavours are supported by the Arts Council with jazz, for example, acquiring an Arts Council Administrator in 1989. The lingering impression, however, is that much of the music that is played and listened to in Northern Ireland receives little attention from the Arts Council. For example, the most commonly heard music on the streets of Northern Ireland is that of the flutes and drums of loyalist and republican marching bands. While concert flute bands receive encouragement from the Arts Council, their more boisterous relatives are largely ignored, despite, or some would say because of, their capacity to enthuse large numbers of working-class people. This attitude to music is replicated throughout the Council's treatment of the arts. Thus, although most forms of the visual arts are promoted, the artistic images most associated with Northern Ireland – the wall paintings on the gable ends of working-class houses – are viewed with suspicion by the guardians of the province's cultural life.

In defence of the Arts Council and other bodies concerned with cultural activity in Northern Ireland, it must be said that increasing interest has been shown in community-based artistic projects. In drama, for example, although a large part of the Arts Council's budget is given to Belfast's Lyric Theatre, formed in 1970 and the only producing theatre in the province, smaller theatrical groups operating within local communities have received growing support. Traditional arts have also been encouraged together with various forms of dance, literature and film. Generally, the Arts Council has pursued a strategy based on the belief that each branch of the arts can help individuals to develop their potential. The degree to which most people are touched by the activities of the Council remains limited. Given the concerns expressed in some quarters about the relationship between culture and political conflict, ironically this in itself may not be the disaster which Arts Council members might suppose it to be.

In its overall approach to the social implications of the arts in Northern Ireland, the Arts Council can be said to reflect an ambiguity which lies at the heart of government policy regarding cultural activities. On the one hand, the Arts Council claims that cultural diversity is a source of strength rather than of division. Thus, there should be a celebration of the different cultures within Northern Ireland. The Arts Council would appear to regard the promotion of traditional culture, including the Irish language for example, as a means to resist globalizing tendencies which are supported by technological innovations and which threaten to culminate in the destruction of all local cultural traditions.

On the other hand, the Arts Council also declares an interest in seeing the arts transcend the divisions in Northern Ireland which emanate from the existence of rival national identities. These apparently mutually exclusive ambitions, namely to promote local traditions and to transcend parochialism, are expressed not only by the Arts Council but by bodies like the Community Relations Council which through its Cultural Traditions Group (CTG) has the task of co-opting culture in the search for greater cross-community understanding. For anyone involved in social engineering by way of the arts the main dilemma is whether cultural activity, in its various forms, is to be used primarily to promote integration or as a vehicle to allow each community to rejoice in those things which make it distinctive, with mutual respect rather than integration being the main objective.

The CTG which was set up in 1988 came under the umbrella of the newly established Community Relations Council in 1990. Its tasks have been to develop better community relations by way of fostering an awareness of cultural diversity in Northern Ireland. Through its various sub-committees the CTG has sponsored conferences on cultural traditions, has subsidized the publication of a wide range of books on local history, politics and crafts and encouraged research into aspects of cultural life through the provision of distinctive fellowships. It has also sponsored the production of material for public broadcasting. The CTG's expenditure in 1993/94 was £343,131. This public patronage has made a valuable contribution to promoting a wider audience for such cultural activity as well as ensuring a permanent record of it. Nevertheless, the CTG has been aware that it treads a difficult shadow line between appearing either to be 'integrationist' or to be celebrating 'division' in society (the 'bucks for bigots' charge). The CTG would be honest enough to admit that there is no clear boundary, liberal enough to place its faith in the educative powers of mutual understanding.

In a society where a parochial fixation with local traditions has been a significant factor in the reproduction of inter-community division over centuries, there may be a strong case for advocating globalization with its intrinsic ability to transcend existing divisions. Unconsciously, perhaps, this argument is supported by the Arts Council in its promotion of high culture which helps to bind some of the people of Northern Ireland, albeit only a middle-class minority for the most part, to an international cultural élite. However, those people who have been most directly affected by the violence associated with the politics of division, namely members of the Catholic and Protestant working-class communities, are seldom exposed to global high culture and are frequently engaged in cultural activities which are as likely to promote division as to unite across the community divide.

Of course, many forms of popular culture are also global. Thus, in Northern Ireland, listening to country music or following soap operas on television are cross-community pastimes, as is watching football on the Sky Sports channel and following an English Premier League team. Many other popular cultural activities, however, merely serve to highlight the very real inter-community differences which exist in Northern Ireland. Sport, for example, while global in its appeal and increasingly in the way in which it is packaged for popular consumption, is not only one of the most prominent activities in the province but also arguably one of the most divisive.

Sport

Sport is a phenomenally popular activity in Northern Ireland. It is played and watched each week by large numbers of people. It also makes an impressive contribution to the local economy. For example, in 1995 there were 8,000 sport-related jobs in the province and the total wealth created by sport-related economic activity was over £100 million. The scale of the income and expenditure of the voluntary sports sector is considerable and is supplemented by financial support from central and local government and from the Sports Council for Northern Ireland which has the responsibility of administering a grant aid budget of £2 million. In addition to its general impact on the social fabric of Northern Ireland, sport has allowed some people from the province to achieve international renown and, by providing opportunities for representatives of the province to appear on the world stage, it helps to consolidate Northern Ireland's distinct geopolitical identity.

Despite its manifest importance, however, sport tended to be ignored until quite recently in studies of Northern Irish politics and society. This omission was partly the result of a more widespread view that, even where it is extremely popular, sport remains marginal to the major concerns of society. In fact, far from being marginal, sport has been increasingly revealed as an important indicator of the character of particular societies and, more than that, as a force for change in those societies, either by exacerbating existing tensions or by playing a positive role in resolving those tensions. In Northern Ireland, nevertheless, the Sports Council itself traditionally encouraged the belief that sport is apolitical and, therefore, not involved either actively or even passively in the politics of division. As the government began to place greater emphasis on community relations initiatives, however, there was a growing recognition by the Sports Council that it could have a role to play. The precise function which sport, like the arts, can serve in terms of cross-community reconciliation is a matter for debate.

It is clearly the case that the world of sport provides us with a window through which we can view Northern Irish society. It can be stated at once that sport offered many people a valuable escape route from the Troubles. It also generated some degree of community integration. For example, of more than 80 sports practised in Northern Ireland, over 75 are enjoyed by members of both major communities and even non-inclusive sports are being developed in the context of integrated education and as vehicles for mutual understanding. Against the Sports Council's positive assessment of its role, however, it can be argued that sport has also been deeply implicated not only in reflecting the divisions around which the Troubles have revolved but also in supporting and even exacerbating these divisions, thereby contributing directly to the political conflict. Furthermore, sport also became a political weapon in the hands of successive British governments and non-governmental agencies which sought to use it to deal with society's problems. First, social control strategies were employed in the 1970s with leisure facilities being provided in an attempt to harness the energies of young people and specifically to distract them from civil disorder. Second, sport increasingly came to be used in a different way as bodies directed their efforts towards social integration or, at best, cross-community understanding. The fact that sport was regarded as having a place in this strategy, however, was itself an implicit recognition of the extent to which it had formerly been involved in the creation of division.

In all societies, sport is implicated in social division. In Northern Ireland as elsewhere, for example, gender is an important factor with the world of sport a predominantly masculine preserve. In addition, social class invariably influences the types of leisure activities in which people engage. It would be wrong to ignore these factors when commenting on the divisive nature of sport in Northern Ireland. On the other hand, since the political conflict in the province owes most to differences of national and religious identity, it is the relationship of sport to these factors which must be the main focus of any attempt to assess the socio-political significance of Northern Ireland's sports culture.

Modern sport arrived in what is now Northern Ireland, as it did in the rest of Ireland, from Britain in the nineteenth century. That is not to deny the existence of games and pastimes which had been enjoyed in Ireland long before the British sports revolution. But the first sports played in a regulated manner in Ireland were of British origin and were played primarily by British people in Ireland, such as soldiers, people closely connected to the British governing élite, such as members of the Anglo-Irish ascendancy, or, eventually, when some of the sports began to lose their aristocratic ties, by members of the Protestant working class in Ulster.

As time went on, these 'British' sports came to fall into two distinct categories. First, there are those which have remained closely linked with Britain, being played primarily in Commonwealth countries, for example, or in Ireland, even after the foundation of the Irish Free State and the severing of political ties with Britain, by an élite which is not exclusively pro-British but remains greatly influenced by Britain's historic role in Ireland. These sports include cricket and rugby union, both of which continued to be organized on an all-Irish basis even after partition had divided the island into two separate political entities. Second, there are sports which originated in Britain and which derived their initial popularity in Ireland from their Britishness but which were to become universally popular. As such, they came to be played throughout Ireland, even by some of those who were and are vehemently opposed to the British presence both before and after partition. The most important of these universal sports in Ireland is association football, although the category also includes boxing, athletics and golf. Like the 'British' sports, many of these are still organized on an all-Ireland basis. Association football, however, significantly as the sport which attracts the greatest working-class interest, followed the boundaries established by partition, with separate governing bodies in the two parts of Ireland. As a result, the game became one of the most powerful cultural identifiers of the presence of two separate political entities on the island.

A third major category of sports played in Ireland, north and south, consists of games organized and administered by the Gaelic Athletic Association (GAA). Formed in 1884 as an element in a broader cultural struggle to resist the spread of British influence in Ireland, the GAA assumed responsibility for revitalizing and in some instances virtually inventing games which could be presented as traditionally Irish. It continues to advance the cause of Gaelic games – hurling, Gaelic football, camogie and handball – throughout Ireland, although since partition it has had to operate in two different political contexts and arguably has been obliged to assume a dual character as a consequence, both consolidating the existence of a 26-county Irish Republic while simultaneously helping to keep alive the idea of ending partition.

The origins and early development of sports in Ireland have important repercussions for their contemporary status in Northern Ireland. Traditional 'British' games, like rugby union, continue to reflect their origins. Although played throughout Ireland, by Catholics as well as by Protestants, they are essentially a Protestant and Unionist preserve in the north – a situation which is maintained by custom and tradition, themselves secured by a divided educational system in which state schools, especially grammar schools, are the principal nurseries for these sports. Thus, although education is also related to social class in Northern Ireland as elsewhere, and this relationship is manifested in terms of sports preference, the most significant aspect of these 'British' games as regards political division is that they are identified with Unionism and attract few Catholic players or followers.

The situation of sports like association football, which originated in Great Britain but which have subsequently acquired a universal character, is very different. Soccer is extremely popular in Northern Ireland with both Catholics and Protestants and, at the senior competitive level, members of both communities play together for the same teams. Ironically, in certain respects, the game is actually more divisive than manifestly exclusive sports like rugby union. This is illustrated by two separate but related phenomena. First, Northern Ireland's national team, although always including Catholic players, has become increasingly supported only by Protestants, some of whom have used international matches to express in highly emotive terms their attachment to Protestantism (or anti-Catholicism) and to the Union. Second, although many Catholics play for Irish League clubs in Northern Ireland and most teams receive some degree of support from the Catholic community, the general ambience of Irish League football is Protestant and Unionist and little or no attempt has been made over the years to alter this situation. Indeed the opposite has been true with clubs supported mainly by Catholics, Belfast Celtic and Derry City, being forced to withdraw from the Irish League in 1949 and 1971 respectively.

The impression created by these phenomena is of a Protestant community seeking to maintain control over a sport in a manner which could be said to reflect Unionist political efforts to maintain the Union in the face of growing encroachment by Irish Nationalists. It should be stated, however, that this is not simply an example of Protestant intransigence. In the case of identification with the national team, for example, it is no coincidence that Catholic support for Northern Ireland began to dwindle at precisely the time when the Republic of Ireland's national side started to enjoy international success for the first time ever, thereby providing an Irish alternative for football-loving northern Catholics. As regards the lack of Catholic involvement in the organization and ethos of Irish League football, the traditional attitudes of the GAA should not be ignored.

Initially the GAA banned its members from playing 'foreign' games, association football included. Even after this rule was rescinded, the Association continued to adopt a suspicious attitude towards soccer, particularly in rural Ulster. It has been helped in its efforts to maintain Gaelic sporting traditions in Northern Ireland by the same divided educational system which has also helped rugby union and cricket to flourish. In the case of Gaelic games, the main training grounds are Catholic schools, especially grammar schools run by the Christian Brothers. Just as 'British' sports contribute to the distinctive identity of the Unionist community in Northern Ireland, so the Gaelic sports movement is of vital importance to the construction and reproduction of a separate Irish Nationalist identity. In addition, the fact that the GAA refuses membership to members of the British security forces is taken by Unionists as evidence that the entire Nationalist community served by the Association is politically subversive.

Conclusions

Naturally not all sports are as involved in the politics of division as the major team games discussed here. Individual sports such as golf and boxing have been more successful in bringing together members of the two communities and forming the basis for harmonious relationships. Recognizing that sport not only plays a part in maintaining divisions but can also help to bring people together, British government ministers, their civil servants and a variety of bodies concerned with community relations arrived at the conclusion by the late 1980s that sport had to be used more subtly than in the past if it was to have a socially beneficial impact. More needed to be done than merely providing leisure centres where young people could let off steam in a controlled environment, perhaps, but not necessarily, with youngsters from the other community. Instead, strenuous efforts have been made to pursue integration through sport and to generate respect for rival sporting traditions. So far, however, these attempts have met with only limited success.

The sports which people play are fundamental to the construction of their identities. As such, they are celebrated by their practitioners and supporters. Perhaps in a changed political environment, the symbolic importance attached to separate sporting traditions will begin to wane. Until then, however, it is to underestimate the intensity of feeling engendered by sports to imagine that they can be enthusiastically pursued in a context in which they are freed from the marks of their birth and early development.

Like the arts and other cultural activities in Northern Ireland, therefore, sport reflects the differences in society and offers us an insight into the extent to which people value their differences. For some, sports provide opportunities to transcend inter-community divisions. For most, however, it will only be when these divisions cease to have political implications that the arts and sport can become neutral spheres of activity.

Further reading

Arts Council of Northern Ireland, *To the Millennium. A Draft Strategy for the Arts in Northern Ireland*. Belfast, 1994.

Bairner, A., 'The end of pitched battles? The peace process and sport in Northern Ireland', *Causeway*, 1(3), Summer 1994.

Bracefield, H., Brett, D. and Henderson, L., 'The arts in Northern Ireland', *Studies*, 80(318), Summer 1991.

Cultural Traditions Group, *Giving Voices*. Cultural Traditions Group, Belfast, 1995.

Sugden, J. and Bairner, A., 'National identity, community relations and the sporting life in Northern Ireland', in L. Allison (ed.), *The Changing Politics of Sport*. Manchester: Manchester University Press, 1993.

Sugden, J. and Bairner, A., *Sport, Sectarianism and Society in a Divided Ireland*. Leicester: Leicester University Press, 1993.

Chapter 21

CHURCHES, SOCIETY AND CONFLICT IN NORTHERN IRELAND
Duncan Morrow

Introduction

For many, Northern Ireland has become synonymous with religious divisions. Numerous surveys have shown that the Northern Irish are among the most loyal churchgoers in western Europe. Over half the population still attend church services at least once a week, while more than 80% retain some attachment to a church. Labels such as 'Protestant' and 'Catholic' are regularly used to identify social groups and as shorthand for specific political positions. The impression is often given that conflict is Northern Ireland is between two groups divided by religious confession.

Churches are not simple institutions with a single, clearly defined meaning. They are both communities of believers, whose actions singly and together make up the totality of each church, and institutions with buildings, administration and professional staff. In public or political debates, the churches are referred to as institutions, identified most closely with the clergy. In the twentieth century, however, religious adherence does not necessarily mean a particular political viewpoint.

Religion, and conflict surrounding religion, has played a role in Irish and specifically Northern Irish affairs since the Reformation. In this, Ireland is not different from most of continental Europe. However, the specific conditions of political and religious movements in Northern Ireland resulted in ingrained communal divisions, where the lines of religious rivalry ran almost parallel to political divisions.

Although some individual Protestants became notable Irish Nationalists and some Catholics remained strongly Unionist, the trend throughout the nineteenth century was towards the consolidation of political divisions on the basis of religious tradition, a tendency which has stretched into the present day. When most Protestants opposed Home Rule for Ireland, the slogan 'Home Rule is Rome Rule' encapsulated the close association of religious and political identities and fears. From the outset, controversy over religion in Northern Ireland was directly linked to political loyalties.

Demography and denomination

The largest denominations in Northern Ireland today remain the descendents of the churches existent in Ireland after the plantation of the seventeenth century. In the interim, numerous other groups have emerged, all of which are usually classified as broadly Protestant. Numerically, the two most significant have been Methodists and Baptists.

In statistical terms, churches in Northern Ireland remain relatively strong. In the 1991 census for Northern Ireland, 89% of people identified themselves as belonging to a specific Christian denomination. Of the total, 38.4% declared themselves Roman Catholics, while 50.6% belonged to a number of different Protestant churches. Nevertheless, raw statistics hide a number of important features.

Although Presbyterians and Anglicans (Church of Ireland) account for over 75% of all Protestants, there are more than 45 separate denominations with more than 100 members in a population of less than 800,000. This contrasts sharply with the Catholic population, unified into one institutional body. As we shall see, this difference has had political as well as religious significance, as the institutional unity of Catholicism has sometimes been seen as threatening when contrasted with the fragmentary nature of Protestantism.

There have been important changes of denominational proportions since Northern Ireland was established in 1921. Immediately after the partition of Ireland, Catholics made up 34% of the population in the north and Protestants 65%. For many years, a higher Catholic birthrate was balanced by a higher emigration rate among Catholics. As a result, the relative proportions in the population changed little. There is some evidence, particularly in relation to migration, that these patterns have begun to change in the 1970s and 1980s. Significantly, interest in changes in denominational proportions is regarded as profoundly important for secular politics.

The 1991 census recorded a rise in the number of those refusing to answer the census question on religion and those claiming no religion, who together accounted for 11% of the population. There has also been a sharp decline in the size of the two largest Protestant denominations. Between 1921 and 1991, the percentage of Presbyterians in the population fell from 31% to 21%. The corresponding figures for the Church of Ireland are 27% and 18%. This has only been partly offset by the rise in the number of those attached to smaller Protestant groups, who now make up 8% of the population (see Chapter 22).

Although Northern Ireland is theoretically and statistically a mixed community in terms of religious denomination, there is increasing evidence that statistical mixing masks increasing separation at local level. These marked religious cleavages, and changes within and between them, have a significance beyond the level of faith or religious adherence. They continue to be used to provide important sociological indicators of political change.

Lastly, although church attendance and membership remain comparatively high, there is evidence of a drift towards secularization. Statistics indicate that, especially in the Belfast area, church attendance in all denominations is declining.

Denominations in Northern Ireland

The largest single denomination in Northern Ireland is the Roman Catholic Church. Organized on an all-Ireland basis, the church is geographically divided into dioceses, each with its own bishop. The senior bishop in Ireland, the Primate of All-Ireland, has his seat in Armagh. Within the boundaries of Northern Ireland, the Catholic Church is a minority. Nevertheless, given that over 95% of the population of the Republic of Ireland are, at least nominally, Catholic, the church is by far the largest on the island of Ireland.

The Catholic Church has long been the largest and most publicly prominent institution within the Nationalist community. Sharing the suffering of the Catholic people of Ireland during the penal laws period, the history of the church was always closely bound to that of the people. The church was the one established institution able to represent popular Catholic views to the British authorities while also able to organize key parts of social life. The clergy became important mediators between a threatened and sometimes hostile community and the British authorities. The resulting high profile of the clergy confirmed for many Protestants that the church was the most important institution for their opponents. At the same time, the church authorities also came under attack from more radical republicans who accused the church of leniency towards the British authorities. Thus the Catholic Church has been accused of being both an organizer for republicanism and an agent of British imperialism.

Since Catholic Emancipation, many Catholics, including many clergy, have contended that religion is not a central feature of conflict in Northern Ireland. Most Catholics have tended to regard political and economic inequity and injustice as the root of the Northern Irish problem. The Catholic Church has negotiated with various governments, British or Northern Irish, over social and economic matters. They have not discussed theology. At the same time, the very fact that the church negotiates or that the church manages schools, social facilities and economic initiatives has raised the profile of the church in public affairs and given weight to those Protestants who argue that the church is the controlling influence in Catholic society. Clearly, the issue looks different from the inside than it does from the outside.

The Roman Catholic Church in Ireland has been regarded as one of the most conservative parts of the Roman Catholic communion. This has had important effects in Ireland, especially during the late nineteenth and early twentieth centuries. In reaction to the rise of secular liberalism in continental Europe, the papacy became increasingly conservative. The infallible authority of the Pope in certain situations was underlined, the veneration of the Virgin Mary was encouraged and, in the *Ne temere* decree of 1909, the conversion of partners in mixed marriages was stipulated together with the requirement that all children should be raised as Catholics. Protestant churches were confirmed as churches 'in error', and, in a famous phrase, 'error has no rights'. All of these had an impact on the relationship of Catholics to Protestants in Ireland, strengthening Protestant concerns. The fact that the Irish Free State, later the Republic, was overwhelmingly Catholic, also meant that many of the laws of the state reflected Catholic concerns and attitudes.

Changes, especially in the 1960s, have also had significant implications for relationships in Northern Ireland. At the second Vatican Council in the 1960s, many aspects of the Roman Catholic Church were reformed. Although inter-communion remained impossible, Protestant churches were declared to be 'separated brethren' and church unity to be a desirable goal. The resultant increase in ecumenical contact with Protestant churches and church people in Ireland, in its own turn, caused difficulties for some fundamentalist Protestants, many of which remain unresolved.

The Catholic clergy today remain important figures in the social life of the Catholic community in Ulster. Many of the physical and financial assets of that community, such as schools, church buildings, youth clubs and social facilities, are managed with direct clerical involvement. In the 1980s, clergy also became involved in the management of a number of employment and training schemes. The vast majority of clergy have consistently opposed political violence in Northern Ireland and among many Nationalists they are regarded as the strongest 'internal' opponents of the IRA. This has again led to accusations from republicans that the church is an agent for Unionism.

The term 'Protestantism' is often used in Northern Ireland as the counterpart of Catholicism. This has some validity when referring to divisions of political loyalty but it is inaccurate when used about the churches. There is no single institution which can claim to speak for all Protestants. Indeed this is one of the most important differences between the two politically divided groups. There is no unified 'Protestant' teaching on church structures or even on central doctrines. Institutional unity, in so far as it exists at all, is provided by political and cultural groups such as the Unionist parties and the Orange Order and not by the churches.

The largest Protestant denomination, the Presbyterian Church, is rooted in Scottish Calvinism, strongly influenced in the nineteenth century by the evangelical revival. Traditionally, the church has had both a liberal wing, which has been at times ecumenical and socially radical, and a larger conservative wing, marked by biblical fundamentalism and hostility towards Catholicism. Although technically an all-Ireland church, Presbyterians are geographically concentrated in Counties Antrim and Down.

The Church of Ireland, once the established church of the whole island, is hierarchical in structure and retains a stronger sense of an all-Ireland purpose. This may stem from the fact of previous establishment. While fundamentalist theological opposition to Catholicism has been traditionally weaker than among Presbyterians, the Church of Ireland has been the home of both landed and working-class Unionists, sometimes with close attachment to the Orange Order. While Anglicanism in other countries has been strongly marked by Catholicism, Anglicanism in Ireland has always been strongly Protestant or low church.

Ulster Methodists, the third largest Protestant denomination, also have strong evangelical roots and a traditional interest in social reform. As the church most removed from political power, they have sometimes appeared less clearly identified in political terms.

Church attendance among Ulster Protestants is considerably lower than among Catholics and has been steadily declining. Despite this decline, the churches have not been replaced by any other mass organizations. Trade unions and political parties remain small. The Orange Order no longer commands the support of previous years and membership of paramilitary groups is concentrated in geographical pockets. As a result, the churches are still by far the largest institutions of civil society.

Support for a partitioned Ireland has been nearly universal among Protestants since 1920. The Protestant clergy in Ulster have generally not had to mediate between their communities and the authorities. Those Protestant clergy who have been prominent in public affairs have become so by virtue of their election to secular office rather than through their church position. Once the Northern Ireland government had made certain guarantees about religious education and church representation on boards of management, the Protestant churches transferred most of their schools into full state control. This contrasts with the position of the Protestant clergy in the Irish Republic, who have sometimes acted as communal guardians.

There have been few controversies about the public role of the Protestant churches, in contrast to debates about the Catholic Church. However, it is usually Protestants who ascribe a religious dimension to communal divisions. In part this is due to the public profile of the Roman Catholic Church, on both sides of the Irish border. In Ireland before partition, Protestantism was a clear identifier of difference. 'Protestantism' was the emotional core of anti-Nationalism and became a unifying secular political identity in Northern Ireland. Until 1920, most Protestants in Ireland spoke of themselves as Irish *and* British, in contrast to Nationalist claims to be Irish, *not* British. After partition, Nationalists in Northern Ireland still proclaimed themselves Irish, an identity seldom, if ever, denied to them by the Irish south of the border. Faced by apparently hostile Irish Nationalism, some Unionists now prefered to describe themselves as British, not Irish, only to find that, except during and immediately after World War II, this met little echo in England, Scotland and Wales. Given this perceived weakness in the emotional bonds of the Union, self-definition still relies on labels such as Northern Irish or, more usually, Protestant. Protestantism can therefore be a label for an entirely secular identity.

The divide between Protestantism as a statement of faith and as a political identity is thin. Many Protestants have always been overtly hostile to Catholicism. In a context of Unionist insecurity about Britain's will to support their position, many have found the radical anti-Catholic and anti-Nationalist commitment of fundamentalist church leaders appealing. In this way, for example, the Reverend Ian Paisley, a minister in the small Free Presbyterian Church, has had a strong appeal for working-class, and often non-church, Protestants.

There is thus an asymmetry in the way in which the churches relate to the communities which sometimes bear their names. The Catholic Church has had a high institutional profile, sometimes apparently negotiating for a community with the government. The repeated experience is that the political negotiations are about social, economic and political questions. Unionist ideological or religious objections to Catholicism tend to be regarded as diversions or unimportant by Catholics. Simultaneously, the Protestant experience is that the Catholic Church is the main political operator within the community from which their enemies come. Protestant churches have been less important as social organizers, but Protestantism, and the anti-Catholic dimension of Protestantism, has been crucial to the political shape and ideology of Unionism at various times.

Churches and society in Northern Ireland

The churches are still the largest voluntary social institutions in Northern Ireland, the focus of important, if sometimes invisible, social networks. The churches also fulfil important cultural tasks even for those with no regular worshipping attachment. Church buildings are often central community resources for young people, women's groups, charities and even sports clubs, especially in rural areas. Only pubs and drinking clubs can claim similar social centrality.

Networks of organizations and clubs provide a substantial part of the social and community infrastructure in Northern Ireland, ranging from youth clubs and women's groups to prayer and bible study groups. About 90% of Northern Irish churches have active choirs. Such minutiae become important when we consider that an average size of 25 members would mean 27,000 church choir singers in Northern Ireland.

Churches are also voluntary economies, collecting and distributing money and benefiting from unpaid labour. Highly paid professionals and tradespeople give freely of their time which is nowhere accounted for. Numerous charities have benefited from this practice. Similarly, many of the Credit Unions, now widespread in Northern Ireland, had clerical and parish involvement.

Church institutions also participate in the administration of major public services, especially in the fields of education, social services, employment and healthcare. The Roman Catholic Church has a controlling interest in most of the schools attended by Catholics in Northern Ireland. Protestant church nominees, while no longer holding the controlling interest, participate on the vast majority of the remaining schools. Many churches have developed social welfare schemes. The Catholic Church also continues to have an important role on the boards of a number of important public hospitals.

Mass unemployment in Northern Ireland in the 1970s led to the expansion of job training and employment schemes under church management. Although the focus on church management was most resented in Catholic areas, posts were distributed fairly evenly between Protestants and Catholics, although smaller Protestant churches are often more active in this sphere than the larger denominations.

As a result, the institutional churches are woven into the fabric of Northern Irish society. Secular–church interfaces are widespread throughout the province. There is no doubt, however, that the churches have tended to reflect that society rather than transform it.

The churches, conflict and inter-community relationships

The churches are part of the historic fabric of Northern Irish society – relatively stable human communities, living side by side but with very little trade in membership. This stability has contributed to the historical importance of churches as the oldest still-existing institutions in Northern Ireland. Churches have been part of the creation and maintenance of community memories, myths and histories. As such, each church has overwhelmingly ministered within one political tradition. The range of experience in each church is not substantially greater than the experience of one side of a political divide. Unionism is the overwhelming political loyalty within Protestant churches as Nationalism is within the Catholic church. As a result, the equation of Catholic with Nationalist or Irish and Protestant with Unionist or British has never been successfully repudiated.

At one level, the preference of Protestants for a nominally Protestant state and of Catholics for a majority Catholic state is not surprising. However, the fact that elsewhere in western Europe, both traditions coexist happily in the twentieth century suggests that this is insufficient reason for this equation of the political and the confessional.

In communities which regard one another with suspicion or hostility, in which the fact of being a Protestant or being a Catholic may be grounds for apprehension or fear, the avoidance of such situations of fear, which may mean the avoidance of one another, is a matter of common sense. Northern Ireland's past and present provides innumerable examples of good reasons for such suspicion. The churches find themselves reflecting these secular experiences of their members.

In Northern Ireland, any mixed Catholic–Protestant group may avoid raising questions whose impact might be so controversial as to break up the group. Churches are not mixed. Churches provide a refuge and comfort. Inter-community work can hardly happen within a single church, only between them. Given their own historical antagonism to one another and strong resistance to treating one another as equals, churches have been slow to lower their defensive ramparts. The churches may not be opposed in theory to changed community relations, but to actively participate in them means jumping over deeply felt historical and doctrinal differences.

Crucially, in Northern Ireland, doctrine has been reinforced by experience. The violent death of a member of a church community is felt by all the members. Inevitably, Protestant churches experience the fear and murder of their members more deeply than the fears and murders of those outside. The same is true for Catholic churches. If such atrocities repeatedly seem to come from the other community, hostility is easily nurtured. Violence therefore reinforces the sense of isolation from one another in the churches.

The churches in Northern Ireland have, to some extent, unwittingly given political and social hostility an institutional shape and an ideological validity. Although the reasons given are different from those of secular society, the inability of churches to treat one another as of equal validity has the same result as similar refusals by other groups in secular society. In effect, church actions towards one another are sufficiently analogous to the actions of secular groups for the attachment of the terms 'Protestant' and 'Catholic' to be used without successful contradiction. The boundary between a refusal to deal with one another equally on grounds of doctrine or on grounds of political enmity is often invisible.

Conclusions

Any picture of Northern Ireland which does not treat the churches seriously is inevitably flawed. While it is certainly true that secularization has begun in Northern Ireland, the churches remain central social and cultural institutions in chaplaincy, in public and private moral and political ideology and in formal and community politics. Churches play a different political role for Nationalists than they do for Unionists but together they are integral to the social fabric.

The labels 'Catholic' and 'Protestant' have continued to be used as shorthand to describe sides in conflict in Northern Ireland. They are likely to continue to do so for some time to come. Usually, Christianity does not provide the explicit grounds for those in conflict. Clergy point to the fact that those in churches tend to be less violent than those outside them. However, in a country which has sustained such a conflict for more than 25 years, the issues in conflict are inevitably underpinned by their central institutions, including the churches, even if the links are indirect. In general, the churches have been unable to put effective distance between themselves and particular political causes. Clergy have tended to share the suffering of their laity rather than transform it.

However, the churches are far from the sole cause of inter-community violence. Once aroused, secular national causes can be quickly considered sufficient justification for enormous cruelty. Nationalist secular strife is often fought with equal fanatical devotion and the same focus on the evil outsider and the traitor. Even if the churches were to fade, the importance of religion may well remain.

Further reading

Boyd, R., *Christianity in Ireland*. Geneva: World Council of Churches, 1987.

Brooke, P., *Ulster Presbyterianism*. Dublin: Gill and Macmillan, 1987.

Bruce, S., *God Save Ulster! The Religion and Politics of Paisleyism*. Oxford: Oxford University Press, 1986.

Daly, C., *The Price of Peace*. Belfast: Blackstaff Press, 1992.

Dunlop, J., *A Precarious Belonging*. Belfast: Blackstaff Press, 1995.

Hickey, J., *Religion and the Northern Ireland Problem*. Dublin: Gill and Macmillan, 1984.

Lee, S. (ed.), *Freedom from Fear*. Belfast: Institute of Irish Studies, 1991.

Lennon, B., *Catholics after the Ceasefire*. Dublin: Columba Press, 1995.

McElroy, G., *The Catholic Church and the Northern Ireland Crisis*. Dublin: Gill and Macmillan, 1991.

Morrow, D., *The Churches and Inter-community Relationships*. Coleraine: University of Ulster, 1991.

Smyth, C., *Ian Paisley: Voice of Protestant Ulster*. Edinburgh: Scottish Academic Press, 1987.

Wilson, D., *An End to Silence*. Cork: Mercier Press, 1986.

Wright, F., 'Protestant ideology and politics in Ulster', *European Journal of Sociology*, 24, 1973.

Chapter 22

THE NUMBERS GAME:
THE DEMOGRAPHIC CONTEXT OF POLITICS
Paul Doherty

Introduction

Politics in Northern Ireland is articulated around the issue of national identity and allegiance, rather than around economic or class issues. The greater number are Unionist and wish to maintain the constitutional status quo, while a minority are Nationalist and aspire to Irish unity. Because of this fundamental division, elections within the province at local government, national and European level tend to be dominated by this question and are in effect referenda on nationality and allegiance.

In other political contexts, so-called 'floating voters' may transfer their votes across political divides and so effect a change of government. In Great Britain, for example, voters may change from Conservative to Labour or vice versa. The floating voter is therefore a prime target for election canvassers, particularly in marginal constituencies where these electors can have a major impact on the electoral outcome. In Northern Ireland, however, voters do not cross the political divide to any significant extent. Shifts of allegiance may occur on either side of the divide, with voters transferring from Ulster Unionist to DUP, for example, or from Sinn Féin to SDLP, but they will only cross the divide on comparatively rare occasions, and then for tactical purposes.

It follows from this that the numerical size of the two communities is of fundamental importance to politics in the province at all levels. This importance is heightened by the fact that the minority is a large one, that it is perceived to be growing, and that in some areas it is numerically dominant. We therefore need to examine the demographic and social geographic context if we are to understand properly the politics of the province, and to do this we need accurate statistics. Official data sources such as the Northern Ireland Census of Population do not record national identity, but we have a good indicator of the two groups in their religious allegiance, which has been recorded in censuses since 1861. For historical reasons, Unionists are almost exclusively Protestant while Nationalists are almost exclusively Catholic, and indeed Protestant and Catholic are labels commonly used to identify the two groups. This chapter will therefore focus on the numbers and distribution of Protestants and Catholics, as indicators of the two communities in the province.

Population numbers

Before considering these issues, however, we need to look briefly at the wider context. The 1991 Northern Ireland Census of Population enumerated 1,577,836 persons, an increase of 2.7% since 1981. Much of this growth can be attributed to a rate of natural increase of about 0.7% per annum in the 1980s, which is largely the consequence of a birth rate which is high by both British and Republic of Ireland standards. Northern Ireland historically has experienced high levels of out-migration caused by the depressed economy, but in the 1980s out-migration fell to an average of about 7,800 per annum, and this fall contributed to the growth in population. Within this picture of general growth, however, the population of Belfast declined, as people moved out to the suburbs and surrounding towns such as Carrickfergus, Lisburn and Newtownards.

Against this background we can now consider the relative numerical strengths of the two communities, starting with the observation that if the minority were small, the politics of Northern Ireland would be very different. In the Republic of Ireland, the Protestant minority only constitutes about 4% of the population and has been in numerical decline for many years. It therefore poses no threat to the majority, the issue of national identity is not in question, and politics can organize on more conventional social and economic lines. By contrast, in Northern Ireland the minority is large and growing: 38.4% were enumerated as Catholics in 1991, compared with 31.4% in 1971. For Protestants this poses a threat. There is a widespread perception that they will eventually be outnumbered by Catholics who would then vote for a change in the constitutional position of the province. This helps explain the siege mentality which is part of the Protestant mind-set. For Catholics the possibility of eventual majority status has helped a growing political self-confidence and a strengthening of Nationalist aspirations, with the realization that time would seem to be on their side. The actual size of the two communities is therefore an important matter, but the *perceptions* of the balance are also important.

Table 22.1 provides a historical perspective: it shows that the proportion of Roman Catholics in Northern Ireland declined until 1937, after which it rose slightly until 1961. The figures for 1971 and 1981 are best disregarded, as these censuses were conducted against a background of terrorist activity and political campaigns not to respond to the religion question. The 1991 census did not experience these problems and can be taken as a good indicator of the religious composition of the population, although 7.3% still refused to state their religion. The 1991 census shows that 38.4% of the population claim to be Catholic, the highest percentage for over 100 years. Discounting the unreliable figures for 1971 and 1981, the Catholic proportion would therefore seem to have risen fairly steadily since 1937. The numerical increase from 1961 to 1991 was 21.7%, which was more than twice the rate of increase of the total population. In addition, the average size of Catholic families is larger than their Protestant counterparts, and they have a younger age profile. It is these facts which give rise to the popular view that the balance of population will in the fullness of time change to favour the Catholics, who will then vote for a united Ireland.

Table 22.1 Religious composition of the population, 1861–1991

Year	Total population	Roman Catholic (%)	Protestant[a] (%)	None (%)	Not stated (%)
1861	1,396,453	40.9	59.0	–	0.1
1871	1,359,190	39.3	60.7	–	0.0
1881	1,304,816	38.0	61.9	–	0.1
1891	1,236,056	36.3	63.5	–	0.2
1901	1,236,952	34.8	65.1	–	0.1
1911	1,250,531	34.4	65.4	–	0.2
1926	1,256,561	33.5	66.3	–	0.2
1937	1,279,745	33.5	66.3	–	0.2
1951	1,370,921	34.4	65.2	–	0.4
1961	1,425,042	34.9	63.2	–	1.9
1971	1,519,640	31.4	59.2	–	9.4
1981	1,481,959	28.0	53.5	–	18.5
1991	1,577,836	38.4	50.6	3.7	7.3

Source: The Northern Ireland Census 1991, Religion Report.

[a] The column headed 'Protestant' is the sum of those indicating their religion as 'Presbyterian', 'Church of Ireland', 'Methodist' or 'Other Denomination'. The classification 'Other Denomination' consists mainly of less numerous Protestant groups such as Brethren and Baptists, but also contains other faiths. These other faiths are numerically small and their inclusion with the Protestants does not substantially distort the overall picture.

Population distribution

While the overall balance of numbers is relevant to the long-term constitutional future of Northern Ireland, the balance at local level is relevant to more immediate issues, namely the control of local councils and the outcome of Westminster and European elections. Figures 22.1 to 22.4 show some key religious distributions in 1991, by local government district (LGD), and they illustrate the highly variable religious geography which is characteristic of the province. (We need to note in passing that this geography is even more variable at a finer scale – in the Belfast Urban Area in 1991, for example, 45% of the population lived in highly segregated areas at the 1 km grid square level, no less than 94.3% of Protestants lived in areas where they were in the majority, and 60.7% of Catholics lived in areas where they predominated.) Figure 22.1 shows that Catholics predominate in the west and periphery of the province, and this has been historically the case. They are relatively less numerous in the urban core which is focused on Belfast, where Protestants predominate.

However, this is not a static picture. There has been a tendency to spatial polarization, that is, an increasing propensity to living apart at all scales, from local government district down to street level. This polarization has been fuelled by

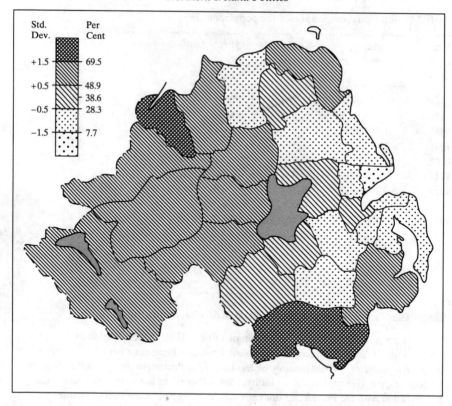

Std.
Dev.

Per
Cent

+1.5 — 69.5

+0.5 — 48.9
      — 38.6
-0.5 — 28.3

-1.5 — 7.7

Figure 22.1 Distribution of Roman Catholics, 1991, by Local Government District

intercommunal tensions since 1969. Figure 22.2 illustrates that while the percentage of Catholics grew in most of the 26 LGDs, it decreased in five, which were all in the Belfast periphery in the east. These five LGDs contain much of the Protestant middle class who commute to Belfast to work. In 1971 four LGDs had Catholic majorities. By 1991 Catholic majority LGDs had increased in number to 11. This has obvious electoral implications, with some councils changing control and others finely balanced at present, but looking set to change as the population balance translates into a changed voting balance in a few years' time. All Catholic majority areas in 1971 became more Catholic by 1991. But only five Protestant majority areas became more Protestant, and these were all LGDs where Catholics were already less than 25% of the total.

Those areas which became Catholic majority areas in 1991 were already more than 40% Catholic in 1971. But if we consider the present situation, there are only two areas currently with between 40 and 50% Catholics, namely Armagh and Craigavon. This suggests that these are the only areas with a prospect of changing their balance in the foreseeable future. Half of the 26 LGDs have experienced above-average growth in their proportion of Catholics. Most of these districts lie in the western peripheral areas of the province where the Catholic proportion is already high. The two which are outside the western periphery are Belfast and

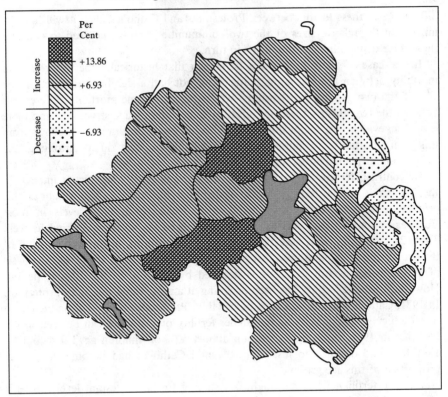

Figure 22.2 Change in the percentage Roman Catholic, 1971–91

Lisburn. Lisburn contains the recent extension of Catholic west Belfast into Poleglass, and this has produced the district's growth in Catholic numbers. The growth in the Catholic population of Belfast is noteworthy, as this LGD contains 17.7% of the population of Northern Ireland, and in political terms it may be viewed as the most important district in the province.

Population prospects

We have seen that the proportion of Catholics in the population has been growing since 1937, and that in a number of local government districts the population balance has changed to a situation of Catholic majority. We therefore have good reason to ask if there is indeed a prospect of Catholics attaining majority status in the province as a whole. While it would be possible to produce a series of population forecasts, for our present purposes the discussion will be confined to an examination of the variables which come into play in forming future population numbers.

The population composition of any area is shaped by the interplay of mortality, fertility and migration. In the Northern Ireland context, if there is a differential in these factors between Protestants and Catholics, then it will have an impact on the relative sizes of the two communities, and so we need to consider these three demographic components in turn.

In the case of mortality, it can be shown that historically the differences in mortality between the two communities have not had a significant impact on the size of the two groups. Furthermore, while there are some mortality differentials between the two groups, these are offset by their differing age structures, and there is no firm evidence of major difference in overall crude death rates. It follows from this that mortality variation plays no significant part in determining the intercommunity population balance.

By contrast, fertility differentials *are* marked and have a significant impact on the balance. Catholic fertility has exceeded that of Protestants throughout this century. In recent years there has been a decline in fertility levels in most European countries, and this has been experienced in Northern Ireland as well. Table 22.2 provides some statistics illustrating this, using a simple fertility ratio of the proportion of persons aged 0–4 per thousand women aged 15–49. On the basis of this statistic, overall fertility has declined by 28.2% over the 20-year period. However, Catholic fertility has been declining at a more rapid rate than Protestant. In 1971, Catholic fertility was 49% higher than Protestant; by 1991 it had declined to 40% higher. The impact of the higher fertility of Catholics can be seen in the fact that in 1971 Protestants made up almost 50% of children aged 0–4, but by 1991 they had declined to just over 40% and Catholics had become the largest proportion of this age group.

Catholic fertility, while still high, is declining to the Protestant level. There is evidence that this decline is more marked in the Belfast area, where average Catholic family size has dropped by almost one-fifth since 1971. If this rate of decline were to be maintained, then the overall Catholic/Protestant fertility

Table 22.2 Fertility levels in 1971 and 1991

	Total population	Roman Catholic	Protestant[a]	None	Not stated
Fertility ratio[b]					
1971	461	574	384	–	581
1991	331	382	273	356	430
Change 1971–91	−28.2%	−33.4%	−28.9%	–	−26.0%
Proportion of 0–4 age group					
1971	100.0%	38.3%	49.9%	–	11.8%
1991	100.0%	45.4%	40.7%	4.3%	9.5%

Source: Adapted from the Northern Ireland Census 1971 and 1991 Religion Reports.

[a] The column headed 'Protestant' is the sum of those indicating their religion as 'Presbyterian', 'Church of Ireland', 'Methodist' or 'Other Denomination'. See footnote to Table 22.1.

[b] Number of children aged 0–4 per thousand women aged 15–49.

differential would disappear by about 2015, and by around the turn of the century in the greater Belfast area. Clearly the rate of fertility convergence is a key influence on the long-term overall balance of Protestants and Catholics. If the Catholic fertility rate declines rapidly to Protestant levels in the manner just described, then a Catholic majority would not appear, although they would constitute a larger proportion of the population than at present. The longer the convergence takes, the more likely it is that Catholics will become the larger group because their fertility will have exceeded that of Protestants for a longer period. The rapid decline in the Belfast area has already been noted, and fertility decline in the Republic has also been rapid, dropping by about one-fifth in the 10 years from 1979. Similar falls in Catholic fertility have been experienced in other parts of the world, notably North America. It is argued that these declines are due to an increasing secularization of the population and a weakening influence of the Church, particularly on the issue of family planning. Other factors that may have a bearing include improved socio-economic circumstances and increased female participation in the labour force. Whatever the reason, clearly the long-standing fertility differential between Catholics and Protestants in Northern Ireland is disappearing, and this has important implications for the likelihood of a Catholic majority.

Given that there has been a fertility differential for such a long time, it begs the question of why a Catholic majority has not been achieved already. Indeed, despite the fertility differential the Catholic proportion in the population has not always increased: it fell from its peak level of 40.9% in 1861 to a low of 33.5% in 1935, and has only subsequently begun to grow. The explanation for this lies in the third demographic component that we have to consider, namely emigration, which has historically acted to counterbalance the effects of differential fertility. High levels of emigration have been a characteristic outcome of the long-standing weakness in the province's economy, but the emigration rates for Catholics have been much higher than those for Protestants. For example, it has been estimated that 58% of the net out-movements in the period 1937–51 were Catholics, and this from a group that composed around 34% of the population at that time. In other words, the high Catholic fertility levels that have existed over a long period of time have been offset by high Catholic emigration levels, and this held back the growth of the Catholic population.

During the 1960s, a period of economic prosperity and peace in the province, the overall level of emigration fell and Catholics made up a lesser proportion of those leaving. However, with the outbreak of 'the Troubles', emigration rose in the 1970s and the province experienced a net population loss. The relative decline in the Troubles in the 1980s, together with slightly improved economic circumstances, brought a reduction in emigration once more, and the population began to grow again. This serves to illustrate the volatile nature of emigration: of the three demographic components it is the most variable and the most subject to influence by external forces. It would seem that Catholics now form a lesser proportion of the outflow than previously, but this proportion is highly variable and dependent on the circumstances prevailing at any given time.

It follows that it is not possible to predict the size of future emigration flow with any confidence, or its religious composition. What is clear is that the political and economic circumstances in the province are major determinants of emigration levels at any given time. In recent years Protestants have dominated the outflow of students, and many who have gone to Great Britain to study do not return, at least in the short term. Equally the high level of unemployment among Catholics encourages emigration from that community. The continuing fall in the student grant may encourage more Protestants to remain in Northern Ireland for higher education, even more so if the current peace continues. And if there is a 'peace dividend' in the form of economic growth, it is likely that emigration will fall and be more evenly balanced in composition. It might be suggested therefore that emigration differentials may be of less significance in the future, and that fertility convergence will be the key factor in determining future population composition, but it must be emphasized that the influence of emigration is particularly subject to varying circumstances in the province.

Having considered the demographic variables, we need to discuss a further issue which impacts on any examination of future population balance. The discussion so far has used the census enumeration of Catholics and Protestants as indicators of the numbers of Unionist and Nationalist voters. However, the last three censuses have recorded a significant number of persons who did not wish to be designated as belonging to any religious group – Catholic, Protestant or anything else. In 1971 and 1981 campaigns were conducted to disrupt the census, and these produced much higher levels of non-statement of religion than had previously been experienced (see Table 22.1). This was particularly marked in 1981, when there was also significant under-enumeration of the population, so that we do not know for certain the size of the population in that year, or its religious composition. The 1991 census was much better: there was no campaign against the census, and there were no significant problems in its execution. There was in fact a positive incentive to answer the religion question on the census return, because religion statistics are increasingly used to allocate resources fairly in the province. It was therefore in the interests of both communities that their numbers were accurately known. There is good reason to believe that the 1991 census was the best enumeration of the population of Northern Ireland for 30 years. In addition to the 7.3% who did not state a religious affiliation, those who claimed to be of no religion were enumerated separately for the first time in 1991, and a further 3.7% fell into this category. (The various non-Christian groups comprise less than 0.5% of the population, and are not considered significant in the context of this discussion.) We therefore have 11.0% of the population who cannot be classified as Protestant or Catholic, and the implications of this need to be considered.

If we look at the spatial distribution of those of no affiliation (Fig. 22.3) and those not stating an affiliation (Fig. 22.4), a very clear geographical pattern is apparent. In both cases, most of the province has average or below-average levels, but the eastern LGDs, focused on Belfast, have above-average levels. The distributions are very similar: low values in the west, higher values in the east around Belfast. Taking the two distributions together, we are looking at those who cannot be classified as either Catholic or Protestant, and these are concentrated in the greater Belfast region. Belfast and its eight neighbouring LGDs all have more

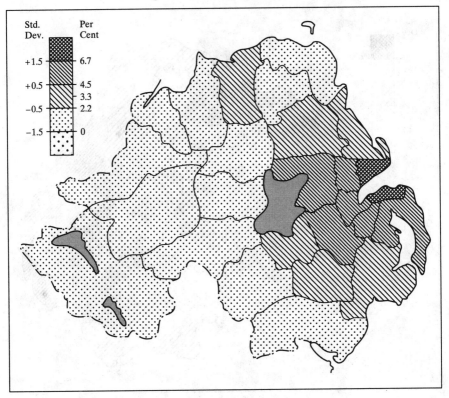

Figure 22.3 Distribution of persons claiming no religious affiliation, 1991

than 12% of their populations either claiming no affiliation, or not stating their religion. North Down has the highest level, 17.5%.

Within these LGDs there is also substantial variation: in the Malone–Stranmillis area, parts of Jordanstown and Holywood, for example, over 20% of the population are neither Catholic nor Protestant. These are all upper-middle-class areas. Again, in both east Belfast and Castlereagh, those in this category outnumber the Catholics. Given the class composition of these areas it is unlikely that the non-statement of religion is due to intimidation or fear, and it is suggested that what we have here may be indicating a movement away from religious affiliation. While church attendance is still high in Northern Ireland, there is evidence of decline among some groups, particularly younger persons from Protestant backgrounds, and this tends to support such an inference.

Two points can be made concerning the Not Stated and No Religion groups. First, their combined size in parts of the urban east of the province seriously weakens any analysis of the population based on the traditional binary Protestant–Catholic classification, and the discussion of the future population prospects must be read in the light of this. Second, it may be that we are seeing the first signs of a fundamental change in the nature of society in Northern Ireland, in the development of a group who view themselves as neither Protestant nor

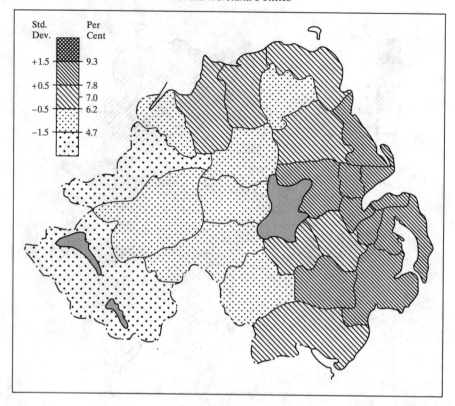

Figure 22.4 Distribution of persons not stating a religious affiliation, 1991

Catholic. If this shift from traditional religious identities is accompanied by a shift from traditional political identities to non-sectarian political parties, this would have an increasing political impact. If these groups have increased in size by the 2001 census, it would indicate that significant change is underway.

Conclusions

In 1970 a series of eight carefully reasoned projections were published which sought to provide estimates of the future intercommunity population balance in the province. The authors predicted that the earliest a Catholic majority might occur would be about the year 2010, but that it was more likely to happen some time after that. However, if we compare these projections with the situation which actually occurred in 1991, the percentage of Catholics in the population was in fact rather less than the lowest value predicted by any of the projections. Without being in any way critical of these projections, it serves to illustrate the difficulty of making such prognostications.

In the present discussion we have seen that the future population balance depends critically on the rate at which the Catholic fertility level converges with that of Protestants, and the future levels and differentials of emigration. The prospect of eventual Catholic majority is not at all certain, especially if Catholic fertility drops rapidly, as it may well do. It seems quite possible that we are moving to a situation of a more even balance of numbers, but with Protestants still in the majority. If this were to occur, there then would be little prospect of a change in the constitutional position. We have also noted the presence of a group who cannot be classified as Protestant or Catholic, and this introduces a further element of uncertainty into the equation.

Finally, our discussion has proceeded on the assumption that Protestants vote Unionist and Catholics vote Nationalist. While this has been true historically, we cannot say with confidence that it will continue to occur, particularly if peace prevails and the province experiences economic growth. These circumstances would enable Catholics to participate on a more equal basis in politics and economic life, giving them a greater stake in the province's affairs than heretofore. They might therefore be less inclined to vote for a united Ireland, as such a constitutional change would lead to a diminution in their socio-economic well-being. If this discussion has served any purpose, it is to demonstrate that the demographic context of Northern Ireland's politics is subject to a number of variable and unpredictable influences, with the only certainty being that we live in interesting times.

Further reading

Compton, P.A., 'The changing religious demography of Northern Ireland: some political implications', *Studies*, Winter 1989.

Compton, P.A., Coward, J. and Wilson-Davis, K.,'Family size and religious denomination in Northern Ireland', *Journal of Biosocial Science*, 17, 1985.

Doherty, P., 'Agape to Zoroastrian: religious denomination in Northern Ireland 1961 to 1991', *Irish Geography*, 26(1), 1993.

Shuttleworth, I., 'Population change in Northern Ireland, 1981–1991: preliminary results of the 1991 Census of Population', *Irish Geography*, 25(1), 1992.

POSTSCRIPT

Chapter 23

FRAMEWORKS AND THE FUTURE
Arthur Aughey and Duncan Morrow

In the summer of 1993, British government priorities in Northern Ireland shifted from the commitment to promote political talks between the main constitutional parties in Northern Ireland. Talks had been held under the Secretary of State for Northern Ireland, Peter Brooke, in the spring of 1991 and resumed under his successor, Sir Patrick Mayhew, in 1992 but they came to an inconclusive stalemate in November of that year. The purpose of those talks had been consistent with the long-stated political objective of both British and Irish governments to marginalize terrorists and their political advocates, particularly the Irish Republican Army (IRA) and its political wing, Sinn Féin. Political agreement between constitutional groups, it was thought, would provide for the conditions of a lasting peace. The last major initiative in Northern Ireland, the Anglo-Irish Agreement of 1985, was based explicitly on this policy.

In the summer of 1993 the policy emphasis was changed. Nationalists in Northern Ireland were increasingly signalling that an IRA ceasefire might be achievable. The common purpose of both governments became the search for an agreement which would enable the incorporation of those hitherto excluded because of their violence or their justification of violence. The achievement of an end to political violence was now understood to be the necessary condition for broader political agreement. The 'talks process' was set aside as the 'peace process' was given priority. The Irish government, with traditional links to constitutional Nationalism in Northern Ireland, broadly embraced this change of emphasis. The British government, on the other hand, initially appeared more cautious.

Following considerable political turmoil in the autumn of 1993, the Prime Minister of the United Kingdom, John Major, and the Taoiseach of the Republic of Ireland, Albert Reynolds, issued the text of a common document on 15 December 1993 at 10 Downing Street which, they hoped, might establish the principles for a political settlement in Northern Ireland.

The precise sequence of events which led up to the Downing Street Declaration, as the joint declaration was immediately called, remains uncertain. However, any understanding has to start not in 1993 nor even in 1992 but as far back as 1988.

The origins of the Downing Street Declaration

In 1988 the leader of the SDLP, John Hume, began a well-publicized exchange with Gerry Adams of Sinn Féin about the way Irish Nationalists might best expand the opportunities provided by the Anglo-Irish Agreement of 1985. Hume argued that the British government was not the main obstacle to Irish unity, as republican ideology had always insisted. Indeed, Hume believed that the British government was 'neutral' on the Union. Furthermore, Hume maintained that IRA violence itself was delaying the process by which Irish unity could be achieved by forcing the British to defend themselves against giving in to terrorism and deepening Unionist hostility to anything which seemed to move Northern Ireland towards Irish unity. It was possible that if Republicans were only willing to end their campaign of violence, the British government might shift from neutrality to being a 'persuader' for an 'agreed Ireland'.

In 1988 Sinn Féin/IRA could not accept Hume's analysis of the situation and the role he envisaged for the British government. The talks broke down without positive conclusion. For the IRA Britain was *the* problem and not part of any solution as Hume believed they might become. However, while the campaign of violence continued unabated there was evidence of a rethink within the republican movement.

In early 1992, Catholic clergy with connections to the Republican movement in west Belfast contacted Hume about developing what they presumed to be a new and hopeful disposition within the IRA towards an ending of violence. In April 1993 it was revealed that Hume had resumed his dialogue with Adams. This was the (public) beginning of what became known as the Hume–Adams dialogue, an initiative the purpose and substance of which dominated political debate in Ireland, North and South, throughout that year. Both men issued a number of joint statements. The first of these statements spoke of an acceptance by the two leaders that 'the Irish people as a whole have a right to national self-determination'. This traditional republican demand was softened somewhat by the qualification that 'the exercise of self-determination is a matter for agreement between the people of Ireland' and that 'a new agreement is only achievable and viable if it can earn and enjoy the allegiance of the different traditions on this island'. The information which the Irish government had on the Hume–Adams discussions encouraged Albert Reynolds, the Prime Minister, to submit a set of principles (the first draft having been made as early as spring 1992) to the British government. He did this in June 1993.

In September 1993, Hume and Adams announced that they had come to agreement on the conditions which could end IRA violence. Hume submitted (or verbally conveyed) a report of that agreement to the Irish government. The so-called 'Hume–Adams' document has not yet been published. At the time it caused considerable confusion and consternation among officials in London, Belfast and Dublin. A renewed upsurge in terrorist activity in the last week of October left 26 people dead and gave a further urgency to events. At a meeting in the margins of a European Community summit in Brussels on 29 October, John Major and Albert Reynolds, while refusing to adopt or endorse the 'Hume–Adams' proposals, committed themselves 'to work together in their own terms on a framework for peace, stability and reconciliation consistent with their international obligations and their wider responsibilities to both communities'. The Brussels statement complemented the six principles previously enunciated by the Irish Foreign Minister, Dick Spring. These were:

1   that the people of Ireland, North and South, should determine their own future without violence or coercion;
2   that determination would come about in the construction of new structures of government in Northern Ireland and in new relationships between North and South and between the two islands. It might ideally lead to Irish unity;
3   that there must be majority consent to a change in Northern Ireland's constitutional status (originally Spring specified *Unionist* consent);
4   that the majority have the right to refuse that consent;
5   that the Irish constitution should ultimately acknowledge that unity could only be by consent (implying amendment of Articles 2 and 3 of the Irish constitution which claim sovereignty over Northern Ireland);
6   that there would be a place at the negotiating table for 'the men of violence' only when they renounced violence.

By early December there were rumours that agreement might not be reached at all, that neither the Irish nor British government could accept the other's formula. At least 18 drafts were passed between officials and ministers of the two governments before both Prime Ministers were certain that they had a declaration which could satisfy their respective needs.

The Downing Street Declaration

By 15 December 1993 both governments felt ready to announce a joint declaration of principles. The Downing Street Declaration consists of 12 paragraphs containing six main points:

1   The British government will uphold the 'democratic wish of a greater number of the people of Northern Ireland on the issue of whether they prefer to support the Union or a sovereign united Ireland'.
2   The British government agrees that 'it is for the people of the island of Ireland alone, by agreement between the two parts respectively, to exercise their right of self-determination on the basis of consent, freely and concurrently given, North and South, to bring about a united Ireland, if that is their wish'; and the Irish government accepts that 'the democratic right of self-determination by the people of Ireland as a whole must be exercised with, and subject to the agreement and consent of a majority of the people of Northern Ireland'.
3   The British government declares that it has no selfish strategic or economic interest in Northern Ireland.

4   The role of the British government will be to 'encourage, facilitate and enable the achievement' of agreement between 'both traditions in Ireland'.

5   The Irish government agrees that 'in the event of an overall settlement' and 'as part of a balanced constitutional accommodation' it will 'put forward and support proposals for change in the Irish Constitution which would fully reflect the principle of consent in Northern Ireland' (i.e. amend Articles 2 and 3).

6   If those groups now supporting violence were to renounce it, they would be free 'to join in dialogue in due course between the governments and the political parties on the way ahead' after they had shown that they intended to 'abide by the democratic process'.

Reception of the Joint Declaration

All the major parties in the Irish Republic and Great Britain generally welcomed the Declaration. In Northern Ireland, both the SDLP and Alliance Party greeted the Declaration as establishing the principles for political progress. The Ulster Unionist Party neither welcomed nor rejected the Declaration explicitly, believing that it contained some positive points, especially on the principle of consent, but expressing concern about the implications of some of the 'green' language. There were some grounds for optimism on the part of both governments that there existed reasonable cross-community acquiescence in, if not support for, the principles of the Declaration. Of the constitutional parties, only the Democratic Unionist Party rejected the Declaration outright. Ian Paisley publicly denounced it as 'appeasement' of the IRA and a 'sell-out' of the Union.

The official position of Sinn Féin was that it would consult widely within the republican movement about acceptance or rejection of the principles. The Downing Street Declaration did not provide enough, however, to make the IRA stop its campaign immediately. Sinn Féin's own demands were much greater than the promises made in the Declaration. They continued to object to what they maintained was a Unionist 'veto' over progress towards Irish unity. Furthermore, they insisted that the British government should persuade Unionists to accept a united Ireland and set some timeframe within which Irish unity would come about.

While Sinn Féin did not have to accept the Declaration (and they have not), the IRA had to end violence before Sinn Féin could enter full discussions about the future of Northern Ireland. Republicans were thus faced with a real choice of continuing the 'armed struggle' and isolation or of ending violence and finding a place in talks. Despite an apparent rejection of the Declaration at Letterkenny in July 1993, the IRA declared a 'complete cessation of military activities' on 31 August 1994. If this was neither a renunciation of violence nor a declaration of a permanent end to terror, it nevertheless transformed the political landscape of Northern Ireland. Loyalist paramilitaries announced their own ceasefire in October. The way was now clear for a further British–Irish initiative.

The Framework Documents

On 22 February 1995 the two governments published their new proposals under the title of *Frameworks for the Future*. These 'Framework Documents', as they were widely known, were the result of more than two years of discussion between officials and ministers of the two governments. As their name suggests, the Framework Documents were formulated as a way of setting the guidelines for discussion about the future of Northern Ireland. Their origin lay in the failure to resolve key difficulties which had emerged during the Brooke and Mayhew talks of 1991–92, especially on relationships between Northern Ireland and the Republic of Ireland. However, ideas and suggestions which were put forward in those negotiations resurfaced in a variety of forms. In particular, the so-called three-stranded approach of the talks – institutional linkage between the internal administration of Northern Ireland, North–South arrangements and a British–Irish Agreement – is the pattern which is followed faithfully in the Frameworks. The precise status of the documents themselves remained unclear. The Irish position appeared to be that the Frameworks represented an effective blueprint which could be submitted to the people ultimately over the heads of the political parties. The British position appeared to be that the documents would give focus and direction to discussion between the parties but would be capable of real amendment and change.

The Frameworks consist of two distinct but related documents. The first, *A Framework for Accountable Government in Northern Ireland*, was described by John Major at the launch in Belfast as the 'British government's ideas – based on discussions with Northern Ireland parties – as to how local people could take far more control over the way Northern Ireland is governed, on a fair and equitable basis'. The second, *A New Framework for Agreement*, was, according to Major, 'a shared understanding – prepared at the request of Northern Ireland parties – between the British and Irish governments, as to how relations in the island of Ireland, and between these islands, might be based on co-operation and agreement to the mutual advantage of all.' It is stressed in the proposals that overall agreement on all issues should be reached by negotiation and that any outcome should be acceptable to the people. The British government repeated its undertaking to submit any outcome of talks to a referendum in Northern Ireland. They further stressed that while the proposals were not a 'blueprint' to be imposed they were 'strongly commended' by the two governments, a formula which seemed designed to keep the precise meaning of the proposals unclear.

The proposals for the internal government of Northern Ireland suggest an Assembly of 90 members to oversee the work of the Northern Ireland Departments. It would operate on a committee system proportionate to the strengths of the parties in the Assembly. The Chair of a Committee would be the head of his or her relevant Department. There would also be a Panel, composed of three directly-elected members, to which would be referred all contentious business. This Panel would act on the basis of unanimity. In other words, each of the largest parties – at present the UUP, DUP and SDLP – would have an effective veto on local legislation.

The second document is concerned with a range of matters: constitutional issues, North/South institutions, East/West structures and the protection of rights. This document sets out in institutional form the principles of the Downing Street Declaration. Both governments propose that any agreement must involve 'a balanced accommodation of the differing views of the two main traditions on the constitutional issues in relation to the special position of Northern Ireland'. The British government intends to modify the Government of Ireland Act of 1920, the basis of its sovereignty in Northern Ireland, while the Irish government would propose changes to Articles 2 and 3 which are the territorial claim to Northern Ireland. A North/South body is envisaged which would involve the Heads of Department from the Northern Assembly and their counterparts in the Irish government. This North/South body would have executive, harmonizing and consultative functions. These functions could be extended without limit on the basis of an 'agreed dynamic'.

Appropriate executive functions for the North/South body are considered to be, for instance, those involving 'a natural or physical all-Ireland framework' and European programmes and initiatives. Those functions considered appropriate for harmonization range from agriculture and economic policy to health and education. All decisions in the North/South body would be by 'agreement between the two sides'. A Parliamentary Forum of elected representatives from Belfast and Dublin is also envisaged.

Proposals for the so-called 'East/West' structures repeat the main provisions of the existing Anglo-Irish Agreement, only this time provision is made for an association of the Northern Ireland Assembly in its deliberations. Arrangements are also proposed for the protection of civil, political, social and cultural rights in both parts of the island of Ireland. If the Northern Assembly were to collapse or fail to perform its functions, direct rule would be re-introduced. However, co-operation already developed in the North/South body would be maintained.

Reaction to the Framework Documents

The principle which the British and Irish governments used to justify the Framework Documents was the principle which has been used to justify every initiative since the beginning of the Troubles: 'balance'. The stated intention of the Documents is 'a balanced accommodation of the differing positions of the two main traditions'. This is sometimes known as trying to 'square the circle' (to use a term of Dick Spring's). The first position to be squared is that Northern Ireland is a part of the United Kingdom because that is the wish of a majority of its citizens and that it ought to remain so for as long as that majority desires it. The second position to be squared is that Northern Ireland should move as rapidly as possible from its present UK status towards belonging to a sovereign united Ireland. Both of these positions have been advanced or defended not only by political but also by military means. In the circumstances of the last few years, as we noted at the beginning of this chapter, it has been the concern to ensure the end of paramilitary operations which has helped to drive the policy of the two governments. In particular, it has been the concern to ensure the end of IRA violence which has influenced the politics of the Framework Documents. There have been four broad responses to these developments in Northern Ireland.

Firstly, most Unionist politicians have interpreted the Frameworks as an appeasement of republican terrorism. Unionist politicians have argued that the Northern Ireland Assembly would be powerless and, possibly worse than powerless, unworkable. It would be a convenient fiction to allow power to be transferred from Westminster to the 'dynamic' North/South institutions. Since the form of the Anglo-Irish Agreement remains essentially intact, Unionists have argued that the Framework Documents involve even greater Dublin interference and influence within Northern Ireland. Both governments deny that the documents entail joint authority. Unionists do not believe them.

Many Nationalist politicians regard the Documents as unsatisfactory but as a meaningful basis for negotiation. While Unionists deplore what is in the Frameworks, Nationalists have welcomed both the language of and the 'dynamic' within the proposals. The Frameworks indicate the intention of the British and Irish governments to 'intensify' their co-operation to achieve the objective of overcoming the 'legacy of division' in Ireland, which can be read as holding out the possibility of a united Ireland in the longer term.

Thirdly, some traditional republicans believe that the Framework Documents represent a betrayal of the Irish people. The 'peace process' is a surrender process by which Ireland's struggle for the ideals of freedom and justice have been abandoned by the present leadership of Sinn Féin and the IRA.

The fourth response, represented perhaps by the Alliance Party and some people in both Nationalist and Unionist camps, has been more ambiguous. Broadly, they accept that special arrangements and phrases and the use of 'green' language is necessary to wean republicans away from violence. It is in everyone's interest that peace be maintained. Some people holding this position emphasize that Northern Ireland should remain part of the United Kingdom but they also accept North/South institutions as a way of recognizing an Irish dimension. They would still be wary of a process of harmonization taking place irrespective of the consent of the majority in Northern Ireland or irrespective of the practicality of such harmonization. In negotiations they would expect full acceptance by Nationalists and the Irish government of the legitimacy of Northern Ireland's place within the United Kingdom on the basis of consent. Those who hold this view and yet are sympathetic to the idea of ultimate Irish unity want to avoid any possibility of overall Unionist control in Northern Ireland. They emphasize that 'parity of esteem' has to be a reality and not merely an aspiration and desire some island-wide focus in public life.

Between civil war and stability

Predicting the future is always a hazardous occupation in politics. Few observers of Northern Ireland politics could have predicted the events of 1993 to 1995. What is clear is that the politics of Northern Ireland have entered a different phase after

1994. The fact of the ceasefires created a substantial break in the rhythm of violence which was the predominant marker of Northern Irish political life for 25 years and we can safely assert that Northern Ireland politics will not return to the *status quo ante*.

Nonetheless, at the time of writing (September 1995), Northern Ireland remains on an uncompleted journey between perpetual civil unrest and political stability. There are many in Northern Ireland who believe that political violence is over for good. There are others who remain unconvinced, believing that this is just a temporary respite. In the context of such uncertainty, there are simply too many variables to try to predict with authority any single outcome.

A number of factors do appear to be significant. Firstly, the ceasefires of autumn 1994 proved to be widely popular in and of themselves. The absence of any final political destination did not seem to distract from the general relief at the ending of fear from political violence. War weariness and widespread alienation from active involvement in political life, at the very least, seem to have taken their toll. Any attempt to return to the armed struggle, from whichever quarter, will have to take this popularity into account.

Secondly, the Downing Street Declaration and the subsequent Framework Documents were greeted with virtually universal approval outside Northern Ireland. No party of significance in either Great Britain or the Republic of Ireland opposed the documents. The historic importance of an agreement on Northern Ireland which encompasses every British and Irish party from the British Conservatives to Fianna Fáil should not be underestimated. This fact makes the task of any party or group in Northern Ireland which opposes the broad thrust of the documents very difficult. This seems to suggest that the three-stranded policy formulated in 1991 and the central place accorded by both London and Dublin to the Anglo-Irish dimension of Northern Irish affairs are likely to be long-term features of all future negotiations. The visit of Prince Charles to Dublin in late May 1995 and the attendance of Sinn Féin representatives at an Irish commemoration of those who fought in the British Army during World War Two further symbolized changing approaches.

Thirdly, the active interest of the US President Clinton in Northern Irish affairs confirmed that Northern Ireland had acquired a foreign policy dimension of potential significance for both Irish and British governments and thus for all internal participants. At crucial moments during 1994 and 1995 it appeared as if the US government was allying itself closely with the position of the Irish government, especially in relation to the access to all major political figures in Washington granted to Gerry Adams. At other times, US pressure on paramilitaries, for example on the decommissioning of weapons, was particularly significant. In adopting such an active posture, the United States made clear that it had a number of economic and political levers by which to influence the Northern Irish political landscape in important ways.

Shifts in paramilitary tactics and the cementing of ties between London and Dublin certainly account for much of the political change. Nevertheless, the public rhetoric of Unionism and Nationalism of various hues remained, and remains, remarkably similar to the rhetoric of pre-ceasefire politics. The Framework

Documents remained highly contentious, especially for Unionists, but also for many republicans. Whether the Documents represented a 'one-way street' to a united Ireland, albeit delayed over 20 years, or underpins partition for the foreseeable future still remains unresolved. In the space between hopes and fears which such unclarity leaves, there is considerable scope for continued dispute and unease. This ongoing unease appears to represent the most likely source of future antagonism.

In the absence of internal agreement, the most likely outcome in the short and medium term is a continuation of the broad lines of government which have prevailed since the Anglo-Irish Agreement of 1985. These are government under direct rule from Westminster, broad and regular consultation between the British government, in particular the Northern Ireland Office, and the Irish government on all areas of contention and controversy, and continuing efforts to transfer powers to a locally elected body. Since the Anglo-Irish Agreement, however, both governments have learnt to make policy as independent as possible of any necessity for the participation of elected Northern Irish representatives in the government of the province. Instead they have made government dependent on their own ability to carry out administrative decisions, whether through the Civil Service or through numerous non-governmental organizations, with all of the implications that such a strategy has for concepts of representative democracy. In the absence of political violence, however, that task seems likely to be considerably less inconvenient to the governments than it has been since 1972.

Further reading

Boyle, K. and Hadden, T, *Northern Ireland: The Choice*. London: Penguin, 1994.

Cadogan Group. *Lost Accord*. Belfast: Cadogan Group, 1995.

Dunlop, J. *A Precarious Belonging*. Belfast: Blackstaff Press, 1995.

Forum for Peace and Reconciliation. *Paths to a Political Settlement in Ireland*. Belfast: Blackstaff Press, 1995.

Frameworks for the Future, London and Belfast: HMSO, 1995.

Lennon, B. *Catholics after the Ceasefire*. Dublin: Columba Press, 1995.

O'Leary, B. and McGarry, J, *Understanding Northern Ireland*. Oxford: Blackwell, 1995.

Ryan, M, *War and Peace in Ireland*. London: Pluto Press, 1994.

Appendix 1

CHRONOLOGY OF EVENTS 1920–95

1920: Passage of the Government of Ireland Act provides for devolved Parliaments to be established in Dublin and Belfast.

1921: First meeting of the Northern Ireland Parliament.

1922: Signing of the Anglo-Irish Treaty between the governments of the United Kingdom and the Irish Free State. Proportional Representation is abolished for local elections in Northern Ireland.

1925: Governments in London, Belfast and Dublin agree that the boundary between the six counties of Northern Ireland and the 26 counties of the Free State should remain unchanged.

1929: Proportional Representation is abolished for elections to Stormont Parliament.

1932: Opening of the new Northern Ireland Parliament buildings at Stormont.

1935: Sectarian riots take place in Belfast.

1937: A new Constitution of the Irish Free State. Articles 2 and 3 of that Constitution claim sovereignty over the entire territory of the island of Ireland.

1939: Outbreak of the Second World War. Northern Ireland is committed to the war effort. The Irish Free State stays neutral.

1941: German bombing raids on Belfast.

1945: End of Second World War.

1949: The Irish Free State becomes a Republic. The British government passes the Ireland Act which proposes that Northern Ireland will remain a part of the UK until its Parliament votes otherwise.

1956: Beginning of the IRA's 'border campaign'.

1957: Publication of the report *An Economic Survey of Northern Ireland* which attempts to identify the major developmental problems of the region.

1962: End of the IRA's border campaign. Fiftieth anniversary of the signing of the Ulster Covenant.

1963: Terence O'Neill becomes Prime Minister of Northern Ireland.

1964: Publication of the Hall Report on the economy advises the attraction of outside industry to Northern Ireland.

1965: Seán Lemass makes the first official visit to Belfast by a Prime Minister of the Republic of Ireland. Publication of the Wilson Plan for economic regeneration.

1966: Fiftieth anniversary of the Battle of the Somme and of the 1916 Easter Rising.

1967: Founding of the Northern Ireland Civil Rights Association.

1968: Holding of the first civil rights marches in Northern Ireland. Formation of the People's Democracy. Unionist government introduces a programme of reforms to meet Catholic grievances on housing and voting.

1969: O'Neill resigns as Prime Minister of Northern Ireland and is replaced by James Chichester-Clark. The Unionist government requests the support of the army to maintain law and order following riots in Derry and Belfast.

1970: Formation of the Alliance Party and the Social Democratic and Labour Party. The Reverend Ian Paisley is elected to Westminster. Principles of the Macrory Report for the reform of local government are accepted. First policeman dies in the Troubles.

1971: Chichester-Clark resigns and is replaced by Brian Faulkner. SDLP withdraw from Stormont. Formation of the Democratic Unionist Party. First soldier dies in the Troubles.

1972: Direct rule is introduced. William Whitelaw becomes the first Secretary of State for Northern Ireland. Publication of a British government Green Paper on the future of Northern Ireland.

1973: UK and the Republic of Ireland join the European Community. Publication of the British government's White Paper on the future of Northern Ireland. Agreement on a 'power-sharing' Executive. Francis Pym becomes Secretary of State. Sunningdale Conference agrees a Council of Ireland to express the 'Irish dimension'. Proportional Representation reintroduced for district council elections.

1974: Election of a Labour government in the UK. Merlyn Rees becomes Secretary of State. In the Westminster elections of February anti-Sunningdale Unionists (United Ulster Unionist Council) win 11 of 12 seats. Ulster Workers' Council 'strike' leads to the fall of the power-sharing Executive. Direct rule resumes. Passing of the Prevention of Terrorism Act.

1975: IRA 'truce' is called and runs from January to September. The Northern

Ireland Convention meets to discuss constitutional matters. In the national referendum on EEC membership a majority of Northern Ireland voters choose to remain within the Community.

1976: Convention is dissolved without agreement. Founding of the Peace People. Roy Mason becomes Secretary of State. Fair Employment Agency is established.

1977: Another Loyalist 'strike' fails to achieve its objectives. The strike leads to a break-up of the UUUC. Unionist politics becomes increasingly a two-horse-race between Ulster Unionists and Democratic Unionists.

1978: House of Commons votes to increase the number of Northern Ireland seats from 12 to 17.

1979: Election of a Conservative government in the UK. Humphrey Atkins becomes Secretary of State. In the first European Parliament elections, Ian Paisley of the DUP, John Hume of the SDLP and John Taylor of the UUP take the three Northern Ireland seats. The IRA murder Lord Mountbatten. Atkins proposes conference on the future of Northern Ireland to a lukewarm response.

1980: Failure of the Atkins conference. First Anglo-Irish summit is held in Dublin. An H-Block hunger strike by republican prisoners, called in October, ends in December.

1981: Beginning of a new H-Block hunger strike by republicans in March. Hunger-striker Bobby Sands wins the Fermanagh/South Tyrone by-election. James Prior becomes Secretary of State. Hunger strike is abandoned in October after the death of 10 republicans including Bobby Sands. Establishment of the Anglo-Irish Intergovernmental Council.

1982: Prior introduces proposals for 'rolling devolution'. Elections are held for the new Northern Ireland Assembly. SDLP refuses to take up its seats.

1983: Establishment by the Irish government of the New Ireland Forum. The Conservative Party wins the general election in the UK. Gerry Adams of Sinn Féin wins the seat of West Belfast.

1984: Publication of the Report of the New Ireland Forum. It proposes options of a united Ireland, a federal Ireland or British–Irish joint authority over Northern Ireland. In the second European Parliament elections the three sitting MEPs are returned. Douglas Hurd becomes Secretary of State. The IRA bomb the Conservative Party conference in Brighton. British government rejects the Forum options.

1985: In the local council elections Sinn Féin wins 11.8% of the vote. Tom King becomes Secretary of State. The Anglo-Irish Agreement is signed. Beginning of Unionist campaign of protest. The 15 Unionist MPs resign their seats to force a test of public opinion in Northern Ireland on the Agreement.

1986: In the Westminster by-elections Unionists increase their overall vote but lose the seat of Newry and Armagh to the SDLP. On 3 March there is a Unionist

'Day of Action' against the Agreement. Unionist-controlled councils obstruct normal business in protest at the Agreement. The Northern Ireland Assembly is dissolved.

1987: A Unionist-sponsored petition against the Agreement receives 400,000 signatures. The Conservative Party wins the UK general election. Beginning of 'talks about talks' for an alternative to the Agreement between Unionist parties and Secretary of State. IRA murder 11 people at the Enniskillen Remembrance Day service.

1988: SDLP begins talks with Sinn Féin. Three IRA members are shot dead in Gibraltar. Irish Supreme Court rules that Articles 2 and 3 of the Republic's Constitution entail a 'constitutional imperative' to reunify the island. A broadcasting ban on direct statements by paramilitary groups is imposed by the British government.

1989: British and Irish governments publish a review of the workings of the Agreement. European Parliament elections are held. Hume and Paisley are elected. Jim Nicholson replaces John Taylor for the UUP. Peter Brooke becomes Secretary of State. Conservative Party conference votes to organize in Northern Ireland. Brooke suggests that the British government might talk to Sinn Féin if it renounced violence.

1990: A new and stronger Fair Employment Act is enacted. First meeting of the British–Irish Interparliamentary Body takes place. Unionists refuse to take up their seats. Brooke attempts and fails to get agreement on arrangements for talks about alternatives to the Agreement. Mary Robinson is elected President of the Irish Republic. The Conservative Party replaces Mrs Thatcher as leader. John Major becomes Prime Minister.

1991: Brooke announces agreement on a formula for 'three-stranded' talks on the future of Northern Ireland. Anglo-Irish Conference is suspended to allow the talks to take place. Talks begin on 17 June and end on 3 July.

1992: Albert Reynolds becomes Prime Minister in the Irish Republic. The Conservative Party wins the UK general election. Gerry Adams loses the West Belfast seat. Sir Patrick Mayhew becomes Secretary of State. There is a three-month suspension of the Anglo-Irish Conference. A new round of political talks takes place from April to November. Progress is made on structures for devolution. After the ending of these talks the British government begins bilateral discussions with the Northern Ireland parties. Mayhew repeats Brooke's statement that Sinn Féin could be included in talks if IRA violence is ended.

1993: Hume and Adams resume their discussions. Irish Foreign Minister Dick Spring proposes a joint framework document with the British government to be put to the electorate over the heads of the Northern Ireland parties. Hume and Adams reach agreement on principles and forward a document to the Irish government. Intensified discussions take place between the British and Irish governments to seek a formula for ending violence. It is revealed that

226

representatives of the British government have been conducting secret discussions with Sinn Féin. The Downing Street Declaration is published.

1994: Sinn Féin demands 'clarification' of the Downing Street Declaration. The British government refuses and then concedes. First meeting of the Northern Ireland Select Committee. European Parliament elections return the three sitting MEPs. First the IRA and then the Loyalist paramilitaries announce ceasefires. Sinn Féin demands inclusion in talks on the basis of their 'democratic mandate'. The British government requires assurance on a permanent end to violence. The Forum for Peace and Reconciliation is established in Dublin.

1995: The British and Irish governments launch the *Frameworks for the Future*. A government minister talks officially to a Sinn Féin delegation. Gerry Adams meets Sir Patrick Mayhew in Washington. Robert McCartney QC wins the North Down by-election as a UK Unionist. Riots at Orange marches during summer. Stalemate over the issue of the decommissioning of paramilitary weapons. David Trimble elected leader of the UUP.

Appendix 2

ABBREVIATIONS

ACAS	Advisory Conciliation and Arbitration Service
ACE	Action for Community Employment
ACNI	Arts Council of Northern Ireland
AIA	Anglo-Irish Agreement
AIIGC	Anglo-Irish Intergovernmental Council
ANC	African National Congress
AOH	Ancient Order of Hibernians
APNI	Alliance Party of Northern Ireland
BBC	British Broadcasting Corporation
CAJ	Committee on the Administration of Justice
CAP	Common Agricultural Policy
CBI	Confederation of British Industry
CCDC	Central Citizens' Defence Committee
CCRU	Central Community Relations Unit
CEC	Campaign for Equal Citizenship
CLMC	Combined Loyalist Military Command
CLR	Campaign for Labour Representation
CRC	Community Relations Council
CSF	Community Support Framework
CTG	Cultural Traditions Group
DANI	Department of Agriculture for Northern Ireland
DCAC	Derry Citizens' Action Committee
DED	Department of Economic Development
DENI	Department of Education for Northern Ireland
DFP	Department of Finance and Personnel
DL	Democratic Left
DOE	Department of the Environment
DPP	Director of Public Prosecutions
DUP	Democratic Unionist Party
EAGGF	European Agricultural Guarantee and Guidance Fund
EC	European Community
ECHR	European Convention on Human Rights
EDG	European Democratic Group

EEC	European Economic Community
ELDR	European Liberal, Democratic and Reformist
EOCNI	Equal Opportunities Commission for Northern Ireland
EP	European Parliament
EPA	Emergency Provisions Act
EPP	European Peoples' Party
ERDF	European Regional Development Fund
ESF	European Social Fund
EU	European Union
FEA	Fair Employment Agency
FEC	Fair Employment Commission
FF	Fianna Fáil
FG	Fine Gael
GAA	Gaelic Athletic Association
GDP	Gross Domestic Product
GNP	Gross National Product
IBA	Independent Broadcasting Authority
ICTU	Irish Congress of Trade Unions
IDB	Industrial Development Board
IFI	International Fund for Ireland
IIP	Irish Independence Party
INLA	Irish National Liberation Army
IPLO	Irish People's Liberation Organization
IRA	Irish Republican Army
IRSP	Irish Republican Socialist Party
ITGWU	Irish Transport and General Workers' Union
ITN	Independent Television News
ITV	Independent Television
LEDU	Local Enterprise Development Unit
LGD	Local government district
LNI	Labour in Northern Ireland
LOL	Loyal Orange Lodge
MEP	Member of the European Parliament
MP	Member of Parliament
NGO	Non-governmental organization
NI	Northern Ireland
NIALRA	Northern Ireland Abortion Law Reform Association
NICE	Northern Ireland Centre in Europe
NICRA	Northern Ireland Civil Rights Association
NICS	Northern Ireland Civil Service
NICVA	Northern Ireland Council for Voluntary Action
NIF	New Ireland Forum
NIHE	Northern Ireland Housing Executive
NILP	Northern Ireland Labour Party
NIO	Northern Ireland Office
NORAID	Irish Northern Aid Committee

NUPRG	New Ulster Political Research Group
OIRA	Official Irish Republican Army
PAF	Protestant Action Force
PANI	Police Authority for Northern Ireland
PD	People's Democracy
PIRA	Provisional Irish Republican Army
PLO	Palestine Liberation Organization
PR	Proportional Representation
PSF	Provisional Sinn Féin
PTA	Prevention of Terrorism Act
PUP	Progressive Unionist Party
RHC	Red Hand Commando
RIC	Royal Irish Constabulary
RIR	Royal Irish Regiment
RSF	Republican Sinn Féin
RTE	Radio Telefís Éireann
RUC	Royal Ulster Constabulary
SACHR	Standing Advisory Committee on Human Rights
SDLP	Social Democratic and Labour Party
SF	Sinn Féin
SPA	Special Powers Act
STV	Single Transferable Vote
TD	Teachta Dála (Member of the Dáil)
TUC	Trades Union Congress
UDA	Ulster Defence Association
UDP	Ulster Democratic Party
UDR	Ulster Defence Regiment
UFF	Ulster Freedom Fighters
UK	United Kingdom
UKREP	United Kingdom Permanent Representation (at EU)
UN	United Nations
UPNI	Unionist Party of Northern Ireland
UTV	Ulster Television
US	United States (of America)
UUC	Ulster Unionist Council
UUP	Ulster Unionist Party
UUUC	United Ulster Unionist Council
UVF	Ulster Volunteer Force
UWC	Ulster Workers' Council
VUPP	Vanguard Unionist Progressive Party
WP	Workers' Party
YTP	Youth Training Programme

BIBLIOGRAPHY

Alexander, Y. and O'Day, A. (eds), *Terrorism in Ireland*. London: Croom Helm, 1984.

Arthur, P., *Government and Politics of Northern Ireland*. Harlow: Longman, 1987.

Arthur, P., 'The media and politics in Northern Ireland', in J. Seaton and B. Pimlott, (eds), *The Media in British Politics*. Aldershot: Gower, 1987.

Arthur, P., 'Three years of the Anglo-Irish Agreement', *Irish Political Studies*, 1990.

Arthur, P., 'The Anglo-Irish Joint Declaration: towards a lasting peace', *Government and Opposition* 29(2), Spring 1994.

Arthur, P., *Government and Politics of Northern Ireland*. London: Longman, 1994.

Arthur, P. and Jeffery, K., *Northern Ireland since 1968*. Oxford: Blackwell, 1988.

Arts Council of Northern Ireland, *To the Millenium. A Draft Strategy for the Arts in Northern Ireland*. Belfast, 1994.

Aughey, A., *Under Siege: Ulster Unionism and the Anglo-Irish Agreement*. Belfast: Blackstaff Press, 1989.

Aughey, A., Hainsworth, P. and Trimble, M. J., *Northern Ireland in the European Community: An Economic and Political Analysis*. Belfast: Policy Research Institute, 1989.

Bairner, A., 'The battlefield of ideas: the legitimation of political violence in Northern Ireland', *European Journal of Political Research*, 14, 1986.

Bairner, A., 'The end of pitched battles? The peace process and sport in Northern Ireland', *Causeway*. 1(3), Summer, 1994.

Bardon, J., *A History of Ulster*. Belfast: Blackstaff Press, 1992.

Bell, G., *The Protestants of Ulster*. London: Pluto Press, 1976.

Bell, P., 'Direct rule in Northern Ireland', in R. Rose (ed.), *Ministers and Ministries*. Oxford: Clarendon Press, 1987.

Bew, P., *Ideology and the Irish Question 1912–16*. Oxford: Oxford University Press, 1994.

Bew, P. and Gillespie, G., *Northern Ireland: A Chronology of the Troubles 1968–1993*. Dublin: Gill and Macmillan, 1993.

Bew, P. and Patterson, H., *The British State and the Ulster Crisis*. London: Verso, 1985.

Bew, P., Gibbon, P. and Patterson, H., *1921–94 Northern Ireland, Political Forces and Social Classes*. London: Serif, 1994.

Birrell, D. and Murie, A., *Policy and Government in Northern Ireland: Lessons of Devolution*. Dublin: Gill and Macmillan, 1980.

Bishop, P. and Mailie, E., *The Provisional IRA*. London: Corgi, 1988.

Bloomfield, K., *Stormont in Crisis*. Belfast: Blackstaff Press, 1994.

Boyce, D.G., *Nationalism in Ireland*. London: Routledge, 1991.

Boyd, J. and Black, H., 'Industrial relations', in R.I.D. Harris, C. Jefferson and J.E. Spencer (eds), *The Northern Ireland Economy; A Comparative Study in the Economic Development of a Peripheral Region*. London: Longman, 1990.

Boyd, R., *Christianity in Ireland*. Geneva: World Council of Churches, 1987.

Boyle, K. and Hadden, T., *Northern Ireland: The Choice*. London: Penguin, 1994.

Bracefield, H., Brett, D. and Henderson, L., 'The arts in Northern Ireland', *Studies*, 80(318), Summer 1991.

Brewer, J.D., 'The public and the police', in P. Stringer and G. Robinson (eds), *Social Attitudes in Northern Ireland. 2, 1991–1992*. Belfast: Blackstaff Press, 1992.

Brewer, J.D. *et al.*, *The Police, Public Order and the State*. Basingstoke: Macmillan, 1988.

Brooke, P., *Ulster Presbyterianism*. Dublin: Gill and Macmillan, 1987.

Bruce, S., *God Save Ulster! The Religion and Politics of Paisleyism*. Oxford: Oxford University Press, 1986.

Bruce, S., *The Red Hand. Protestant Paramilitaries in Northern Ireland*. Oxford: Oxford University Press, 1992.

Bruce, S., *The Edge of the Union, The Ulster Loyalist Political Vision*. Oxford: Oxford University Press, 1994.

Buckland, P., *A History of Northern Ireland*. Dublin: Gill and Macmillan, 1981.

Butler, D., *The Trouble with Reporting Northern Ireland. The British State, the Broadcast Media and Nonfictional Representation of the Conflict*. Aldershot: Avebury, 1995.

Cadogan Group, *Lost Accord*. Belfast: Cadogan Group, 1995.

Centre for Research and Documentation (CRD) Belfast Community Forum on Policing, *Policing in a New Society*. Belfast: CRD/BCFP, 1995.

Committee on the Administration of Justice (CAJ)/Hainsworth, P., *The Stalker Affair: More Questions than Answers* (2nd edition). Belfast: CAJ Pamphlet No. 10, 1988.

Community Development Review Group, *Community Development in Northern Ireland: Perspectives for the Future*. Belfast: WEA, 1991.

Compton, P.A., 'The changing religious demography of Northern Ireland: some political implications', *Studies*, Winter 1989.

Compton, P.A., Coward, J. and Wilson-Davis, K., 'Family size and religious denomination in Northern Ireland', *Journal of Biosocial Science*, 17, 1985.

Connolly, M., *Politics and Policy-making in Northern Ireland*. Hemel Hempstead: Philip Allan, 1990.

Connolly, M., 'Learning from Northern Ireland: an acceptable model for regional and local government', *Public Policy and Administration*, 7(1), 1992.

Connolly, M. and Loughlin, S. (eds), *Public Policy in Northern Ireland: Adoption or Adaptation?* Belfast: Policy Research Institute, 1990.

Coopers and Lybrand, *Northern Ireland Economy Review and Prospects*. Belfast, 1994.

Coulter, C., 'The character of Unionism', *Irish Political Studies*, 9, 1994.

Cultural Traditions Group, *Giving Voices*. Cultural Traditions Group. Belfast, 1995.

Curtis, L., *Ireland: The Propaganda War, the British Media and the Battle for Hearts and Minds*. London: Pluto Press, 1984.

Daly, C., *The Price of Peace*. Belfast: Blackstaff Press, 1992.

Darby, J. and Williamson, A., *Violence and the Social Services in Northern Ireland*. London: Heinemann Educational, 1978.

Davies, C. and McLaughlin, E. (eds), *Women, Employment and Social Policy in Northern Ireland: A Problem Postponed?* Belfast: EOCNI, 1993.

Dickson, B., 'The legal response to the Troubles in Northern Ireland', in P.J. Roche and B. Barton, (eds), *The Northern Ireland Question: Myth and Reality*. Aldershot: Avebury, 1991.

Dickson, B. (ed.), *Civil Liberties in Northern Ireland* (The CAJ Handbook, 2nd edition). Belfast: Committee on the Administration of Justice, 1993.

Dickson, B., 'Criminal justice and emergency laws', in S. Dunn (ed.), *Facets of the Conflict in Northern Ireland*. Basingstoke: Macmillan, 1995.

Doherty, P., 'Agape to Zoroastrian: religious denomination in Northern Ireland 1961 to 1991', *Irish Geography*, 26(1), 1993.

Dunlop, J., *A Precarious Belonging*. Belfast: Blackstaff Press, 1995.

Elliott, S., 'Voting systems and party politics in Northern Ireland', in B. Hadfield (ed.), *Northern Ireland: Politics and the Constitution*. Buckingham and Philadelphia: Open University Press, 1992.

Equal Opportunities Commission, *A Matter of Small Importance? Catholic and Protestant Women in the Northern Ireland Labour Market*. Belfast: EOCNI, 1995.

Farrell, M., *Northern Ireland: The Orange State*. London: Pluto Press, 1976.

Forum for Peace and Reconciliation, *Paths to a Political Settlement in Ireland*. Belfast: Blackstaff Press, 1995.

Foster, J.W. (ed.), *The Idea of the Union*. Vancouver and Belfast: Belcouver Press, 1995.

Frameworks for the Future. London and Belfast: HMSO, 1995.

Greer, S., *Supergrasses: A Study in Anti-terrorist Law Enforcement in Northern Ireland*. Oxford: Clarendon Press, 1995.

Guelke, A., 'Policing in Northern Ireland', in B. Hadfield, (ed.), *Northern Ireland: Politics and the Constitution*. Buckingham and Philadelphia: Open University Press, 1992.

Hadfield, B., *The Constitution of Northern Ireland*. Belfast: SLS Publications, 1989.

Hadfield, B. (ed.), *Northern Ireland: Politics and the Constitution*. Buckingham and Philadelphia: Open University Press, 1992.

Hainsworth, P., 'The European Election in Northern Ireland', *Irish Political Studies*, 10, 1995.

Harris, R.I.D., Jefferson, C. and Spencer, J.E. *The Northern Ireland Economy; A Comparative Study in the Economic Development of a Peripheral Region*. London: Longman, 1990.

Hickey, J., *Religion and the Northern Ireland Problem*. Dublin: Gill and Macmillan, 1984.

Holland, J. and McDonald, H., *INLA Deadly Divisions*. Dublin: Torc, 1994.

Hughes, E. (ed.), *Culture and Politics in Northern Ireland*. Milton Keynes: Open University Press, 1990.

Johnson, D., 'The Northern Ireland economy, 1914–39', in L. Kennedy and P. Ollernshaw (eds), *An Economic History of Ulster 1820–1939*. Manchester: Manchester University Press, 1985.

Kennedy, D., *The Widening Gulf: Northern Attitudes to the Independent Irish State*. Belfast: Blackstaff Press, 1988.

Knox, C., 'Sinn Féin and local elections: the government's response in Northern Ireland', *Parliamentary Affairs*, 43(4), 1990.

Kramer, J. and Montgomery, P. (eds), *Women's Working Lives*. Belfast: EOCNI, 1993.

Lee, S. (ed.), *Freedom from Fear*. Belfast: Institute of Irish Studies, 1991.

Lennon, B., *Catholics after the Ceasefire*. Dublin: Columba Press, 1995.

Loughran, C., 'Armagh and feminist strategy: campaign around republican women prisoners in Armagh Jail', *Feminist Review*, 23, 1986.

Lyons, F.S.L., *Ireland since the Famine*. London: Fontana, 1973.

Mallie, E., *The Provisional IRA*. London: Corgi, 1988.

McAllister, I., *The Northern Ireland Social Democratic and Labour Party*. London: Macmillan, 1977.

McElroy, G., *The Catholic Church and the Northern Ireland Crisis*. Dublin: Gill and Macmillan, 1991.

McKay, M. and Irwin, G., *Cooperation in Local Government: A Study of Local District Councils and Power-sharing in Northern Ireland*. Belfast: Institute of Irish Studies, 1995.

McKeown, C., *The Price of Peace*. Belfast: Blackstaff Press, 1987.

Miller, D., *Don't Mention the War. Northern Ireland, Propaganda and the Media*. London: Pluto Press, 1994.

Morrow, D., *The Churches and Inter-community Relationships*. Coleraine: University of Ulster, 1991.

Moxon-Browne, E., 'The impact of the European Community', in B. Hadfield (ed.), *Northern Ireland: Politics and the Constitution*. Buckingham and Philadelphia: Open University Press, 1992.

Nelson, S., *Ulster's Uncertain Defenders. Protestant Paramilitary and Community Groups and the Northern Ireland Conflict*. Belfast: Appletree Press, 1984.

Northern Ireland Economic Council, *European Community Structural Funds in Northern Ireland Report 94*. Belfast: Northern Ireland Economic Development Office, 1992.

Northern Ireland Office (NIO), *Policing in the Community: Policing Structures in Northern Ireland*. Belfast: HMSO, 1994.

O'Connor, F., *In Search of a State: Catholics in Northern Ireland*. Belfast: Blackstaff Press, 1993.

O'Day, A. and Alexander, Y. (eds), *Ireland's Terrorist Trauma. Interdisciplinary Perspectives*. Hemel Hempstead: Harvester Wheatsheaf, 1989.

O'Dowd, L., Rolston, B. and Tomlinson, M., *Northern Ireland: Between Civil Rights and Civil War*. London: CSE Books, 1980.

O'Halloran, C., *Partition and the Limits of Irish Nationalism*. Dublin: Gill and Macmillan, 1987.

O'Leary, B. and McGarry, J., *Understanding Northern Ireland*. Oxford: Blackwell, 1995.

O'Leary, C. *et al.*, *The Northern Ireland Assembly 1982–86*. London: Hurst, 1986.

O'Malley, P., *Uncivil Wars*. Belfast: Blackstaff Press, 1983.

Owen, A.E., *The Anglo-Irish Agreement: The First Three Years*. Cardiff: University of Wales Press, 1995.

Patterson, H., *The Politics of Illusion: Republicanism and Socialism in Modern Ireland*. London: Hutchinson Radius, 1989.

Pollak, A. (ed.), *A Citizens' Inquiry: The Opsahl Report on Northern Ireland*. Dublin: Lilliput Press, 1993.

Purdie, B., *Politics in the Streets: The Origins of the Civil Rights Movement in Northern Ireland*. Belfast: Blackstaff Press, 1990.

Rhodes, R., *Beyond Westminster and Whitehall*. London: Unwin Hyman, 1988.

Rolston, B. (ed.), *The Media and Northern Ireland, Covering the Troubles*. Basingstoke: Macmillan, 1991.

Roulston, C., 'Women on the margin: the Women's Movement in Northern Ireland 1973–1988', *Science and Society*, 53, 1989.

Rowthorn, B., 'Northern Ireland: an economy in crisis', in P. Teague (ed.), *Beyond the Rhetoric: Politics, the Economy and Social Policy in Northern Ireland*. London: Lawrence and Wishart, 1987.

Rowthorn, B. and Wayne, N., *Northern Ireland: The Political Economy of Conflict*. Oxford: Polity Press, 1988.

Ryan, M., *War and Peace in Ireland*. London: Pluto Press, 1994.

Ryder, C., *The RUC: A Force Under Fire* (2nd edition). London: Mandarin, 1992.

Schlesinger, P., *Media, State and Nation. Political Violence and Collective Identities*. London: Sage, 1991.

Seldon, A., *UK Political Parties since 1945*. London: Philip Allan, 1990.

Shuttleworth, I., 'Population change in Northern Ireland, 1981–1991: preliminary results of the 1991 Census of Population', *Irish Geography*, 25(1), 1992.

Simpson, J. V. (ed.), *Northern Ireland and the European Community: An Economic Assessment*. Belfast: Commission of the European Communities, 1988.

Simpson, J. V., *Northern Ireland: A Region of the European Union*. European Commission in the United Kingdom. London: HMSO, 1994.

Skar, O. and Lydersen, B., *Northern Ireland: A Crucial Test for a Europe of Peaceful Regions?* Oslo: Norwegian Institute of International Affairs, 1993.

Smyth, C., 'The DUP as a politico-religious organization', *Irish Political Studies*, 1, 1986.

Smyth, C., *Ian Paisley: Voice of Protestant Ulster*. Edinburgh: Scottish Academic Press, 1987.

Smyth, M. and McCullough, W.A., 'Northern Ireland: a case study in the economics of survival', *Studies*, 80, Summer 1991.

Stalker, J., *Stalker*. London: Penguin, 1988.

Sugden, J. and Bairner, A., 'National identity, community relations and the sporting life in Northern Ireland', in L. Allison (ed.), *The Changing Politics of Sport*. Manchester: Manchester University Press, 1993.

Sugden, J. and Bairner, A., *Sport, Sectarianism and Society in a Divided Ireland*. Leicester: Leicester University Press, 1993.

Teague, P., 'Multinational companies in the Northern Ireland economy', in P. Teague (ed.), *Beyond the Rhetoric: Politics, the Economy and Social Policy in Northern Ireland*. London: Lawrence and Wishart, 1987.

Teague, P. (ed.), *The Economy of Northern Ireland: Perspectives for Structural Change*. London: Lawrence and Wishart, 1993.

Todd, J., 'Two traditions in Unionist political culture', *Irish Political Studies*, 2, 1987.

Tomlinson, M., *Twenty Five Years On: The Costs of War and the Dividends of Peace*. Belfast: West Belfast Economic Forum, 1994.

Townshend, C., 'The process of terror in Irish politics', in N. O'Sullivan (ed.), *Terrorism, Ideology, and Revolution*. Brighton: Wheatsheaf, 1986.

Whyte, J., *Interpreting Northern Ireland*. Oxford: Clarendon Press, 1990.

Wichert, S., *Northern Ireland since 1945*. Harlow: Longman, 1991.

Williamson, A. and Acheson, N. (eds), *The Voluntary Sector in Northern Ireland*. Basingstoke: Avebury, 1995.

Wilson, D., *An End to Silence*. Cork: Mercier Press, 1986.

Wilson, D. and Game, C., *Local Government in the United Kingdom*. London: Macmillan, 1994.

Wilson, T., *Ulster: Conflict and Consent*. Oxford: Oxford University Press, 1989.

Wright, F., 'Protestant ideology and politics in Ulster', *European Journal of Sociology*, 24, 1973.

Wright, F., *Northern Ireland: A Comparative Analysis*. Dublin: Gill and Macmillan, 1987.

INDEX

abortion, Northern Ireland Abortion Law Reform Association (NIALRA), 144

abstention, Nationalist policy of, 40, 41, 42, 45, 61, 118

accountability
of local government, 96–7
of local policy networks, 154
of police, 109
under direct rule, 90–2, 96–7

Action for Community Employment (ACE), 152–3

Adams, Gerry, 25, 27, 46, 79, 80, 119–20, 214, 220

agriculture, changes in, 122, 124, 135, 150

Agriculture department (DANI), 89, 132

Alliance Party, 70, 81
responses to 1990s peace initiatives, 216, 219
support of EU, 131
support of power-sharing, 22, 25, 81
women in, 141, 145

Ancient Order of Hibernians (AOH), 149

Anglicans, 191, 193–4

Anglo-Irish Agreement (1985), 26–7, 60, 80, 87, 118–20, 213
Unionist opposition to, 26–7, 35, 36–7, 77, 100, 107, 119

Anglo-Irish Intergovernmental Council (AIIGC), 25, 118

Anglo-Irish relations, 60
1920s-60s, 113–14
1969–74, and start of 'the Troubles', 115
1974–9 Labour government policy, 116
1980–5 summits and Conservative government policy, 117–18

see also Anglo-Irish Agreement; Downing Street Declaration; *Frameworks for the Future*

Anti-Partition League, 42–3

arts, 182–5

'B' Specials, 103, 104

Belfast, 3, 201, 203, 206–7

'Belfast Action Teams' (BATs), 153

Belfast Telegraph, 177, 178

Bleakley, David, 53, 62

'Bloody Sunday', 18

borders
EU and cross-border cooperation, 136
role of police in boundary disputes, 103
see also partition

Boundary Commission, 40, 41

British Army, 16, 17, 104, 105

British government
1990s talks with NI political parties, 27, 119–20, 213
control and censorship of media, 175–6
economic policy, 50
and Government of Ireland Act (1920), 6, 85
initiatives for political stability in NI *see* Anglo-Irish Agreement; Constitutional Convention; Downing Street Declaration; *Frameworks for the Future*; power-sharing
policy of devolution and non-interference, 6, 8, 85– 6, 113
public expenditure in NI by, 9, 33–4, 38, 43, 92, 122–3, 126, 134, 152–3
role in NI policy-making, 92, 148, 151–2
see also Anglo-Irish relations; direct rule

farming *see* agriculture
Faulkner, Brian, 17, 18, 22
fertility rates, 204–5
Fianna Fáil, 35, 41, 42, 113
Finance and Personnel department (DFP), 89, 132
Fitt, Gerry, 22, 45, 54, 79, 80
FitzGerald, Dr Garrett, 25, 116
football, 187–8
Frameworks for the Future (1995), 120, 217–18
responses to, 36, 78, 218–19, 220–1
Free Presbyterian Church, 75, 194
'Friends of Ireland', 117

Gaelic Athletic Association (GAA), 187, 188
government
Framework document proposals for NI Assembly, 217, 219
Northern Ireland Assembly (1982–6), 25, 61, 92, 118
Unionist in NI state (1920–72), 6–8, 9–10, 11–12, 14–16, 32–4
see also British government; Irish Republic; local government
Government of Ireland Act (1920), 6, 85, 122, 218

Haughey, Charles, 26, 117
health
Health and Social Services department, 89, 97, 98
internal market in NHS, 150
Healy, Cahir, 42
Heath, Ted, 17–18
Home Rule, 1912–14 conflict over, 4, 5
housing, Northern Ireland Housing Executive (NIHE), 97, 98, 151, 154–5
Hume, John, 43, 45–6, 54, 70, 73, 80, 130
talks with Gerry Adams, 27, 80, 119–20, 214
hunger strikes, 24–5, 78, 118, 163
Hunt Report (1969), 104

identity, political and religious, 34–5, 190, 191, 194, 196, 199
Industries Development Act, 124
industry, 3, 23, 50, 121–2, 123–5
informers, 'supergrass' system, 106

integration, 36, 63
cultural activities as means of, 181, 182, 184–6, 188–9
International Fund for Ireland (IFI), 119
internment, 17, 20, 45, 104, 105
IRA *see* Irish Republican Army
Ireland Act (1949), 9
Irish Congress of Trade Unions, Northern Ireland Committee (NIC-ICTU), 51–2, 150
Irish Independence Party (IIP), 71
Irish Labour Party, 53–4
Irish National Liberation Army (INLA), 162
Irish National Volunteer force, 5
Irish Nationalist Party, 4
Irish News, 177, 178
Irish Northern Aid Committee (NORAID), 117
Irish People's Liberation Organisation (IPLO), 162
Irish Republic
Catholic majoritarianism in, 35, 200
government censorship of media, 175, 176
government initiatives for political stability in NI *see* Anglo-Irish Agreement; Constitutional Convention; Downing Street Declaration; *Frameworks for the Future*; power-sharing
party constitution of parliament in, 67
relationship with Britain *see* Anglo-Irish relations
relationship with NI, 18, 87, 136, 218
relationship with USA, 114, 116–17, 220
sovereign identity and desire for unity, 113–14
women in politics in, 141
Irish Republican Army (IRA)
1920s Unionist policy in response to, 6, 7
1960s re-emergence and split, 17, 44, 54, 161–2
1969–70 emergence and growth of Provisional IRA, 17, 20, 44, 161–2, 175
1980s violence carried out by PIRA, 25, 26, 27
1994 ceasefire, 46, 80, 214, 216
funding by NORAID, 117
link with Sinn Féin, 46, 54, 78, 163
origins of, 161–2